HITLER'S
HENCHMEN

HITLER'S
HENCHMEN

GUIDO KNOPP

SUTTON PUBLISHING

First published in 1996 by C. Bertelsmann Verlag GmbH, Munich.
This English translation first published in 2000 by
Sutton Publishing Limited · Phoenix Mill
Thrupp · Stroud · Gloucestershire · GL5 2BU

This paperback edition first published in 2005

In collaboration with Peter Adler, Christian Dieck, Peter Hartl, Rudolf
Gültner, Jörg Müllner

Research: Bettina Dreier, Klaus Sondermann

Translation: Angus McGeoch

Guido Knopp has asserted the moral right to be identified as the author
of this work.

British Library Cataloguing in Publication Data
A catalogue record for this book is available from the British Library

ISBN 0 7509 3781 5

Typeset in 10/12.5pt Galliard.
Typesetting and origination by
Sutton Publishing Limited.
Printed and bound in England by
J.H. Haynes & Co. Ltd, Sparkford.

CONTENTS

PICTURE CREDITS

LIST OF ILLUSTRATIONS

FOREWORD:
PERFECTLY ORDINARY GERMANS?

We cannot conceive of the Third Reich without Hitler. And once he was gone, deprived of its evil centre of gravity, it disintegrated like a chimaera. The Reich's murderous existence depended solely on him. Without him it became a ship of the dead.

But the dictator was reliant on henchmen who dedicated themselves entirely to serving him. They, the paladins of his court, were supporters, indeed guarantors of his power: Hitler's willing executives – and executioners. They put into effect whatever the despot commanded, and sometimes rather more.

It is far from the truth to say that Hitler's Reich was a weak dictatorship headed by a work-shy drifter, who let things run away with him, who only occasionally intervened in the power-structure of the Nazi regime and had to be forced into committing his evil deeds. Hitler knew perfectly well that none of his henchmen would ever dare to try doing anything that did not conform with his objectives.

Goebbels, Göring, Himmler, Hess, Speer, Dönitz – six careers whose effect upon the workings of the dictatorship varied greatly. The psychological profiles of all these men do, however, help us to find an answer to the question of 'how it could have happened'. Were they criminals of a very special kind? Were they equipped with the same criminal energy that possessed their chief? Or were they 'perfectly ordinary Germans' who by reason of particular circumstances and chance events were able to build extraordinary careers, which put them in a position to commit extraordinary crimes?

*

Goebbels, Göring, Himmler, Hess, Speer, Dönitz – six of Hitler's henchmen, six executors of his power. Without them and many others Hitler would not have been able to maintain his dominance.

But not until the present day has it been revealed that the actual 'writing on the wall' of his dictatorship, the original sin of the twentieth century, was not the war with its very obvious horrors, but the crime which was concealed within it: Auschwitz, the synonym for mass-murder on an industrial scale. The war, terrible as it was for those who lived through it, is retreating further and further into the sober pages of historical evaluation – and now, after more than half a century, appears more like a cloak beneath which the Holocaust could be hidden and carried to its conclusion.

Of course, those who were directly implicated were not just Hitler's henchmen but also many other accomplices: probably as many as half a million Germans were guilty through their involvement.

In addition to those, how many more knew or suspected what was going on, but remained silent? A survey carried out for Second German Television in 1996 produced some very surprising figures. One question was: did you know anything about the annihilation of Jews in concentration-camps? One might have supposed that the death-camps were pretty well isolated and that news of the terrible things happening there scarcely penetrated into the world beyond. But among Germans over sixty-five years old no less than 8 per cent stated that they had 'themselves found out about' the extermination-camps. Applied to the whole wartime population that represents 6 million Germans! Nineteen per cent of those questioned said that at the time they had heard of the killing of Jews and of the concentration-camps. Again, if we apply that percentage to Germany's wartime population, we get this appalling result: 22 million either had direct knowledge of or had heard about the extermination of Jews in the camps.

Yet knowing about something is not necessarily the same as condoning it. The American historian Daniel Goldhagen (author of *Hitler's Willing Executioners*) believes that hardly a single German was plagued by moral scruples. But if that were true, how do we explain other contemporary evidence, such as Victor Klemperer's diary entry on the day in 1941 when the wearing of the Star of David by Jews was made compulsory? Klemperer, himself a Jew, noted that some excitable youths jeered at him, but more often he encountered gestures of friendliness and even of shame on the part of non-Jewish Germans. Some of the people of Dresden made it clear to him that they were not happy about the way Jews were being treated. But they also showed him their fear of being denounced themselves for showing the smallest gesture of human solidarity. Is that the reaction of a people obsessed by an 'all-consuming anti-Semitism'? Goebbels himself confessed to the armaments minister, Albert Speer, that the introduction of the Star of David was not having the desired effect: 'Everywhere people are showing sympathy for the Jews. This nation is simply not mature, it is full of idiotic sentimentality.'

The Nazi regime was extremely interested in the way public opinion was moving. Numerous authorities – the SD (security service), the police, the civil service and the judiciary – all produced weekly reports on the mood of the people. These reports were compiled at a local and then regional level, and the essential points were fed into the Reich reports of the SD. The latter were published, but without the regional and local breakdowns. A research project by the universities of Stuttgart and Jerusalem (led by Eberhard Jäckel and Otto Dov-Kulka) has now published a comprehensive review: thousands of individual reports – the only scientifically reliable primary source from which to judge what Germans knew, how much they knew and what they made of the information. In the following paragraphs I will quote from these sources.

The first thing to emerge from them is that the anti-Jewish Nuremberg Laws were widely accepted by the population. What the Germans did not accept were uncontrolled pogroms. From hundreds of reports about the *Reichskristallnacht* in November 1938, we find that the Germans took a rather poor view of these violent excesses. For example the chairman of the town council in Minden, Westphalia, writes: 'There is an embarrassed silence about the action ordered by the Party; opinions are seldom voiced openly; people are ashamed.'

Another report states: 'The mood of the population and the broad mass of the Party is dejected.' According to a report from Stuttgart on the November pogrom: 'The action against the Jews gave rise to very widespread criticism. It was pointed out that the destruction of Jewish shops and even of synagogues was in no way intended in the Four Year Plan.' Here the argument was not a moral but an economic one. In individual cases, conscious acts of support for the Jews were heard of; thus an eighty-one-year-old retired colonel, a member of the Nazi Party, was reported as having sent a bunch of flowers to a Jew after 9 November, as a token of his deep sympathy.

It was not like that everywhere and it was certainly not true of all Germans. But there was a widespread feeling of shame. How did the population react to the deportation of their Jewish fellow-citizens from October 1941 onwards? The reports tell us that the branding of Jews with the yellow star in the previous month was often the subject of criticism: 'The identification of Jews is being rejected.' Then there was mounting criticism of operations which could no longer be read about in the papers. In one report from Westphalia we read:

> People are saying that Jews were being forced to work in former Soviet factories, while elderly and sick Jews were ordered to be shot. It was incomprehensible that human beings could be treated so brutally. Whether Jew or Aryan, they were all God's creation.

And in another report:

> It could be observed that a large proportion of the older *Volksgenossen* [national comrades] are generally very critical of the measures to deport Jews from Germany. Within churchgoing circles it is being said openly that the German people must surely one day be prepared for the punishment of God.

How much horrifying detail had penetrated to the Germans at home is shown in a report by the SD in Erfurt:

> The wildest rumours are circulating about operations by the Security Police in the occupied eastern territories. For instance,

stories are being spread among the population that the Security Police have been given the task of exterminating Jewry in the occupied areas. Jews, it is said, are being rounded up and shot in thousands, having first had to dig their own graves. These shootings are said sometimes to be on such a scale that even members of the firing squads have had nervous breakdowns.

That was a pretty accurate description of what was actually happening. But the fears and concerns of ordinary Germans give the lie to any theory that 'the Germans' were indifferent or insensitive – to say nothing of the presumption that the Holocaust had been greeted with enthusiasm. One claim, in a report from Minden, was that

There is a lot of talk among the people that Germans in the United States are obliged to wear a swastika on their left breast for identification purposes, in the same way that Jews are identified here in Germany. The Germans in America are having to pay a heavy price for the mistreatment of the Jews in Germany.

In 1943 a mass-grave of Polish officers, shot by the Soviet secret service, was found at Katyn, a discovery which the Nazis used as the basis for anti-Soviet hate-campaigns. However, the Gestapo noted that 'a large part of the population found this propaganda strange or hypocritical, because far greater numbers of Poles and Jews had been liquidated by the Germans'. Is this the reaction of a people who regarded the 'Final Solution' as a national project?

The findings from these unpublished sources and from the recent opinion survey are more or less identical: many Germans knew quite a lot; they suppressed it, even tolerated it, but to a large extent they did not want it to happen. This is the view held, incidentally, by the overwhelming majority of the 1,285 people questioned.

In 1996 30 per cent of Germans said they were convinced that their contemporaries at the time had known about the murder of the Jews, whereas 62 per cent held the opposite view. A mere 1½ per cent stated that in their view the slaughter of the Jews was supported by most Germans. Around 22 per cent believed there was 'a tendency to tolerate' it. And only 6 per cent of Germans in

1996 held the view that the killing of Jews 'tended to be condemned' by the majority of Germans. The people are sometimes shrewder than historians think.

Would that there had been more 'condemnation'! When Cardinals Faulhaber and Galen used their pulpits to denounce as murder the 'T4' programme, which the regime dressed up as 'mercy killing', Hitler had the programme stopped. In Berlin, early in 1943, the non-Jewish spouses of Jews who had been listed for deportation to death-camps staged a public protest outside the collection centre. This became known as the Rosenstrasse Incident, and resulted in the release of many of those registered for deportation. In Germany, at least, the regime wanted to avoid attracting public attention. Everything was supposed to run in a calm and orderly manner – right up to the gas-chamber. Could similar focused protest in Germany and abroad have even prevented the Holocaust, or at least brought it to an end sooner? No one dared put this to the test.

Who bears the responsibility for the crime of the twentieth century, the murder of Europe's Jews? We put this question, as well, to German respondents in 1996. Nearly 70 per cent replied Hitler; the next largest number (37 per cent) said his henchmen; followed by 32 per cent who said the SS. Only 20 per cent replied that 'the Germans as a whole' were to blame for the killing of the Jews. It is striking to note here that young people under thirty were more inclined to lay part of the blame on 'all Germans' (35 per cent), whereas only 5 per cent of those over sixty-five took that view.

However much of the blame 'the Germans' as a whole should accept, without Hitler the Third Reich would have been inconceivable. This does not mean the shifting of guilt onto one individual. Yet it was his criminal energy which released the criminal energies in others. Hitler held his henchmen in a firm grip. They carried out what he decided – or what in their view was the Führer's intention. The killing of the Jews was not the result of the bureaucratic processes of a dictatorship going berserk, but an official crime deliberately staged by Hitler. Hitler not only initiated the killings, he managed them – through powers delegated to Himmler. Without Hitler there would have been no invasion of the Soviet Union, without Hitler no Holocaust.

This does not amount to an acquittal for his henchmen and accomplices. For Hitler's Holocaust was put into effect by the many 'little people' – willing executioners – who later pleaded that they were forced to obey orders. They were not psychopaths, but perfectly ordinary Germans from a population of supporters and hangers-on.

However, the murders they committed were no more a predetermined and logical product of German history than Hitler himself was. There is no straight path running from the battlefields of Flanders to Auschwitz. There is no direct route taking us from Luther, via Bismarck, to Hitler. Nothing in history is inevitable. That is certainly true of Hitler's so-called *Machtergreifung* (seizure of power) which in truth was more of a *Machterschleichung*, sneaking into power by devious means. Although there was always the possibility that it *could* happen that way, it did not *have* to happen.

The disgrace remains: millions of Germans looked on and looked away. Millions knew enough, certainly, to know very well that they did not want to know any more. Hundreds of thousands of Germans proved to be Hitler's willing executioners. Yet what drove them was not only and not principally a murderous anti-Semitism. It was the opportunity which a satanic regime offered them to realize their basest, most unpleasant urges – and not just against Jews.

That was possible in Germany, and if there, then why not everywhere? History has proved that genocide in the twentieth century has not been exclusive to Germany. Millions met their death in Stalin's *gulag*, in Turkey, in China and Cambodia. What makes the Jewish Holocaust so unique is the industrial efficiency with which it was planned and carried out.

Those of us who were born after the war cannot be held responsible for Auschwitz. But we are responsible for the memory, for preventing it from being obliterated or suppressed. That does not mean collective guilt, but it does mean collective responsibility.

It is necessary to consider how 'perfectly normal people' under very specific conditions become criminals, when a criminal government encourages them to do so. What makes a person inhuman? Pondering that question also means preventing, for all time, man from being the 'wolf of man'. Bosnia and Rwanda were only yesterday.

All the lessons of Germany's Holocaust, all the pictures and the reports have not been able to change human nature. But they can prevent the same thing ever happening again, at least in Europe. I think that is service enough.

CHAPTER ONE

THE FIREBRAND: JOSEPH GOEBBELS

KNOPP/HARTL

I have now learnt abstinence. And a boundless contempt for the common herd.

There is a curse hanging over me and women.

Here is a man who knows the way. I want to be worthy of him.

Hitler talks to me in a very friendly, confidential way. How fond he is of me as a person, too . . .

I suppose it will always be one of the biggest jokes about democracy that it has itself presented its deadliest enemies with the very means by which to destroy it.

The Bolshevists can teach us a lot, especially about propaganda.

It was rather a good thing and helpful to us that at least some of the Jews thought: Oh well, it won't really be as bad as all that.

This plague of Jews must be wiped out. Completely and utterly. Nothing must be left of them.

Now, let the nation arise, let the storm break!

We will go down in history as the greatest statesmen of all time.
Or else the greatest criminals.

Goebbels

You know of course that I am not very keen on this exaggerated anti-semitism. But nor can I really say that the Jews are particular friends of mine. However, I don't think they can be got rid of by insults and polemics or even by pogroms, and even if this were possible, it would be most ignoble and inhuman to do so.

Goebbels to Anka Stalherm, 1919

He has taught us again the old German virtue of loyalty; we are going to stand by him until victory or defeat. Let us thank Destiny for having given us this man, the helmsman in our hour of peril, the apostle of truth, the leader into freedom, the confessor, the zealot, the voice calling us to arms, the steadfast hero, the emblem of Germany's conscience.

Goebbels on Hitler, 1924

Germany longs for this one man, as the earth thirsts for rain in summer. O Lord, show the German people a miracle! A miracle!! A man!!!

Goebbels, 1924

Soon he will listen only to his generals, and things will get tough for me.

Goebbels, 1938

Why can't women be our equal in every way? Can they be educated to it? Or are they simply inferior? Only in rare cases can women become heroines!

Goebbels, 1925

Men of Dr Goebbels' type have always been alien to me, though I have refrained from passing judgement. But today he is the most hated man in Germany. At one time we used to complain about Jewish managing directors sexually harassing their female employees. Now Dr Goebbels is doing it.

Himmler, 1939

We Germans may not know much about living, but when it comes to dying – we're fabulous!

Goebbels, 1932

If I'd told those people to jump from the third floor – they'd've done it!

Goebbels after his 'Total War' speech at the Sportpalast, 1943

This is the secret of propaganda: those whom the propaganda is aimed at must become completely saturated with the ideas it contains, without ever realising that they are being saturated. Obviously the propaganda has a purpose, but this purpose must be so cleverly and innocently disguised that the people we intend to influence simply do not notice it is happening.

Goebbels addressing senior radio executives, 1933

The rhetorical gifts and organisational talents this man displayed were unique. There was nothing he did not seem capable of. The party members were absolutely devoted to him and the SA would willingly have been cut to pieces for him. Goebbels, well, he was just our Goebbels.

Horst Wessel, 1926

To hell with this loud-mouthed propaganda boss, Goebbels by name. The man who, crippled in body and soul, deliberately and with inhuman malice strives to elevate the lie to godlike status, the sole master of the world!

Thomas Mann, 1933

The press today is no longer the enemy but is working alongside government. Today press and government are in fact pulling in the same direction.

Goebbels, 1934

He was without doubt the most intelligent of them all. He was an academic, as you could clearly tell from his choice of words and way of speaking. Unlike Göring, Himmler and Bormann, he possessed the ability to distance himself to some extent from day-to-day events. He wasn't self-centred and he was no coward. He told Hitler what he thought, even when he believed the war was over – and Hitler always listened to him. To me, Goebbels was a propaganda genius and I believe it can equally well be said that he made Hitler as that Hitler made him. He was a very complex personality – completely cold. Where National Socialism was at its worst – in its anti-Jewish measures in Germany – he was the driving force.

Speer, 1979

* * *

As Paul Joseph Goebbels, the undersized 29-year-old philology graduate, stepped out into the forecourt of Munich's massive central station on 8 April 1926, a chauffeur was already waiting for him in a supercharged Mercedes with gleaming chrome. Thanks to the 'gigantic' roadside posters advertising the appearance of 'Dr Goebbels' in the *Bürgerbräu* beer hall the following day, the drive to the hotel turned into a triumphal procession for the newcomer.

'What a splendid reception!' he enthused in his diary. Then, in the evening, when his fatherly host appeared in person to pay his respects to the visitor, Goebbels finally achieved a state of bliss: 'Hitler telephoned. Wants to welcome us in person.' He exulted in his diary: 'He arrives in a quarter of an hour. Tall, healthy, full of vitality. I like him so much. He is embarrassingly kind to us.'

Hitler generously put his limousine at the guest speaker's disposal for a spin around Lake Starnberg before the initiation began the following evening in the Bürgerbräukeller: 'I give it everything I've got. They cheer, they roar. At the end Hitler

embraces me. There are tears in my eyes. I'm in a kind of heaven.'
A wave of ecstasy floods through Goebbels' diary: 'I bow down
before the greater man, the political genius!' Later he adds
another verse to the hymn of praise:

> He is a genius. The unquestioned creative instrument of a
> divine destiny. I stand before him in a state of shock. But *he* is
> like a child; kind, good, compassionate. Yet catlike, cunning,
> clever, agile; and like a lion, huge and roaring. What a chap,
> what a man!

To the young admirer, Hitler was more than a father-figure or
exemplar. Fired with zeal, Goebbels elevated the backroom demagogue into the Messiah and Redeemer in human form. In Hitler
his ill-defined search for religious faith had found an icon. 'What
one believes in is immaterial; the important thing is *believing*.'
These were the words Goebbels put into the mouth of Michael
Voormann, the hero of his bombastic attempt at novel-writing.
Having abandoned both Catholic piety and left-wing
revolutionary exuberance, he now worshipped with glowing faith
an earthly deity who would become the *leitmotiv* of his existence
and was already filling his failed career with a new purpose.

'I am gladly departing this life, which has been nothing but hell
for me,' Goebbels had cried out in his testament to posterity at the
age of only twenty-two. Yet this theatrical exit was postponed to a
later date and he was forced to continue his meagre existence as a
student. A small bursary from the Catholic Albertus Magnus
Society, occasional earnings as a tutor, endless loans from friends,
visits to the pawnbroker, and most of all the money which his
father donated from his meagre income, all helped to keep the
literature student's head more or less above water. When necessary
he just went without meals for a few days. Wherever his student
wanderings took him – Bonn, Würzburg, Freiburg, Munich and
Heidelberg – the spectre of poverty was his constant companion.

His experience of terrible shortages in Germany after the First
World War combined with his personal penury to shape his vision of
a world in which men of ability became the victims of sinister
machinations. 'Isn't it monstrous,' he wrote in frustration to his

boyhood sweetheart Anka Stalherm in 1920, 'that people with the most brilliant intellectual gifts languish in poverty, because the rest are squandering, blowing and wasting the money that could help them?'

In this Goebbels was portraying himself: he felt that he was destined for higher things, was convinced his future was to be a famous writer, an idealist who would change the world. His first steps in life had in fact led him single-mindedly up the social ladder. He was born on 29 October 1897 in the small Lower Rhineland town of Rheydt, the third son of a bookkeeper who had doggedly worked his way up from blue-collar to white-collar status. For this gifted boy, attending the town's high school meant crossing what was in those days still a very rigid class barrier. He enjoyed the privilege of piano lessons and an education in the humanities. As the brightest pupil in his year the university doors were open to him. For the son of a lower middle-class family this success was both a satisfaction and a compensation. For it was not only his humble origins that permanently labelled him an outsider. 'Why had God made him in such a way that people mocked and scorned him?' he made his fictional Michael Voorman complain. 'Why could he not love himself and love life as others did?' It was this cry of self-hate and self-pity which would reverberate to the end of his life. From his childhood he was denied access to the world of the carefree and the undamaged; as a sickly four-year-old he contracted osteomyelitis in the right leg. Despite all the efforts of doctors, growth of the limb was stunted. And for the rest of his life he had to drag the affected foot behind him in an unsightly orthopaedic shoe. While others played, danced or enjoyed sport, the crippled boy always remained on the sidelines. In 1914, excited by the general euphoria of war, he presented himself for an army medical check, only to be wearily waved aside by the doctor. 'When he saw the others running, jumping and romping about,' Goebbels confessed in *Michael*, 'he berated his God for . . . doing this to him; he hated the others for not being like him; he even mocked his mother for being happy to have such a cripple.'

In the solitude of his attic room he learned to hate with a passion: to hate himself in all his ugliness, to hate the others who did not take him seriously, despised him or else smothered him with pity, and lastly to hate the whole of mankind. 'I have now learnt abstinence,' he wrote in his journal of the soul, 'And a boundless contempt for the common herd!'

The malign delight with which he later dissected the weaknesses of others, the vengeance with which he pursued opponents and colleagues alike, the mistrust which led him to suspect treason and plotting all around him, and his incapacity to feel pity – all had their origin in those early days of humiliation. At the same time experience taught him to play down his physical shortcomings by behaving in a particularly assertive way.

> He never lost control. He was calculating and cold. Ice-cold and diabolical.
>
> *Otto Jacobs, stenographer*

It was no coincidence that he cut quite a figure on the stage. With forceful phrases and sweeping gestures he was able to spellbind those around him. He used his repartee and mental acumen to divert attention from his appearance. The success which was denied him on the sportsground and the field of battle, he seized with relentless energy in the classroom and at his desk. In November 1921 Goebbels' ambition to rise in the world was crowned with success: he graduated in the faculty of philology at Heidelberg and was now 'Herr Doktor'. For hours he practised a flamboyant signature, now embellished with academic credentials. Never again would he sign his name without adding his full title. In his home town of Rheydt the neighbours greeted him on the street with respect. For the 24-year-old Goebbels, graduation from university brought social recognition and personal triumph. Yet, far from gaining employment and status, he found himself back in the attic of his parents' house. On its own, his academic title did nothing to free him from material hardship. In the next two and a half years the struggling young man became painfully aware that even 'Doctors' have to earn their keep and write job applications. In his little study the obscure writer filled reams of paper with poems, articles and tracts – but the outside world paid him precious little attention. Apart from the reprinting of six of his essays in the *Westdeutsche Landeszeitung*, the public completely ignored the prolific recluse.

It seemed, therefore, like an admission of total defeat when he was forced to seek gainful employment in a Cologne branch of the Dresdner Bank. Instead of addressing an illustrious audience, his resonant voice was now heard shouting out share-prices on the trading-floor.

His detested duties in the 'Temple of Materialism' reinforced his disgust at the 'hectic dance around the Golden Calf'. 'You talk of capital investment,' Goebbels raged in his diary over speculation during the runaway inflation of 1923 'but behind these fine words lurks nothing but a bestial hunger for more. I say bestial, but that is an insult to animals, for an animal only eats until it has had its fill.' The fertile soil of anti-capitalism brought forth the first shoots of anti-Semitism. His latent prejudice, something frowned on by the Catholic lower middle-class, hardened into a sinister conspiracy theory. In 'the Jews of international finance' Goebbels discovered the perfect scapegoat, both for his personal penury and for the economic hardships of his time. For him Jewish finagling was not only at the heart of Western materialism – the very 'spawn of evil' – but also of international Marxism. The men pulling the strings in both worlds had a common ambition to remove every trace of national autonomy. Fed by the relevant writings of the period, Goebbels distilled from the murky philosophical brew the 'inexorable logic' that only a 'life-or-death struggle' against 'international Jewry' would open the way to a better world.

As yet he apparently found no contradiction between this belief and his acquaintance with actual people of Jewish descent. The Heidelberg literary historian, Friedrich Gundolf, whom Goebbels greatly admired, was Jewish, as was his supervisor, Professor Max von Waldberg, and a close family friend was a Jewish lawyer who gave literary advice to the budding poet. When his fiancée, a teacher named Else Janke, revealed that her mother was Jewish, he was taken aback, but did not end the relationship – at least not immediately. When Goebbels later rose to be a spokesman for the Nazi Party, he threw out his bride-to-be as a tiresome leftover from his youth.

At first, however, it was he who was out on the street. After only nine months his career as a bank employee came to an abrupt end. In order to conceal the disgrace from his family, he continued to commute to Cologne for weeks without a job, until his lack of funds forced him to reveal the truth.

'As a result of a slight nervous disorder brought about by an accident and overwork, I was obliged to give up my employment in Cologne.' That was how he described his failure in a neatly written letter to the Berlin publishing house of Mosse, applying for an editorial position. But all his euphemism was in vain. The applicant was turned down, as he was by the long-established *Vossische Zeitung* and the liberal *Berliner Tageblatt*. His rejection by the metropolis fitted perfectly into his view of the world; the owners of these publishing houses and their featured journalists were obviously Jewish. The whole world, which denied him access to a livelihood, appeared to him 'Jew-ridden'.

Goebbels complained in his diary:

I live in a permanent state of nervous agitation. This miserable, cadging existence. I rack my brains to find a way out of this undignified situation. Nothing seems to work, nothing *can* work. First of all one has to put aside everything that can be called an independent viewpoint, moral courage, personality or character, if one is to count for anything in this world of patronage and careerism. I count for nothing. A big zero.

But in the Bavarian capital, Munich, the itinerant political preacher did count for something. Reports of Hitler's unsuccessful putsch in 1923 roused the deskbound dropout from his lethargy. With growing enthusiasm Goebbels followed the chief protagonist's stage-managed appearances at his trial in Munich for high treason. He said later, in obeisance to his new prophet:

The words you spoke there are the catechism of a new political faith amid the despair of a collapsing and godless world. You did not remain silent. God gave you the voice to express our suffering. You put our torment into words of redemption, formed sentences of trust in the miracle to come.

Inspired by a belief in miracles, Goebbels accompanied an old schoolfriend now and again to public debates and meetings of the 'Popular Socialist Bloc' in his home province of Rhineland-Westphalia. Through the murky 'mixture of cowardice, nastiness, self-importance and naked ambition' which he found there, an illuminating shaft of light penetrated the gloom of his existence: he could become a political commentator! The *Völkische Freiheit* (National Liberty), the splinter party's campaign sheet, published in the industrial town of Elberfeld, was prepared to print the polemical essays of 'Dr G.' – albeit without payment to begin with. Before long almost the entire contents of the paper were being written by Goebbels and shortly afterwards he took over the editorship – 'with idealism and without thanks' but nonetheless with great satisfaction as his reward: 'I am just the tiniest bit happy. The first visible success from my efforts,' noted the editor in his diary. 'Now I am back on top again.'

> Hitler has arrived. He shakes me by the hand. He is still completely worn out from delivering his great speech. Then he goes on talking here for another half-hour. With wit, irony, humour, sarcasm, but also with seriousness, intensity and passion. This man has all the qualities of a king. A born tribune of the people. The coming dictator.
>
> *Goebbels, 1925*

Working for the Party also gave the new member the experience of success on the speaker's platform. It took iron nerves to survive the laughter that initially greeted the appearance of this gaunt and undersized speaker with the disproportionately large head, but after that he was able to cast his spell over the audience. The strangely fascinating timbre of his voice, which could penetrate the loudest barracking, the precise and telling phrases, which were nevertheless comprehensible to every last Party member, the unbridled aggressiveness and biting wit left his audience in rapt silence. With his convincing appearance of inner passion he succeeded in carrying his public with him. He himself remained completely cold, while carefully studying every reaction.

With unfailing instinct he found the turns of phrase which at the right moment touched a nerve among his listeners. Now flattering, now caustic, now beaming, now troubled, he drew from his repertoire on each occasion the tone which best matched the mood in the hall. He garnered the greatest approbation when he attacked his opponents with biting sarcasm; his success was assured whenever he turned the shouts of critics and hecklers back on themselves in stinging ripostes. Every speech was a Herculean labour for him; hoarse, exhausted and streaming with sweat, he would finally stagger from the rostrum. Each gesture was painstakingly rehearsed, every jab of the finger applied with deliberation. The script showed the delivery of the speech in minute detail, the content devised in the seclusion of his study. His target was certainly not the integrity, honesty or good sense of the masses, but it *was* their intelligence. He relied on the effect of wordplay, jokes and disarming arguments. With these he could stir up his listeners, transport them and astonish them. But he did not send them into ecstasy. Whereas Hitler's appearances drove his supporters into an almost sexual delirium, Goebbels seduced them with psychologically calculated persuasiveness. 'I am becoming a demagogue of the worst kind,' he assured himself with pride.

> The essence of propaganda is – I might almost say – an art. And the propagandist is in the truest sense of the word an artist in popular psychology. His most important task is to keep his finger, daily and hourly, on the pulse of the people and to adapt his measures to the heartbeat.
>
> *Goebbels, 1935*

In a group of political agitators not overprovided with brilliant orators, this gifted speaker was soon getting himself talked about. Local branches queued up to book him and very soon Goebbels, now promoted to *Gau* (district) manager, was performing nightly to Party rooms and assembly halls up and down the country. It was not long before the little doctor's pulling power came to the attention of Hitler, recently released from prison in Landsberg

Castle. It was Gregor Strasser, the Nazi Party organizer in northern Germany and Goebbels' mentor, who had told Hitler about the able agitator, and the latter looked with favour on the acolyte, scarcely nine years younger than himself: 'He stood there in front of us. Shook my hand. Like an old friend. And those big, blue eyes. Like stars. He is glad to see me,' Goebbels was moved to write in his diary for 1925. The man who greeted him was, in his eyes, without question 'the coming dictator'. The unequal friendship between the two men was in no way marred by the fact that Goebbels was known as an exponent of the left, socialist wing of the Party.

In 1926 the internal dispute between the right-wing southern element of the party and the leftists of northern Germany came to a head at a conference in the Bavarian town of Bamberg. The hopes of the 'revolutionary' wing all rested on the eloquent doctor. But he kept a low profile after a monologue by Hitler that lasted for hours, and remained silent 'as though he had been pole-axed'. The *Führerprinzip* (principle of sole leadership) made all debate superfluous. Any reservations he had about the 'damned sloppy management' at the Party headquarters in Munich were put in the shade by the radiance of his new idol. 'Adolf Hitler, I love you because you are at once great and simple.'

Yet it was not Hitler's simplicity that tipped the balance. The penniless son of a petty-bourgeois was much more flattered and pleased by the outward pomp and splendour with which his fatherly patron proceeded to pay court to him in Munich. And Hitler had an ulterior motive in this, for he had bigger plans for the resourceful young agitator: as the new *Gauleiter* of the Berlin–Brandenburg region Goebbels' task would be to raise the Nazi flag in the extremely hostile territory of Germany's 'red' capital city. True, the chosen candidate hesitated at first and played hard to get, but in reality he had recognized this as a chance of a lifetime: a position with a future and an assignment which appealed to his fighting spirit. On 7 November 1926 he left Elberfeld for Berlin – it was a journey with no return ticket.

In the metropolis with a population of millions the new *Gauleiter* commanded a pitifully small fraternity of just 300 members. It had absolutely no popular support but merely a

It was impossible to see into Goebbels' heart. He always wore the same poker-faced expression. We just couldn't make him out. I think he really believed in his own phrases – and in the possibility of ultimate victory. He had fallen for his own slogans.

Dietrich Evers, picture-editor on Wehrmacht propaganda

pronounced desire to tear itself apart. With full authority from Hitler, and an iron fist, Goebbels separated the brawling factions and imposed his leadership. He founded a 'victim support society' to collect money, and a school for training young speakers. But none of this attracted any public attention.

'Berlin needs sensation like a fish needs water,' the self-taught politician realized. 'That's what this city lives on and no political propaganda will succeed if it has not recognized that fact.' Consequently, Goebbels never missed an opportunity to grab the headlines. As venues for his parades and meetings he deliberately chose the communist strongholds in industrial suburbs and relied on the effect of the fighting in halls and streets which this would provoke. To this end he recruited his own mobile strike force. Their orders were to create the greatest possible disturbance: 'In riots, when damage to property exceeds 400 Marks, the riot damage law comes into effect. I just mention that in passing,' were the ringleader's disingenuous instructions to his bully-boys.

Once, when the demagogue was in the middle of a racist tirade, a heckler shouted: 'You don't exactly look like a good Teutonic lad!' Foaming with rage, Goebbels gestured to his hit-men to give the troublemaker a lesson he wouldn't forget. It was unfortunate that the man they beat up later turned out to be an evangelical pastor. For Berlin's Chief of Police this incident provided a welcome pretext to outlaw Goebbels' brown-shirts.

But the latter made a virtue out of the ban. The SA troop was transformed into apparently innocent little groups such as the 'All Nine' skittle club, the 'High Wave' swimming association and the 'Old Berlin' ramblers, and the Party parades were moved to venues beyond the city limits. Since the ban had silenced

Goebbel's voice, he replaced it with another organ: a campaign paper with the unambiguous title of *Der Angriff* (The Assault). Its attacks were now constantly aimed at one man: Berlin's Deputy Police-Chief, Bernhard Weiss. As a determined defender of the democratic system Weiss was right at the top of Goebbels' hit-list. But that was not the only reason he was targeted. The brownshirted racists picked out Weiss as the prototype of those they hated most. Under the pejorative name of 'Isidor' he became the object of a disgraceful campaign of ridicule and slander which thrived on widespread anti-Jewish prejudice. Berliners laughed at the malicious – and mostly quite unfounded – stories and the crude caricatures. Thanks to 'Isidor', Goebbels also became famous. Why should he be worried by the long-drawn-out defamation trials – they simply brought him even greater publicity.

Admittedly this notoriety did not gain him any electoral advantage. After the Party had been allowed to re-form on 27 February 1925, the Nazi Party (NSDAP) achieved precisely 2.6 per cent of the Berlin vote in the elections of 1928. Yet for Goebbels himself the elections meant a big leap upward: now at last the one-time pauper could hobble up the steps of the national parliament, the Reichstag. The democratic mandate gave Goebbels an effective public arena in which to attack democracy itself. He sneered in the *Angriff*:

I am not a member of the Reichstag, I am simply a Possessor of Immunity, a Holder of a Free Travel Pass. What has the Reichstag to do with us? . . . We were elected to *oppose* the Reichstag, and we will indeed carry out our mandate in the way our voters intended us to . . . We are entering the Reichstag in order to equip ourselves from the arsenal of democracy with the weapons of democracy . . . We come not as allies, not even as neutrals. We come as enemies! As the wolf descends on the flock, so do we come.

His newly won immunity protected the anti-parliamentary parliamentarian from pursuit by the courts of law, and he used the speaker's rostrum for harangues against the republic, while his official allowances filled the coffers of the local Party. However, the real political battle was taking place on the streets. The more massively the economic crisis swelled the ranks of the unemployed and the dispossessed, the more extreme became the animosity between the opposing political forces.

> What a nation! In tearing itself apart it kills the last remnants of national identity. In any other country the masses would rise up in violent protest. Poor old Germany! What riff-raff! What a rabble! The Jews have certainly got the measure of us!
>
> *Goebbels on the lynching trials in 1928*

The bloody brawls not only provoked a continuous outcry from the press, they also furnished a steady supply of ammunition for propaganda. Goebbels always arranged to pack the first few rows in front of the rostrum with SA toughs, whose heads were ostentatiously swathed in bandages. An even greater draw, he thought, would be some 'genuine martyrs' from his own camp. With exaggerated emotion and regardless of the actual circumstances of death, Goebbels placed a hero's wreath on the head of every SA man who lost his life. Each burial was staged as a major propaganda event. The death-worship reached its climax when the twenty-three-year-old Horst Wessel was shot dead in a seedy milieu of pimps and prostitutes. For Goebbels the death of the young terrorist meant the birth of a heroic myth. 'One of us has to set an example and offer himself as a sacrifice,' he declaimed beside the open grave. 'Then so be it, I am ready!' Acting swiftly, he arranged for a pamphlet of doggerel written by Wessel to be turned into a rousing anthem, which was later to become part of the basic ritual repertoire of the Third Reich.

The anthem was even pressed into service when Goebbels met his communist adversary, Walter Ulbricht, on the platform for a face-to-face duel of words. First the 'Horst Wessel Song' clashed discordantly with the 'Internationale', then punches flew. The debate was drowned out by the hideous din of an indoor battle in which over a hundred people were injured. When the occasion arose, however, the *Gauleiter* did not hesitate to make common cause with the 'red rabble' against the republican government. Many of his methods, such as the unison chanting of slogans, mass-demonstrations, lurid placards, party cells in the factories and door-to-door leafleting, had in any case been copied from his political opponents.

In his black leather jacket and with a tremor in his voice, the gaunt figure, like a Roman 'tribune of the people', addressed workers in their meeting-rooms and became a champion of the 'little man'. He exploited the hardship of the masses as fuel for his inflammatory speeches. He pinpointed the economic crisis as proof of the bankruptcy of the 'system' and of its policy of total compliance with the Treaty of Versailles. Following a simple and constantly repeated formula, he put the blame on the capitalists and Jews who held 'decent, honest Germans' in a stranglehold. Like a preacher he affirmed his congregation in their faith in a 'national resurrection' and in Hitler as their Saviour. But all the time the political prophet felt nothing but cold contempt for the disciples who hung on his words: 'The masses remain what they have always been: stupid, gluttonous and forgetful.'

In his dealings with Party colleagues he soon became adept at employing the whole apparatus of power and intrigue. The opportunist who mouthed ideologies, but never absorbed them, always knew how to side with the majority at the right moment. When his devoted Berlin SA troops led by Walter Stennes staged an open revolt against the Party HQ in Munich, his initial sympathy quickly evaporated and on Hitler's orders he struck back. 'I will fire the traitors with a bang,' he boasted in his diary, and then rigorously 'cleansed' the Party of its rebellious faction. Once again his fear of losing Hitler's protection prevailed over other ties of loyalty. He proceeded with equal ruthlessness when instructed to do away with his former campaign comrades, the brothers Gregor and Otto Strasser. Hitler himself had given him *carte blanche* for the 'ruthless purging' from the Party of all those 'rootless scribblers and muddle-headed armchair bolshevists'.

In gratitude for his unquestioning loyalty and brilliance as an agitator, the master promoted his vassal to be the NSDAP's Head of National Propaganda. The wearisome round of general elections in the dying days of the Weimar Republic offered

Goebbels ample opportunity to display his skills as an organizer, propagandist and orator. In a wave of restless activity he masterminded the election campaign, which covered the entire country, and spread a rallying message presenting Hitler as an omnipresent saviour, soaring over Germany in an aircraft. Goebbels himself was scarcely able to snatch a moment's rest.

Confiding to his diary, the exhausted Goebbels wrote:

> One hardly has time to think. We are carried the length and breadth of Germany by train, car and aircraft. We arrive in a city half an hour before we are due to begin, sometimes even later, then we step on to a platform and speak. . . . When the speech is over, one is in such a state that one feels as if one has just been taken out of hot bath fully clothed. Then we get into a car and drive for another two hours.

Despite all the hardship and the shortage of funds, this punishing programme provided the arch-publicist with one of the happiest periods of his life. In a party which was built on propaganda, he was seen as the man of the hour. On the speaker's platform he had the opportunity to indulge his passion for self-promotion. With placards, banners and leaflets, with gramophone records, films and press campaigns, with demonstrations, parades and mass rallies he could pull out all the stops on the mighty Wurlitzer of audience-manipulation. And most important of all, as Hitler's companion and adviser, he could spend all his time within touching distance of his master. He was needed, he was famous, and he was being rewarded: both with sweeping election victories and with the encouraging praise of his 'Führer'.

Yet for all that, his success still did not earn him comradeship in the brown-shirt ranks. In a party that had adopted the emblems of muscularity, an upright bearing and blond hair, rather than mental ability, Goebbels, the malformed intellectual, carried a double handicap. Both his brain and his affliction branded him throughout his life as an oddity, to be eyed with suspicion. 'I have few friends in the party: Hitler is almost the only one,' he confided to his diary. 'He agrees with me on everything. He will stand right behind me.'

> What first struck me about Goebbels was that there was
> something puppet-like about him. Not in his movements –
> they were those of a demagogue. But when he opened his
> mouth wide, and that was his speciality, he reminded one
> rather of a marionette.
>
> *Stéphane Roussel, French foreign correspondent*

The 'boss' did exactly that, even when, late in 1931, Goebbels went to the altar with Magda Quandt, née Ritschel, who was already expecting his baby. By acting as their witness, Hitler gave his blessing to the marriage, thus making it not only acceptable in Nazi eyes but also a prestigious boost in every respect for the man on his way up. The bridegroom could now boast a wife from the best of families, who until her divorce had been married to one of Germany's wealthiest industrialists and who had committed herself, shapely body and gullible soul, to the Nazi Party. The change in marital status was underlined by a change of accommodation: the imposing and elegant Quandt residence on the Reichskanzlerplatz became a rendezvous for the Nazi elite and a second home for Hitler, who found there a substitute for the family he never had.

On 30 January 1933, in the Hotel Kaiserhof which stood opposite his house and served as the Party's election headquarters, Goebbels experienced the triumphant culmination of his ceaseless efforts: the Germanized Austrian, Adolf Hitler, was appointed Reich Chancellor, the Weimar Republic slunk out of the back door, and Goebbels exulted: 'It is impossible to describe what we feel in our hearts. You want to cry and laugh.'

In reality he felt more like crying. For while the brown-shirted battalions celebrated the 'Seizure of Power' with a grandiose torchlight procession, the propagandist who dreamed it up was sunk in a deep depression: contrary to Hitler's 'formal' promise, there was no place for a rabble-rouser in the government of 'national retrenchment'. So he had to settle for harnessing the national broadcasting service for his purposes in a final electoral battle. More than any politician of his era, Goebbels recognized the huge potential for influence which this medium presented. He would only allow Hitler to appear in cities which had local transmission facilities. And the Führer's broadcast speeches were always preceded by Goebbels at the microphone giving a glowing description of the atmosphere among the audience. With a sense of mission he made sure that throughout the land it would be impossible not to hear the message of national revival. Naked violence and officially sanctioned terrorism, especially after the burning of the Reichstag, did whatever else was necessary to cement Hitler's sole domination of the country. Once the new political masters had got rid of their conservative coalition partners, the drummer was also allowed to join the procession. The little man from Rheydt had completed the first lap: On 14 March 1933 Goebbels was officially sworn in as 'Minister of National Enlightenment and Propaganda'.

> The Minister of Propaganda always signs himself 'Dr Goebbels'. He is the one educated man in the government, which is to say the quarter-educated man among illiterates. The impression of his intellectual potency is remarkably widespread; he is often called 'the brains' of the government. If so, then the demands on him must be modest indeed.
>
> *Victor Klemperer, Jewish novelist (Diary), 1934*

Inwardly, he would rather have sworn a different oath than that of warding off misfortune from the German people. 'One day the sword of our wrath will whip down upon the evil-doers and strike them to the ground in their bare-faced arrogance,' he prophesied darkly in the diary. To the notorious misanthrope the completion of the 'national revolution' had always meant more than the exchange of ministries and posts. For him the hour of victory would also be the hour of reckoning.

But to begin with other calculations determined his agenda. Following plans which had been lying ready in a bottom drawer, Goebbels took only a few days to carve out a ministry which was unparalleled in German history. Never before had such a massive frontal assault been mounted on people's consciousness.

In a neo-classical palace on Wilhelmplatz, to which he later added a severely functional new wing, the minister gathered a posse of young Party members, who were highly educated but lacked any administrative experience. Carefully assigned to departments for propaganda, film, radio, theatre, art, music and the press, they swamped the country with a publicity campaign the like of which had never been seen before. Goebbels' stated objective was clear: 'We are going to work on those people until we've got them at our feet.'

Having seized the reins of government, their job was now to gain mastery over public opinion. The messages were simple and memorable: 'You are nothing. Your nation is everything.' – '*Ein Volk, ein Reich, ein Führer.*' – 'The Jews are our misfortune.' The pernicious ideologies harked back to the Dark Ages, but the means of dissemination were ultra-modern. Cinema screens were used to project feelings of hope and elation. Loudspeakers in public areas and inexpensive radio-sets with the *Volksempfänger* (People's Receiver) label – popularly known as 'Goebbels' Gab' – enabled the new masters of the land to create an aura of omnipresence in the media. The vast geometry of mass rallies, the mystic symbolism of the flames, colours and banners, and the calendar of pseudo-religious festivals, scarcely allowed the *Volksgenossen* (national comrades) a moment to reflect for themselves.

Anyone who still trusted their own intelligence had difficulty in filtering a picture of reality from the flood of misleading reports, euphemisms and half-truths. Goebbels possessed the necessary guile to recognize that the most effective means of clouding people's awareness was not the obvious lie but manipulation of the truth. And he was convinced he could bend the masses to his will. He instructed his Nazi colleagues:

This is the secret of propaganda: those whom the propaganda is aimed at must become completely saturated with the ideas it contains, without ever realizing that they *are* being saturated. Obviously the propaganda has a purpose, but it must be so cleverly and innocently disguised that the person we intend to influence simply does not notice it.

To achieve this the opinion-former needed assistance. Unlike film, radio and news services, which were open to unlimited abuse from the outset, the terrain of the press first had to be ploughed up and resown to suit the purposes of the regime. Only some 5 per cent of newspapers initially flaunted the swastika. The covert appropriation of the remaining titles would continue right through to the end of the war. To begin with, therefore, the new controller of the press adopted a more effective approach: he nationalized the journalists. By law, editors became servants of the state. They required a licence and were subject to official directives. Instead of open pre-publication censorship, the desired tone of press reporting was achieved through detailed regulations governing language, which were implemented with eager obedience. Although Goebbels liked to compare the press to an orchestra playing the same tune on different instruments and with varying dynamics, in fact the sound that came from the newspaper offices was thoroughly tuneless and monotonous. The desks of the soloists whose virtuosity had once enhanced the press of the big cities, were already empty. 'There must be a thorough clear-out here as well,' the conductor had ordered as soon as he had the baton in his hand. 'Many of the people sitting here forming public opinion are utterly unsuited to the task. I'll soon weed them out.'

With the ban on all Jews from creative professions, which drove the country's intellectual elite into exile, the disabled hack satisfied his desire to avenge himself for those years of humiliation. With a speech loaded with pathos he inaugurated the burning of literary works which he himself could not hold a candle to. By instigating a wave of mindless violence the former pauper wanted to get even with Jewish businessmen for the material success that had been denied him. 'I am the most extreme of radicals,' the would-be Robespierre asserted. 'A new breed. Man as revolutionary.' Yet after only one day the regime abandoned the boycott. From now on the marginalizing of the Jews would be effected by pseudo-judicial means.

With a diabolical instinct the agitator made the strategy of cynical deception his own, advising his initiates in 1935:

If my propaganda put across the idea that 'the Jews have absolutely nothing more to lose!' – then you would hardly be surprised if they fought back. No, you must always leave things open. Like, for example, the masterly way the Führer did in his speech yesterday: '*We hope that – er, with these Jewish laws, a tolerable relationship between the German and the Jewish peoples can be brought about.*' Now that's what I call neat! That's real skill! But if he had immediately gone on to say: 'So much for *today*'s laws; but don't imagine that is the end of it; next month [. . .] there will be new laws, and *they* will have you back begging in the ghetto' – well, it would be no great surprise if the Jews mobilized the entire world against us. If, however, we give them a chance, the possibility of *some* kind of life, then the Jews will say to each other: '. . . Hey, guys, calm down a minute, *maybe* it'll be okay!'

The propaganda managers greeted their boss's exposition with glee.

In public the shadows of the racial policy were cleverly banished by sparkling pyrotechnics. In the cinema, on radio, on postcards the Germans were presented with the image of the venerable Field-Marshall von Hindenburg in Potsdam – standing for the conservative elite – offering a hand of welcome to the corporal from Austria. Millions of workers were seen, on 'their' new public holiday, to be celebrating the illusion of a 'national reconciliation' that crossed class barriers. The formerly unemployed were seen shouldering their shovels and marching into the 'Battle of Labour', to build endless ribbons of asphalt across the country. Germans acknowledged with religious fervour that the solitary figure enthroned above the uniform ranks of men and women was no longer just Hitler, nor even the Chancellor, but the *Führer* – a numinous being, not of this world. This leadership cult was Goebbels' most effective piece of propaganda – yet ironically he, the disciple, was as deluded by the self-created myth as was his master.

Goebbels stressed time and again that the population *en masse* is actually female. By that he meant that most people develop a more maternal instinct towards physically weak individuals than towards blond, blue-eyed giants.

Wilfred von Oven, Goebbels' personal adviser

The master of ceremonies could certainly not complain about being under-employed. In September 1933 he had an opportunity, as Germany's delegate to the League of Nations in Geneva, to display his talent for publicity to a foreign audience. But he would have dearly loved not only to glorify Hitler's policy but also to share in formulating it as adviser and Foreign Minister. The Master would certainly lend an ear to the eager advice of his apprentice – but he alone determined the course to be taken. Thus the Minister of Propaganda had to settle for a continuing turf-war with the Foreign Office and other departments over areas of responsibility and the direction of policy. When one of his Party rivals put the little doctor in his place, he could only go running to their Führer, who in fact preferred to give his support even-handedly in all such disputes.

Goebbels knew that only Hitler's patronage guaranteed his own survival among this pack of wolves. That is why, on 30 June 1934, he hurried in fright to his master's side on hearing that the head of the SA, Ernst Röhm, had been arrested and his top brass, along with dozens of other *personae non gratae*, had been executed. His reward was to be given the task of putting the best possible spin on the wilful murder of some 200 political opponents of the regime, namely as being necessary to crush a threatened *coup d'état*.

Nevertheless, Röhm's accomplices and the 'Jewish gutter-press' abroad presented only moderately attractive targets for Goebbels' impassioned tirades. The 'fighting days' were Goebbel's greatest period. Now that political opposition had been suppressed, and the shouts of '*Heil Hitler*' drowned out any disrespectful interjections, his own verbal assaults gradually subsided into silence. The battle with the Church remained a sideshow. Doggedly, the one-time altar-boy turned his aggression against the clergy who were refusing to accept a complete takeover by the state, with its substitute creed. With Hitler's blessing, as always, he fabricated horror stories about moral depravity in Church institutions and launched a series of prosecutions against priests and members of monastic orders. But unfortunately for him, he gained no popularity this way. The mood of the people, for him the indispensable barometer of his campaigns, was stubbornly negative. The repulsive exercise had to be cancelled.

As the years passed, the aggressive agitator transformed himself into the director of a gigantic dream factory producing beautiful make-believe. Referendums showed almost unlimited support for the regime. The drummer retreated into the background.

Goebbels made up for this creeping atrophy of his importance in the ranks of the leadership by energetically accumulating status-symbols in his private life. In 1936 he and his family moved to an imposing country house on the picturesque Schwanenwerder peninsula that juts into the Wannsee lake near Berlin. The previous owner had been Jewish, and Goebbels had borrowed the purchase price of 350,000 marks from Max Amann, Hitler's aide and owner of the Nazi newspaper, the *Völkischer Beobachter* (*National Observer*). The money was an 'advance' against the posthumous publication of his diaries twenty years after his death. Later he forced the Jewish owner of the adjoining property to sell it to him for a pittance, so that he could enlarge his own estate. To enhance his showplace, the successful social climber added a two-seater Mercedes sports-car to his fleet of vehicles and treated himself to a large, and by his own admission, 'rather expensive' yacht, to moor alongside his motor-cruiser, the *Baldur*.

> He radiated something which made all women flock to him. It was something that can hardly be described.
> *Barbara von Kalkreuth, sculptress and friend of the Goebbels family*

To the man of iron will and rigorous conscience such outward extravagance seemed entirely appropriate in view of the great sacrifices he was forced to make as a leading public figure. He instructed his Nazi colleagues:

If I were to spell out to you just how much I have to go without in my life, because I am who I am, then I could prove to you that eighty per cent of the things other people can do, I myself am not free to enjoy. I can't go into a restaurant, can't go into a hotel, can't go into a bar, can't go to a variety show, can't just get in my car and drive off into the blue, can't go for a walk in the street, can't devote myself to my family, and if I buy myself a new suit, I first have to check: Is this a Jewish firm?

On this point, Goebbels did not in fact need to worry. The white outfits that the Minister wore by choice were custom-made by a tailor who, needless to say, was a member of the Nazi Party. Goebbels' hands were always carefully manicured and he took instruction in social etiquette from his aristocratic aides. Thus equipped, the uncrowned king of Berlin used the occasion of the 1936 Olympic Games to invite more than 3,000 guests from all over the world to a reception on the magnificently appointed Peacock Island in the Havel Lake. The glittering and extravagant party was intended to divert some of the attention away from the great sporting spectacle and towards the man who had been instrumental in organizing it. But due to the presence among the distinguished guests of some veteran thugs from the 'fighting days', the night of elegance degenerated into an orgy of drinking and punch-ups which scandalized polite society.

Undeterred, the *arriviste* continued to work on his image as a 'man of the world'. In friendly Italy, ruled by his admired 'Duce', Mussolini, he delighted in attending film festivals in the guise of Germany's emissary. Back home he arranged with the Chief Burgomaster of Berlin to be given an apartment block beside the Bogensee Lake, north of the city, but soon found this 'too small and impractical'. So it was enlarged to form a small complex of five spacious, country house-style buildings. The main residence alone contained twenty-one rooms, a private cinema, air-conditioning, hot-air heating, five bathrooms, a tapestry costing 25,000 marks, windows that could be lowered electrically and a bar. Though situated in a protected area of scenic beauty where building was forbidden, his neighbour Hermann Göring, in his capacity as Reich Master of Forests, generously looked the other way. Unfortunately it was not possible to overlook the 2.26 million Reichsmarks that the project cost. However, as luck would have it, the construction client also held the post of head of the recently nationalized film industry. And so Ufa, the film company, obligingly footed the bill.

Goebbels was quite happy to leave the financing of his third home to the state. For the ministerial palace in the government district was there – as he lectured the sober men from the accounts department – so that he could meet the 'representational obligations which are imposed on me to a steadily increasing degree', and for this noble purpose the total sum of 3.2 million Reichsmarks did not seem excessive. Half a million marks were estimated just for decorating the ground floor and the private suites. On the first site visit the client was far from satisfied with the results, as can be seen from his five-page list of complaints. However, thanks to a minor adjustment to his departmental budget at the expense of the art and theatre funds, all the Minister's desired alterations could be catered for.

> Long talk with Magda. She is very loving and sweet to me. And I love her very much too. It is so good to possess someone who belongs to one totally.
> *Goebbels, shortly before his affaire with Lida Baarova, 1938*

These prestigious properties formed a fitting backdrop for the public presentation of an exemplary family idyll. His wife Magda fulfilled her motherhood quota in true accordance with Nazi doctrine and 'presented the Führer' with six children: Helga (born 1932), Hilde (1934), Helmut (1935), Holde (1937), Hedda (1938) and Heide (1940) were just as blond, obedient and credulous, as the Reich's publicity chief could wish. Dressed in white they had walk-on parts in 'Uncle Führer's' favourite performance as a lover of children. Visitors to the house were greeted with a coy chorus of 'heils', and the press presented the children, together with the Minister and his lady, as the showcase family of the Third Reich.

The opportunities for harmonious group photographs were admittedly rather few and far between. The industrious propaganda boss was usually at his desk from early morning until late in the evening, and quite often at weekends. His diary was filled with film premieres, receptions, studio visits and foreign trips. And any time that remained was devoted less to his marital duties than to his almost obsessive desire for other women. 'Every woman attracts me madly,' he confided to his diary as early as 1926. 'I prowl around like a hungry wolf. And yet I'm as shy as a kid.'

> Marriage would be agony for me. The voice of Eros speaks loud within me!
>
> *Goebbels, 1926*

Later the skirt-chaser was freed from this embarrassment by the fact that most of the women he targeted were dependent on his goodwill. When it came to handing out film roles, he had the last word; he could make or break careers. Yet it would be wrong to attribute his amours purely to the 'aphrodisiac of power'. The literate Lothario knew just how to dazzle women with quickfire repartee, wit and compliments.

It is true that he probably placed less value on successful conquest than on having a reputation as a seducer. Stéphane Roussel, who was then the female Berlin correspondent of *Le Matin*, recalls:

> In those days Berlin was a city of rumour. Our job wasn't always easy. Getting hold of information and then passing it on, were both dangerous. But one thing was easy to get a handle on, because Goebbels wanted people to talk about it: Goebbels, the ladykiller. We got the smallest details about his affaires with actresses, especially filmstars. You were meant to know that this or that woman had once spent a night with the great little Goebbels.

It mattered not whether an invitation to tea at his country house was merely restricted to polite conversation or whether it actually led on to something else. It was important to the seducer only that the rumour factory treated him as a Casanova. He orchestrated a whispering campaign on his own behalf. How much he would prefer to be known as the 'Babelsberg Buck' (after the film studio he frequented) than as a club-footed Mephistopheles! In the guise of Don Juan he could overcome his complexes and with no false modesty place himself among the great men of history. 'Louis XIV of France, Charles II of England, and even the victorious Napoleon,' he announced boldly, 'took as many women as they wanted, and yet their people idolized them.'

My film, *The Voice from the Ether*, was an incredible success. I was summoned to the Ministry of Propaganda. Goebbels was attractive and charming. We walked for a bit and then he invited me out for a drive. Well, of course he then made . . . advances. I thought it was appalling and acted so hysterically that he gave up. Before I was driven home, he just said to me: 'You'll never make a career like that.' Soon afterwards we heard that the filming had been suspended.

Anneliese Uhlig, actress

For him, affaires were just another status-symbol; and the women themselves no more than decorative accessories. In his sweeping disdain for them he was equal with Hitler, writing as Goebbels the novelist:

It is the woman's task to be beautiful and bear children. That is by no means as harsh and primitive as it sounds. The female bird preens for her male and hatches eggs for him. In return the male brings back food. At other times he stands guard and wards off the enemy.

But even this doughty Papageno was not immune to romantic emotion. In one case a brief assignation turned into a fateful love-affaire. *Hour of Temptation* was the highly appropriate title of the film which drew Goebbels' attention to the Czech actress, Lida Baarova. Then the old routine started: flowers, invitations, film parts and flattering words. After wavering at first the twenty-two-year-old Lida, who at the time was still engaged to the actor

Gustav Fröhlich, rather took to the mighty Minister who was courting her. And for Goebbels it was like a second springtime. Whenever possible, he took the young woman to his country retreat on the Bogensee, where they would not be disturbed. He tried his hand, unsuccessfully, at home cooking, played the piano to her and lost his head in a schoolboy romance. The studio chief even went as far as putting into production a feature film with Lida in the starring role. It was to be a thinly disguised version of their own love-story, but unsurprisingly it was swiftly vetoed. The couple began quite brazenly to appear in the limelight at film premieres, until the affaire was not only the talk of the town, but also raised official eyebrows. As was inevitable, his wife, who for her part did not always consider marital fidelity the ultimate virtue, got wind of his activities, and initially an attempt was made to arrange a *ménage à trois*. But this threesome with Magda's young rival could not last. Goebbels' vows of loyalty proved to be a deceptive ploy and his distraught spouse finally considered divorce.

> Last night another long talk with Magda, which was nothing but humiliation for me. I will never forget what she did to me. She is so hard and cruel.
> *Goebbels, during his affaire with Lida Baarova, 1938*

However, in the Third Reich decisions of this kind could only be made at the top. The Minister's rivals at Hitler's court had in any case taken every opportunity to convey full details of Goebbels' piquant affaires to the supreme arbiter himself. The Master tended graciously to overlook the loose lifestyle of his disciple. But a divorce scandal? How would that play, so soon after the furore created by the marriage of his Defence Minister, Werner von Blomberg, to a former prostitute? An amorous entanglement with a Czech woman, just when the dictator was planning the occupation of her homeland? A Propaganda Minister prepared to resign and emigrate, at a time when he needed to put on a show of strength to the rest of the world? For Hitler it was out of the question.

He pronounced an edict, which rang like a knell in the ears of the wayward lover. He commanded that Goebbels and his wife reach a reconciliation and strictly banned any further contact with Lida Baarova. The budding diva's film career came to an abrupt end. From now on Gestapo agents and bugging-devices recorded their every movement. The separated pair both toyed with thoughts of suicide and Goebbels' diary was saturated with lachrymose self-pity: 'It is almost as though I am living in a dream. Life is so hard and cruel.'

The relationship between Hitler and Goebbels was much less coloured by personal feelings than, say, that between Hitler and Speer. Hitler admired Goebbels very much, and rated his ability highly. But there was no note of friendship there. Hitler knew Goebbels' weakness: that he often exploited his position to get his hands on actresses. And that was utterly foreign to Hitler's nature.

Traudl Junge, Hitler's secretary

Not only did people grudge him his happiness in love, now he even risked losing the grace of the Almighty – and that to the undisguised joy of his opponents. Catastrophe had struck. At the centre of power Goebbels saw himself being sidelined. Receptions and talks were now being held without him. The little doctor was simultaneously frightened and impressed by his Master's chilling decree. Yet there was no question but that he must bow to this verdict. Hitler's goodwill was more important to him than any inner emotional yearnings. 'I will be adamant,' he vowed to his diary, 'though my heart is close to breaking. And now a new life begins. A life that is hard, cruel and devoted only to duty. My youth is now at an end.'

After a brief period of grace, Lida Baarova was deported to Prague with Goebbels' consent. A little later, the unfortunate woman would see German troops marching into the city. And on the Berghof, under Hitler's eye, the estranged couple concluded a new marriage contract. Although the affaire would be forgotten by the world, Goebbels' reputation was at an all-time low.

The relationship between Goebbels and Hitler did not always remain the same. During the Czechoslovakian crisis, for example, Goebbels played no part at all. It was clear even then that he would not face a major hostile engagement. Early in 1939 he invited me to a meal. When the conversation turned to Poland, he suddenly went very quiet and said to me: 'I am rather afraid it will go wrong. And if it does, then God help us.'

Heinrich Hunke, Head of the Foreign Department in the Ministry of Propaganda

Others would be made to atone for his misdeeds. The opportunity to present himself once more as a zealous and fanatical henchman arose at the annual commemoration of Hitler's amateurish attempt at a *coup d'état* in 1923. In Munich, on 9 November 1938, the assembled 'old campaigners' received the news that a junior diplomat in the German embassy in Paris had been shot by a young Jew named Herschel Grynspan, who wanted to protest about the deportation of his parents. This was ideal tinder for the political arsonist; it gave him the chance to vent his hate against the 'criminal Jewish rabble' and pose as the most radical of hell-raisers, as he had done in the old 'fighting days'. Carefully staged riots broke out, disguised as spontaneous outbreaks of popular indignation – these had been his speciality, ever since the days when his accomplices in Berlin had attacked 'Jewish-looking' passers-by, or ruined a showing of the pacifist film *All Quiet on the Western Front* by releasing stink-bombs and white mice.

Viewed a film made in mental institutions as a justification for the Sterilisation Law. Appalling material. But brilliant shots. Just looking at it makes the blood run cold. Making those people infertile can only be a blessing.

Goebbels, 1936

This time the incitement had deadly consequences: 'I immediately issue identical instructions to the police and the Party. Then I give a brief talk on the subject to the party leadership.' Such was the laconic version of his inflammatory speech that Goebbels committed to his diary, adding 'Thunderous applause'. The Nazi assault units knew what was expected of them. Throughout the Reich, SA men in civilian clothes set fire to synagogues, demolished and looted Jewish-owned shops, beat up and killed members of the ostracized minority. Over 20,000 people were loaded onto trucks like cattle and shipped off to concentration-camps. An internal Party report later noted that 'the verbal instructions of the Head of Reich Propaganda were well understood by all the party leaders present to mean that the Party should not be seen as the initiator, but in reality was to be responsible for organizing and carrying out the action.'

The man pulling the strings took a furtive delight in the widespread devastation that he had sparked off, noting in his diary with a *frisson* of pride:

> I make for the hotel and see a blood-red sky. The synagogue is on fire. We make sure the fire service does just enough to save the surrounding buildings. Apart from that, let it burn. The shock-troops have done an awesome job. . . . As I drive to the hotel, I hear the shattering of window-panes. Bravo, bravo! The synagogues are burning like great blast-furnaces. German property is not at risk.

But the reputation of the regime *was* at risk. So the fire-raiser earned no praise, only harsh criticism for his excess of zeal and the uncontrollable violence. Himmler, the Gestapo Chief and his Deputy, Heydrich, felt their authority had been infringed, Göring complained about the damage to the economy, and Hitler was concerned about Germany's image abroad. The removal of the Jews from public life should be carried out 'noiselessly' by bureaucratic regulation. From then on it was done that way. As the worldwide protests soon ebbed away, Goebbels was once again on top of things. True, Hitler kept his henchman well away from the business of government, but he needed him to prepare the population mentally for the coming war.

According to the *vox populi*, which means, for example, my rather talkative barber, the general mood is going rapidly downhill. There have even been complaints about high party functionaries apparently made in a tone and with a lack of caution that are quite unheard of: 'Complaints about what, particularly?' I asked. 'About everything!' was the answer. 'Joseph' [Goebbels] was said to be the chief offender. But the whole mix-up of party and state couldn't go on like this. Then all this big-noise posturing, with Goebbels again at the top of the list.

Ulrich von Hassell, German diplomat and anti-Nazi

On Hitler's fiftieth birthday, Goebbels' propaganda team presented the head of state as a military commander bent on war, taking the salute at the greatest parade of armed forces in German history, which took place along Berlin's newly built east–west thoroughfare. The martial display acted like a call to arms. The promoter received the signals with a show of confidence: 'The goddess of victory gleams in the blazing sunshine. A wonderful portent.'

In reality Goebbels was not at all comfortable with the thought that a war in the west might shatter the structure they had so carefully created. The man he suspected of pushing Hitler into war was the Foreign Minister, Joachim von Ribbentrop. In consternation he watched as his adversary forged the pact in Moscow between the arch-enemies Hitler and Stalin. Although he proclaimed the pact as a 'brilliant move in the propaganda game', and affirmed his faith in the 'genius of the Führer', the alliance with 'World Enemy Number One' seemed to him nonetheless 'rather strange'.

The same was true of Hitler's determination to go to war. The Propaganda Minister, it is true, followed his instructions and used fabricated reports of Polish atrocities to prepare the ground for the subjugation of Germany's eastern neighbour, whom Hitler had once personally assured of his peaceful intentions. Secretly, however, he hoped that the Western powers would show restraint and not declare the invasion to be a *casus belli*.

At the same time, the pint-sized civilian hoped he would not disappear from Hitler's view behind the epaulettes of the top military brass. The self-deception was in vain. London and Paris declared war on the Reich, and Goebbels, 'downcast and turned in on himself', as an observer remarked, was momentarily assailed by doubts about the 'infallibility' of his Führer.

These anxieties were soon dispelled, not only by the 'lightning victories' of the *blitzkrieg* and the paralysis of the French and British, but also by a bomb which had exploded nine months previously. The bomb in question had been constructed and placed by a courageous south German cabinet-maker named Georg Elser. It went off on the evening of 8 November 1939 in Munich's *Bürgerbräukeller* – just a few minutes after Hitler had prematurely left the hall. His credulous acolyte saw in the coincidence a sign of providence: 'He stands under the shield of the Almighty,' Goebbels mused in his diary. 'He will not die until his mission has been fulfilled.'

The 'mission' of the warlord included the liquidation of Poland's elite, the enslavement of its workforce and the corralling of its Jewish population into ghettoes. Once again Goebbels wanted to see for himself, and used a tour of inspection in occupied Poland to stoke up his racial hatred. His personal witnessing of the misery caused by the German reign of terror in Lodz is described in his diary as cynically as if he had been visiting a zoo – while always intent on seeking confirmation of his loathsome prejudice:

> Drive through the ghetto. We get out of the car and look at everything thoroughly. It is indescribable. These are not even human beings, they are animals. Therefore our task is not a humanitarian but a surgical one. We have to make amputations here. Quite drastic ones.

That is why on the following day he had nothing more urgent to do than once more to display to the Führer his credentials as an

overzealous anti-Semite: 'To see the Führer. I report on my Polish
trip, which interests him very much. Most of all, he agreed fully
with my exposition of the Jewish problem. The Jew is a waste
product. More of a clinical than a social matter.' He had no need
to convince his mentor on this point. At a time when the military
were setting the pace, Goebbels believed that turning Hitler's
declaration of war on Jews into an administrative policy was *his*
territory, somewhere he could score some points. Furthermore,
the job appealed to the paper-pusher's thirst for revenge. He
noted for posterity:

> I protest to the Führer about the fact that under the food
> rationing programme Jews are treated exactly the same as
> Germans. That will be abolished right away, I tell the Führer
> about our film on the Jews. He makes some suggestions. The
> main thing is that at this moment the film is a very valuable
> propaganda tool for us.

The film, entitled *The Eternal Jew*, was the most poisonous
concoction ever turned out by a propaganda factory. People were
put on a par with rats. Destruction by word and image was the
precursor of their physical annihilation. 'An anti-Semitic film of the
very sort we wanted' was the delighted verdict of the man whose
film industry had hitherto been more concerned with distractions
and entertainment.

Goebbels also provided suitably martial propaganda to
accompany Hitler's military campaigns. Every attack was greeted
with a drum-roll of publicity. The minister stoked up resentment
against British 'plutocrats' and French 'warmongers' and as the
situation required he mobilized morale or diverted attention from
invasion plans. The opinion-formers were not only targeting the
domestic population. Cleverly designed leaflets, foreign-language
broadcasts and secret transmitters in enemy territory were all
aimed at undermining the fighting spirit of the opposition. The
battle of words was waged with particular bitterness against
Britain. The British Prime Minister, Winston Churchill, appeared
in a distorted image as a corrupt whisky-toper in the grip of the
'Jewish plutocratic clique'. Goebbels was in his element. Now he

had an adversary again. Now he could attack and respond to attacks as he did in the glorious 'fighting days'. And now he had victories to proclaim.

> He knew how to put people into a trance-like state of fervour. He was a master of the lie, a cynic – and out of all the top Nazis he was definitely the most intelligent and eloquent.
>
> *Bert Naegele, war reporter*

In 1940, when Hitler returned in triumph to Berlin from signing the armistice with France at Compiègne, the very place where the German Army had laid down their arms in 1918, his trusty squire prepared for him a reception without compare. The war-leader, whom many now regarded as a supernatural figure, rode over a sea of flowers and past unending ranks of jubilant Germans. The humiliating capitulation of the First World War now seemed gloriously avenged. 'The shame has now been erased. We feel as if reborn,' an exultant Goebbels told his diary. Also erased were the worries and fears which had plagued him since the outbreak of war: 'What we have carried out at the behest of a higher historical destiny, is the judgement of God. The Führer is very human and touchingly kind. He is the greatest historical genius we have ever possessed. It is an honour to be permitted to serve him.'

However, the honour of being made privy to his Führer's plans continued to be denied him. While Hitler had long been working on plans for the invasion of the Soviet Union, Goebbels was still bemoaning the pact with the 'sub-human Bolshevists'. When the Soviet Foreign Minister, Vyatcheslav Molotov, visited Berlin late in 1940, the most insecure member of the 'master race' professed disgust at the appearance of the guests from Moscow. 'Not a single distinguished face. It's as if they wanted fully to confirm our theoretical views about the nature of Bolshevist ideology.' He vetoed the printing of anything in the newspapers which might suggest appreciation of Russia's culture or way of life and alerted his spin-doctors 'not to allow into

Germany any hint of Bolshevist leanings or conviction'. In his condemnation of the East he was a loyal follower of the Führer. Both were waiting impatiently for the real ideological crusade to begin: 'Sooner or later we must settle matters with Russia. When, I don't know, but I *do* know it will happen.'

It was in March 1941 that Hitler put Goebbels in the picture. In preparing for the greatest military invasion of all time, the war-leader was more than ever dependent on support and diversionary tactics by his propaganda department. The initiate, full of pride and eager for the fray, noted:

> The big operation then comes later: against R[ussia]. It is being very carefully camouflaged, only a very few know about it. It will begin with extensive troop-movements to the *west*. We will divert suspicion to every quarter except the east. A dummy operation against England will be prepared, and then we head off like lightning in the other direction. No holds barred.

In this game of deception a special role was assigned to the Minister of Propaganda. He wrote an article for the official Nazi paper, *Völkischer Beobachter*, about the occupation of Crete, which was laden with allusion and suggested between the lines the possibility of a landing in Britain. Then, before the copies were distributed he had them confiscated with a great kerfuffle. From this, foreign observers were intended to conclude that the author had not been able to resist disclosing Germany's war-plans. With this stage-managed revelation of an impending invasion on the one hand, and a flood of conflicting and misleading reports on the other, the propaganda coup seemed to be a success. Even in Moscow there was total surprise when, in the early hours of 22 June 1941, the invasion of the Soviet Union began.

'The breath of history is audible,' wrote Goebbels poetically in his diary. 'A great and wonderful age, in which a new Reich is born. Not without birth-pangs, it is true, but it rises towards the light.' The midwife had done his preparatory work thoroughly. Shamelessly stealing the fanfare chords from Liszt's *Preludes*, he had a 'signature tune' composed to introduce special reports on 'Operation Barbarossa'. In great secrecy he had 800,000 copies made of Hitler's clarion call to his unsuspecting 'national comrades'. And this time it was his turn to provide the Germans with a plausible explanation of the war. 'Psychologically speaking, the whole business presents some problems. Parallels with Napoleon etc.,' he had earlier reasoned, rightly, in view of the risky expansion of the war in a vast second front against the former pact partners. 'But that can be overcome with anti-Bolshevism.'

This was a subject in which he was well versed. His propaganda sold the invasion to a sceptical population as 'Europe's crusade against Bolshevism'. In a 'deed which will change world history,' the Führer had barely averted an 'annihilating Mongol onslaught'. The legend of Hitler's pre-emptive strike had the effect of concealing the true ideological nature of this campaign of destruction. In his diary Goebbels was more frank: 'The thing we have fought against all our lives, we are now about to wipe out.' He banished any fears with a show of confidence: 'Bolshevism will collapse like a house of cards. We are embarking on a series of victories without equal,' he persuaded himself. 'I rate the fighting capacity of the Russians very low, even lower than the Führer does. If ever an action was a sure thing, then it's this one.'

> It was hammered into us by propaganda that the Russians were primitive people, who were dirty and had no culture. When I went to fight in 1945, I thought the Russians were animals who you had to kill quickly, before they killed you.
> *Karl-Heinz Bialdiga, member of Hitler Youth and Volkssturm*

But the only sure thing was that, after the first few weeks of success, this prognosis proved to be self-delusion. Only a month after the launch of the assault, a subdued Hitler admitted his fatal miscalculation to Goebbels:

The Führer gives me a detailed appreciation of the military situation. In the past few weeks it has at times been critical. It is clear we have completely underestimated Soviet strike-power and particularly the arms and equipment of the Red Army. We weren't even close to getting a picture of what the Bolshevists had at their disposal.

This revelation cast the first shadows over the aura of infallibility surrounding 'the greatest military leader of all times': 'The Führer is inwardly very aggrieved that he let himself be so misled by reports from the Soviet Union about the Bolshevists' potential. . . . He has suffered badly from it. We are now in a major crisis,' wrote Goebbels, while his newsreels blanketed the German population with triumphant reports of victory. The campaign got bogged down in the autumn mud and was defeated by the sub-zero temperatures of winter. Outside Moscow the German troops had no chance against well-armed Siberian units. In their supreme arrogance the German High Command had failed to provide their men with adequate winter clothing and equipment.

For the little doctor the crisis was good for business. As a would-be Army Commander in an ill-fitting uniform the inexperienced civilian was a figure of fun. But as field chaplain to the nation he could win his laurels. He believed he could make up for the military failures in the field by rousing the spirit of the nation with his oratory. He saw that the moment had finally come to transform an indifferent society into a 'community of destiny' acting with a single purpose. In a large-scale campaign he had wool and winter clothing collected by the ton as 'a Christmas present from home for the lads at the Front'. Instead of a mood of victory he demanded self-sacrifice, echoing the 'Blood, sweat and tears' slogan of his secretly admired adversary, Winston Churchill. Those who are not fighting at the front, he insisted, must work tirelessly at home to equip and supply the armed forces.

It is our aim to annihilate the Jews. Whether we win the war or are defeated, this goal must and will be achieved. Should the German army be forced to retreat, on its way it will destroy every last Jew on earth.

Goebbels, prior to 1944

This applied especially to the Jewish citizens of his *Gau*:

> I will put the ultimate demand to them, either to play their part
> in the labour organisation, and soon, or else to accept that, with
> 78,000 Jews in total, food rations will only be provided for the
> 23,000 of them who are working. If that brings the Jews to the
> edge of starvation, then we'll soon get them to work.

In reality, he was less concerned to exploit the hated minority than to
achieve their public humiliation. Since 'strong sentimental
objections' had delayed his project to 'make Berlin into a Jew-free
zone', awaiting death was to become a hell for the Jews. More
inventive and more treacherous than any other anti-Semite, Goebbels
dreamed up an endless stream of discriminatory measures: step by
step, he banned Jews from owning bicycles, typewriters, books,
gramophones, refrigerators, cookers and radio sets, from travel on
public transport, entry into cinemas, opera-houses, public baths and
parks, and finally even drove them from their own homes. From his
hate-filled brain came the notion of publicly branding the persecuted
race with a yellow Star of David. He triumphantly reported in his
diary how Hitler had given in to his insistence. Goebbels wanted to
enhance his reputation as a fanatical racist – now that he knew the
plans for murdering Jews in the rear of the Eastern Front were being
put into effect. He was all too precisely informed that the 'final
solution to the Jewish question' meant millions of deaths by
asphyxiation, writing in his diary on 27 March 1942:

> From the *Generalgouvernment* [German-administered Poland]
> Jews are being deported eastward, starting with Lublin. The
> procedure to be adopted is pretty barbaric and not to be
> described in more detail. Not many of the Jews themselves will
> be left. In broad terms it can be stated that 60 per cent of them
> have to be liquidated, while only 40 per cent can be put to
> work. The former *Gauleiter* of Vienna, who is carrying out this
> operation, is doing so with circumspection, using a method that
> does not attract too much attention. A sentence is being carried
> out on the Jews, which is admittedly barbaric but which they
> fully deserve.

Even in public the Minister of Propaganda made no secret of what he knew. His infamous attempt to justify this genocide could be read almost word for word in the glossy and prestigious weekly magazine, *Das Reich*, on 16 November. Referring back to Hitler's verdict of annihilation at the beginning of the war, Goebbels wrote in his column: 'We are now seeing the fulfilment of this prophecy and a fate awaits the Jews which, though hard, is more than deserved. Sympathy or even regret over this is entirely inappropriate.'

Goebbels was fully aware that this crime of millennial proportions would in the end destroy all bridges to the community of civilized nations. He saw there was no turning back and so for him the war now had only one purpose – to postpone the final day of reckoning – true to the dictates of his master: 'The Führer says: right or wrong, we have to win. It is the only way,' he noted in his diary, adding: 'We have put so much into it anyway that we *must* win, otherwise our whole nation, with us at the head of it, and everything that is dear to us, will be wiped out.'

In the last few months it was absolutely clear to Goebbels that there was no hope of victory. Even so, he and Hitler never abandoned the idea that the alliance between the western powers and the Soviet Union could not survive in the long run. Admittedly neither believed in a victory, but they hoped at least for a tolerable peace settlement.

Wilfred von Oven, personal adviser to Goebbels

His colleagues could, in this event, rely on Goebbels to arrange his own exit. He knew he had nothing more to lose and made this a theme of his propaganda. All or nothing, victory or destruction – the Propaganda Minister's answer to the débâcle on the Russian Front, which was now obvious in Stalingrad, was in the phrase 'total war': no one could any longer escape involvement in the war machine. Those who could not prove that their employment was 'war-essential' were forced either to enlist or to work in arms manufacture. An additional million-strong army recruited in this way was expected to turn the war round in a 'decisive battle'. Yet the amateur strategist still found no support for his crude visions. His principal weapon was still the word.

So it was that on 18 February 1943, in his famous, or rather notorious Sports Palace speech, he sought popular endorsement for his obsessional concept of 'total war'. At his command were the psychological skills with which to steer the carefully selected audience in the direction he wanted. Using all the tools of rhetoric, he ran the gamut from flattery to condemnation; with promises and threats, mockery and hate, he mobilized pride, envy and fear, and in a constantly intensifying performance of high drama, he literally robbed his audience of their powers of reason. At the end he posed ten rhetorical questions which evoked not merely approval but a wave of ecstasy. With the same calculating coldness that he had applied to planning and rehearsing every detail of his performance, the orator later privately gave this dismissive verdict on his audience: 'If I had recommended that they go and jump from the roof of a tower-block, they would have done it.'

With this speech of speeches he assured his position as the Reich's Number One demagogue. While the rest of the leadership figures were keeping their heads down and Hitler had gone virtually silent in public, the agile agitator was constantly on the move, handing out medals to air-raid wardens, arranging special rations for people bombed out of their homes, rallying munitions workers to meet their quotas and preaching self-sacrifice on the radio. To show an example himself, Goebbels would only invite guests to his house if they surrendered their food-coupons in return for the meagre fare. His wife, with whom he was once more reconciled, courted publicity by taking the tram to work every day at the Telefunken factory.

Daily wartime life and nights of bombing drove the last traces of peace from the country. Yet Goebbels' totalitarian obsession was still far removed from reality. Not until the attempt on Hitler's life, on 20 June 1944, after which Hitler started suspecting betrayal all around him, did the Führer's loyal follower move to the centre of power. In Berlin he crushed the attempted coup with ruthless finality. His ambition had been finally realized. As 'Reich Director for Total War Deployment' he now had wide-ranging powers to stamp out the last remnants of civilian social life and to comb industry and commerce for reserves for the Front and munitions production. Goebbels himself described this function as 'war dictatorship'.

Although bureaucracy and personal string-pulling reduced the effectiveness of this recruitment campaign, the Germans were nonetheless now getting some idea of the real meaning of the term 'total war'. Hastily assembled reserve battalions could do nothing to halt the collapse of the German Front in the east or the advance of the Allies in the west – they could only prolong the agony.

Personally, even Goebbels scarcely had any illusions that the fiction of a final victory could be maintained, stating in his diary in mid-1944:

> The situation in the east causes me ever greater concern. Surely it must be possible in the end to halt the Front somewhere. If it goes on like this, the Soviets will very soon have reached our East Prussian frontier. I keep asking myself desperately, what the Führer is doing about it.

But with his public appearances Goebbels turned the myth of an imminent change in fortune into a widely held creed. Never short of a telling simile, he likened the war now to a feverish sickness, now to a marathon race, now to the changeable weather, in order to paint a convincing prospect of the 'final victory'. Since no amount of massaging could make reports from the Front bolster up this hope, Goebbels seized upon a new propaganda weapon, one which reality could not tarnish: he encouraged a belief in miracles. First he promised a secret 'wonder-weapon', which had the advantage that the most miraculous effects could be ascribed to it, since it had never yet been deployed. He then prophesied the imminent collapse of the Allied alliance, which, as in the Seven Years' War of the eighteenth century, would turn the tables in Germany's favour. Even at the end, when Soviet troops were already pressing in among the ruins of Berlin, he promised the liberation of the city by the fabled 'Wenck Army' (named after its putative commander), which existed on paper only.

Hitler's birthday! Hearing Goebbels' speech, the first I had voluntarily listened to, I wondered whether this was utter madness or simply guile; was he coolly playing a double game? Party chiefs are committing suicide, well over half of Germany is occupied, the Eastern Front is moving irresistibly westward . . . and Goebbels speaks as though victory is in sight.

Ursula von Kardorff, journalist and diarist of the Third Reich period, later anti-Nazi (Diary, 20 April 1945)

The more palpable the prospect of defeat, the fewer were those who gave credence to such promises. For most people what mattered was their own struggle for survival. The most gullible victims were to be found among those who had never heard any other message. The youngest in the population still trusted his words, allowed themselves to be dazzled by Goebbels' meretricious imagery and roused by his militant slogans.

When members of the Hitler Youth and elderly men marched past his outstretched arm carrying *Panzerfaust* grenade-launchers, Goebbels could at last feel like a soldier. The *Volkssturm* was the *Gauleiter*'s last contingent. With it he hoped to stage the defence of 'Fortress Berlin' as a heroic finale to his 'total war'. In the dying days of the war this epic but futile last stand would cost tens of thousands more lives. The organizer of the carnage had long since lost all touch with reality. His last piece of propaganda was his own legend. In order to give posterity an idea of his importance he had all his diaries committed to microfilm and shipped out of the capital.

As I was typing Hitler's will, Goebbels suddenly came in. I was shocked by his appearance. He was deathly pale and with tears in his eyes he said to me: 'Frau Junge, the Führer wants me to leave him, to take over a function in the new government. But I can't do that. I'm *Gauleiter* of Berlin. My place is at the Führer's side. I cannot abandon him.'

Traudl Junge, Hitler's secretary

After the other paladins had withdrawn from the city, he wished to portray himself as the last man of loyalty, standing obedient to his Führer to the end. In order to be as close to him as possible, he moved with his entire family into Hitler's gloomy bunker beneath the Reich Chancellery. At last he had achieved what he had longed for all his life: he had his master all to himself. Together with him he wanted to go down in history as the 'martyr' of his mania.

But Hitler upset his calculations by appointing him, in his political testament, to be his successor as Chancellor of the ramshackle Reich. The designated executor was thus not permitted to escape his responsibilities by committing suicide! He now had to brace himself for the darkest chapter in Germany's history. For a moment Goebbels was thunderstruck. But once Hitler had died by his own hand on 30 April, the ex-Führer had no further say in the execution of his instructions.

Goebbels, in an addendum to the testament, justified his own contemptible suicide:

In the maelstrom of betrayal that surrounds the Führer during these critical days of the war, there must at least be someone who will stand by him unquestioningly and to the death, even if that contravenes a formal command, however rational the thinking behind it, that is expressed in his political testament. For the first time in my life I must categorically refuse to follow an order from the Führer. My wife and my children join me in this refusal.

There was quite a scene in the bunker when we heard them say: 'The children are staying here!' Women from the kitchen and the office all came and pleaded on their knees with Frau Goebbels for the sake of the children. Hanna Reitsch, the pilot, came as well and wanted to fly the children out of Berlin. Frau Goebbels refused. Then the day came when Frau Goebbels prepared the children for their death, in my room. She put them in little white dresses and combed their hair, then went outside with them. Goebbels was not present. Dr Stumpfegger then went out to them, and Dr Naumann said to me: 'They'll get something sweet to drink and it'll all be over.' So then Stumpfegger administered poison to the children.

Rochus Misch, radio-operator in Hitler's bunker

The children were never asked. They could have had no inkling that their father, after his own utter downfall, had condemned them to death as well. They were to be the last victims of his blind fanaticism.

CHAPTER TWO

THE NUMBER TWO: HERMANN GÖRING

KNOPP/MÜLLNER

From the first moment I saw and heard him, I fell for him, hook, line and sinker.

I have no conscience! Adolf Hitler is my conscience.

Every bullet that leaves the barrel of a police pistol is my bullet.

Each time I face Hitler my heart drops into my boots.

I'm really a Renaissance man; I love magnificence.

I decide who is a Jew.

Anyone who tortures animals offends German national sentiment.

I wouldn't like to be a Jew in Germany.

It's terrible – Hitler has gone mad.

At least for twelve years I lived decently.

One day you will lay our bones in marble coffins.

Göring

Hermann will either be a great man or a criminal.

Franziska Göring, about her son, c. 1903

On Sunday 30 August Captain Göring's demands for a larger dose of Eudokal (a morphine derivative) became more and more urgent and he insisted on a quantity he himself had decided on. At about 5 p.m. he forced open the medicine-cupboard and took out two ampoules of 2 per cent Eudokal solution. Six nurses were unable to stop him and he adopted a threatening attitude. Captain Göring's wife was present and insisted that we give him what he asked for; she feared that in his rage the captain could kill someone.

Sister Anna Törnquist of the Aspuddens nursing-home, where Göring was treated as a patient in 1925.

You are a great intellect and a great man. You mustn't let people get you down. I love you so much, with body and soul, that I couldn't bear to lose you: and being a morphine addict is the same thing as committing suicide – every day you lose a little bit of your body and of your soul. You are in the grip of an evil spirit and an evil power, and your body is gradually wasting away. Rescue yourself and by doing so save me too.

Carin Göring, letter of 26 January 1927

Away with 'General' Göring, that hygiene-obsessed hangman with his three hundred uniforms, who wallows in lip-smacking gluttony and a bestial relish for the life-and-death power that a crazy destiny has dropped in his lap, and daily smears his horrific name across death-warrants on young people who, driven to desperate resistance for the sake of a political creed – however misguided – are many hundred times better than him.

Thomas Mann, 1933

The SA was nothing but a mob of gangsters and perverts! It's a damned good thing I got rid of them, otherwise they'd have done for us.

Göring, 1934

I dream of having an air force which, if ever the hour should strike, will descend on the enemy like an avenging host. Our opponent must feel he is beaten even before he has crossed swords with you.

Göring addressing young Luftwaffe officers in 1935

I may as well say it, since the war is over: The *Reichsmarschall* has been under the permanent influence of morphine. I have seen, when discussions were protracted and the effect of the morphine wore off, how the *Reichsmarschall* would fall asleep in a meeting. And he was commander-in-chief of the Luftwaffe!

Helmut Förster (General der Luftwaffe), May 1945

Göring arrives. The repulsive old roué. Wants to be a general. Why not straight to field-marshal? Göring's got fancy ideas. He rubs everyone up the wrong way with his arrogant rank-pulling. I hope the fat slob leaves soon.

Goebbels, diary, 1933

We've got to stop going for broke.

Göring to Hitler, 1938

All my life I've gone for broke.

Hitler's reply

We ought to be happy if after this war is over Germany has kept its 1933 frontiers.

Göring, 1942

Mein Führer! The supplying of the 6th Army in Stalingrad from the air is personally guaranteed by me. You can rely on it.

Göring, 1942

I hereby charge you with the task of making all necessary preparations, from an organizational standpoint, for a comprehensive resolution of the Jewish question in the German sphere of influence in Europe. In as far as this impinges on the jurisdictions of other central authorities, they are to be involved.

I further require you to present, at an early date, an overall draft plan of the organizational, practical and material measures to be taken in anticipation of carrying out the intended final solution of the Jewish question.

Göring to Heydrich, 31 July 1941

I have never expressed my approval of one race describing itself as master-race over another, but have only stressed the difference between races.

Göring before the Nuremberg War Crimes Tribunal, 1946

When I take an oath of allegiance, I cannot break it. Even for me it was hellishly hard to keep, I can tell you! Just try playing the crown prince for twelve whole years, always devoted to the king, even though disagreeing with many of his political actions, but incapable of doing anything about it and having to make the best of the situation.

Göring at Nuremberg, talking to the court psychologist, Gustave Gilbert, 1946

* * *

The prisoner Hermann Göring is not prepared for this, but his manner does not betray the fact. He looks drowsy, sunk in his chair in the first row of defendants, with his hands over his eyes. Now and then he raises his head to look briefly to his left. There, on the back wall of courtroom 600 of the justice building in Nuremberg, a cinema screen hangs between two massive portals. The room is in semi-darkness, only the dock and the judges' desk are theatrically lit by spotlights. Silence reigns. It is an appalled, numbing silence, broken by occasional sobbing or sighing, as though the whole court were having a nightmare. But Göring remains impassive. He has turned away from the images shown in filmed exhibit 2430-PS, but on his headphones he listens through an interpreter to the American commentator's description: 'In this concentration-camp near Leipzig over 200 political prisoners were burned alive. Other prisoners, originally numbering 350, were shot as they rushed out of the barracks . . .' For an hour the official evidential film of the American indictment on 29 November 1945 documents the crimes committed in the concentration-camps – acts of murder, for which Hermann Göring too, the second most senior figure in the Third Reich, bears responsibility. He dismisses them brusquely and hides behind the mask of the bluff but honest citizen taking refuge in cynicism. 'It was such an enjoyable afternoon,' he later complains in his cell. 'My telephone conversation about the Austrian business was read aloud and we all laughed about it. And then this ghastly film came on and simply spoilt everything.'

The unbearable films not only ruin Göring's mood. Above all they destroy the brazen illusion that it is possible with duplicitous words to cover up, indeed deny, unprecedented crimes. Göring would still be given the opportunity in 58 hours of cross-examination to deploy his rhetorical talent, charm and sheer *chutzpah*. But in the face of these images words have no power. He is probably aware of this and retreats into a shell of feigned ignorance. Göring acts the innocent. The once authoritative figure claims to have known nothing of mass-murder, even though he was involved in every act of inhuman violence, even though he had signed almost every anti-Jewish law, decree and death-warrant, and had authorized Reinhard Heydrich, the head of the *Reichsicherheitshauptamt* (Chief Office of National Security), to prepare the 'comprehensive resolution of the Jewish question'.

Göring removes his headphones, when it is proved that he contributed to the enslavement and slaughter of eleven-and-a-half million human beings. No, he can remember nothing.

'The higher one is placed,' he tries to convince a Defence Counsel, 'the less one sees of what is taking place at a lower level.'

'Did you learn nothing of the atrocities which the whole world knew about?' insisted the court psychologist, Gustave Gilbert.

'Oh, one heard no end of rumours, but of course one didn't believe anything of the sort.'

'Ugh, those mass-murders!' he explodes at one point. 'The whole thing is a damned disgrace. I would rather not speak of them, or even think about them.'

The question of the extermination of the Jews has stayed in my memory. Göring was present at two critical meetings and had signed certain documents. In the trial he first of all took the responsibility for it upon himself. But then he disputed everything and said that he had not intended it to be like that, that he believed the Jews had all emigrated and that he had not been aware of extermination-camps. That was quite unbelievable: the whole pose of the man now fell apart. In the end he looked pitiful.

Göring was the most interesting figure at the Nuremberg Trial. He either sat upright or lounged back, resting his arm somewhere. His body-language showed that he wouldn't stand for any nonsense. Even with his gestures and facial expressions he made sure that people had to pay attention to him.

Susanne von Paczensky, observer at the Nuremberg Trials

He also demands silence on the subject of his own guilt from his associates sitting with him in the dock or when being interrogated about genocide in the witness-box. Göring continues to believe he has authority over others and flies into a violent rage when SS General Erich von dem Bach-Zelewski speaks openly about mass-murder. For a brief moment he seems to lose all self-control, he leaps to his feet and can only with difficulty be restrained by the guards, as he splutters:

My God, that filthy bloody double-crossing swine! That cheap scoundrel! God damn him to hell! The dirty, numbskulled sonofabitch! He was the most notorious murderer of the whole damned bunch. The disgusting, stinking *Schweinehund*! Selling his soul to save his filthy neck!

Here we get an unfamiliar image of Göring. The baggy riding-breeches and the bluish grey jacket without medals or insignia flap like windless sails around the body of a man who once weighed 300 pounds. In prison he has lost 80 pounds. He is now free of his morphine addiction and after the cold-turkey cure appears to be in the best of physical shape. This Göring no longer resembles that 'vacantly smiling mollusc', described by the American prison Commandant, Burton C. Andrus, at the start of his incarceration. In the Nuremberg courtroom his eyes once again betray that cold determination which smoothed Hitler's path to power and ruthlessly eliminated his political opponents. He behaves almost with the confidence of a victor even though he knows that the gallows await him. The trial will be Göring's last public appearance and he is absolutely determined to leave a memorial to National Socialism and to himself – not as the 'Second Man' after Hitler but, as the American newspapers are calling him, the 'Number One Nazi'.

> I was the only man in Germany, other than Hitler, who had my *own* authority, not derived from him. The people just needed someone to love, and the Führer was often too distant from the masses. So they latched on to me.
>
> *Göring at the Nuremberg Trial, 1945*

As Hitler's designated successor he was made for the role of embodying the regime of terror in the dock. Once Hitler had slunk away from his responsibilities the weight of accusations fell chiefly on Göring, as Hitler's 'most loyal champion': Subversion of peace, preparation for a war of aggression, crimes against humanity – Göring accepted these charges calmly. 'The victor,' he noted on the indictment document 'will always be the judge and the defeated always the accused.' He wanted to appear before the tribunal self-assured, serene and superior, but like any actor he was stricken with stage-fright. 'The slight tremor in his hands and his strained facial expression were signs of his nervous tension,' observed Gilbert before the start of the trial, 'and he began a dress-rehearsal of his part as the agonized nobleman about to go on stage for the last act.' On the second day of the hearing, after months of waiting in his cell, the curtain finally rose. 'Before I answer the question of the court, as to whether I plead guilty or not guilty . . .' Göring managed to say, before immediately being instructed by the presiding judge to offer his plea without further ado. Only then did Göring say: 'I plead not guilty to the charges as stated.'

At Nuremberg he wanted to go on playing the role he had played in the Nazi Reich, as the Number Two man. He tried to manipulate his fellow-prisoners. He reminded them of their duty to stand up for Hitler. During the lunch-break he always told them how they should behave and what they should say during the trial. On some of the defendants – Ribbentrop, Sauckel, Streicher – he certainly exercised an influence. Others – Schacht, Speer and Frank – were against him and preferred to organize their defence independently. In the end they complained about him and at that point Göring became isolated from the others.

William Jackson, son and assistant of the Chief Prosecutor at Nuremberg

The defendant would have ample opportunity to play the part of persecuted innocence and to give account of a life characterized by status-seeking and acquisitiveness, by insatiable hunger for luxury, power and recognition. From being a fighter pilot in the First World War he had risen to Commander-in-Chief of the Luftwaffe, economic supremo and 'Minister of Everything', who collected offices, honours and works of art as other people collect stamps – a glittering personality to whom many labels were attached: puffed-up, conceited clothes-horse; coldly calculating criminal; morphine addict and misguided officer. A confident talker, socially at ease, he represented the jovial face of the Third Reich: popular, portly and pitiless – a cold tyrant dressed up as a philanthropist; a 'perfumed Nero', whom Hitler at first called a 'friend', then condemned as a 'failure', because the Luftwaffe could not keep his promises, and, as the war headed for catastrophe, he gave himself up to good living, strutting around in make-believe uniforms, remote from reality and a prey to drugs 'He was skilful, cunning, cold-blooded, courageous and had an will of iron,' was how the French Ambassador, André François-Poncet described him. 'And he was a cynic. Though capable of chivalry and magnanimity, he could be implacably cruel.' Göring saw himself in a friendlier light: 'I am what I have always been: the last Renaissance man.'

A penchant for pomp and pageantry had been part of his character since childhood, since the years spent in Schloss Mauterndorf and Burg Veldenstein, the properties of his wealthy, half-Jewish godfather, Dr Hermann Ritter von Epenstein. The latter had invited the Görings and their children to live with him – not without an ulterior motive, since young Hermann's mother Franziska was his mistress. Von Epenstein cultivated a colourful, romantic lifestyle and from him Göring inherited a love of medieval masquerade. On the battlements of 'his' castle he dreamed of knights and princesses, posed as Robin Hood, or as a Boer General in the South African War that was currently raging, whose adventures interested him far more than his tedious school work or the petty strictures of boarding school in Ansbach. He skipped lessons, was disobedient and ran away several times. As his mother commented: 'Hermann will either be a great man or a criminal.'

It was only his training-officers at the cadet college in Berlin's Lichterfelde district who succeeded in harnessing Göring's exuberant temperament with Prussian discipline and parade-ground drill. The military academy turned the recalcitrant youth into an ambitious and hard-working cadet. It seems to have been a relief to him to get away from his parents and their strange *ménage à trois* with his godfather. In 1911 he passed his examinations with the award of 'excellent'. He was now a lieutenant, aged nineteen, proudly wearing the Kaiser's uniform and with an entrée to elegant Berlin society. However, the young officer looked for excitement in the air, rather than on the sofa or the dance-floor. When the First World War broke out he joined the Imperial flying corps, qualified as a pilot and in 1916 engaged in his first air battles. He gained a reputation as a daredevil. Thanks to his courage in action he was very soon given command of a fighter flight. There was admittedly some muttering among his colleagues that Göring had exaggerated the number of enemy planes he had shot down. Nevertheless, in recognition of his eighteen attested 'kills', on 2 June 1918 Kaiser Wilhelm presented the air ace with the highest German decoration for outstanding bravery, the *Pour le Mérite* – a distinction which he would exploit for a long time to come. Ennobled by heroism, Göring displayed the so-called 'Blue Max' with as much pride as another status-symbol: the walking-stick belonging to the legendary 'Red Baron', Manfred von Richthofen, whose much-feared 'Richthofen Circus' Göring led as its last Squadron Commander.

To the very end the elite of German pilots fought, and incurred heavy losses, against enemy superiority in the skies. Yet no death in action dealt such a heavy blow to the corps as the sudden news of the armistice. All their sacrifice seemed to have been in vain. Never would Göring be able to come to terms with it. When the squadron met for the final time in the town hall *Bierkeller* of Aschaffenburg, he swore an oath before his fellow-officers: 'Our hour will come again!'

For the time being, however, the Treaty of Versailles banned military aviation in Germany. To escape the ignominy Göring fled to Sweden, where he made a hit with aerobatic displays and earned a living as a parachute salesman and air-taxi pilot. On a Swedish aristocrat's estate he fell head over heels in love with the attractive Carin von Kantzow. This rather emotional daughter of a Swedish officer was in fact married, but was so bowled over by the brash charm of the German flying-ace that she abandoned her husband and son and followed her lover to Germany, where they were married in 1922.

In the new Weimar Republic a thirty-year-old retired Air Force captain faced an uncertain future. For want of anything better to do, and with no great enthusiasm, Göring studied history and economics at Munich University. But rather than wanting to acquire academic knowledge, the battle-hardened pilot longed for comradeship, acts of heroism and a 'strong man' who would restore Germany to her former might. Göring met this new 'Kaiser' one autumn day in 1922 at a demonstration in Munich's Königsplatz. From the start he was fascinated by this man, and shortly afterwards was sitting opposite him at one of his 'consultations'. The man would give a new direction to his life and told him exactly what he wanted to hear: Versailles was a disgrace, Jews and communists were to blame for everything, the Fatherland had to be saved. Göring trusted this Hitler to liberate Germany from the yoke of the victorious powers. 'From the first moment I saw and heard him,' he wrote two years later, 'I fell for him, hook, line and sinker.' And Hitler, too, was glad to have met the highly decorated veteran. 'Splendid! A war-hero with the *Pour le Mérite* – just think of that! Excellent propaganda value! And what's more, he's got plenty of money and won't cost me a penny.' Göring's reputation promised to be useful to the fledgling Party. The bluff hero and the fanatical demagogue – it was like a devil's pact. When Hitler put his new associate in charge of the SA, Göring made this emotional promise: 'I place my destiny in your hands, through good times and bad, though it may cost me my life.'

Göring took only a marginal interest in Hitler's Party and its programme and as head of the SA derived little satisfaction from the unglamorous daily routine. It is true that he quickly turned the rundown *Sturmabteilung* into a potent private army, but he preferred to apply himself to the pleasanter aspects of his office, had his first Ruritanian uniform tailored and looked down with contempt on the 'Bavarian beer-swillers and backpackers' of the NSDAP. He was patronizing in his treatment of 'Party enthusiasts' like Rudolf Hess or Alfred Rosenberg, and so it is hardly surprising that he remained without real power within the party. Ideology he dismissed as 'junk' – Adolf Hitler was his party. For him he was ready to risk his life. With him he would take power in the Reich.

I follow only the leadership of Adolf Hitler and of God Almighty!

Göring, 1933

On 9 November 1923, a gloomy, wet and cold day, the choice between power and powerlessness would be made on the streets of

Munich. Just before midday a column of SA and shock-troopers moved off and marched towards Odeonsplatz. At its head walked Hitler, Göring and General Ludendorff, the ageing warhorse of 1914–18. The cheers and shouts of '*heil*' from the onlookers led them to hope that their bid for power might succeed. But when they were within a few yards of the Feldherrnhalle war memorial, a shot rang out followed by a salvo that raked the street. The Bavarian police were aiming at the first row of marchers. The exchange of fire lasted sixty seconds. Fourteen of the rebels and three policemen were killed. Hitler flung himself to the ground. Göring received several shots in the groin and lay severely wounded and motionless in the roadway. After several seconds he regained consciousness and dragged himself, bleeding heavily, out of the line of fire. SA men hoisted him into a car and took him to the house of a Jewish furniture-dealer named Ballin, where he received makeshift treatment. After that he was on the run from the police. Accompanied by Carin he crossed the border into Austria, where doctors at the Innsbruck hospital injected him for the first time with morphine – the drug which made him an addict, but for a short time allowed him to forget the pain. The failure of the Munich *Putsch* had stopped his political career in its tracks. The government of Bavaria circulated his description and issued a warrant for his arrest. Unlike Hitler, however, he remained at large, though the racking pain from his injuries was, despite the morphine, almost unbearable. Both Göring's personal doctor, Dr Ramon von Ondarza, and his long-serving nurse attested after the war to a severe injury to his testicles. As a result of this bullet-wound Göring believed himself to be sterile.

From his prison-cell in Landsberg Castle Hitler sent word to the exile in Austria, ordering him to go immediately to Italy and make contact with Mussolini, who had appointed himself dictator of that country little more than a year earlier. Göring's agreeable manner and dazzling rows of medals were intended to seduce the *Duce* into giving the shattered 'Movement' across the Alps a helping hand to the tune of 2 billion lire. Some hope. Mussolini did not even receive Hitler's importunate emissary. While Göring's property in Germany was confiscated and Ernst Röhm took over the SA, the unhappy couple returned penniless and disillusioned to Carin's parents in Sweden. But of course Hermann Göring could not escape the pain of his wounds. Almost every day he took morphine injections. Once a slim, good-looking man, he soon became bloated and fat, suffered from poor memory and from the compulsion to take the drug in order to make life bearable. When withdrawal symptoms set in Göring sometimes lost all self-control and on one occasion even tried to take his own life.

> 2 September to 7 October 1925:
> Patient disruptive, in a depressed state, moaned, cried, was anxious, continually asking for things, touchy and quickly aroused; downcast, garrulous, feels he is a victim of 'Jewish conspiracy'; thoughts of suicide; exaggerated withdrawal symptoms; tendency to hysteria, self-centred, exaggerated self-confidence; hates Jews, has dedicated his life to the struggle against Jews, was Hitler's right-hand man; hallucinations; attempted suicide (hanging and strangulation); utters threats, has secretly obtained an iron weight as a weapon; visions, voices, self-accusations.
> *From Göring's medical report at the Långbro mental nursing home, Sweden, 1925*

Things could not go on like this: in a nursing-home for patients with severe nervous disorders at Långbro near Stockholm, the addict tried to win the battle against the drug and thus relieve his wife Carin of the appalling pressure. 'Being a morphine addict,' she implored him in a letter, 'is the same thing as committing suicide – every day you lose a little bit of your body and of your soul.' With increasing desperation she observed how Göring apparently lacked the strength and will to overcome his dependence. 'You are in the grip of an evil spirit and an evil power, and your body is gradually wasting away. Rescue yourself and by doing so save me too!'

Göring was stuck with the morphine habit. 'A brutal hysteric with a very weak character,' is how a Swedish medical report described him. He was a depressive, the doctors declared, a suicide risk, self-obsessed and a 'Jew-hater'. Nonetheless the patient was released on 7

October 1925, with no symptoms of mental disturbance, according to Professor Olov Kinberg. Officially Göring had been pronounced cured. But in fact he was a sick man – an addict, who daily injected himself with up to 50 milligrams of morphine. No one but Carin would know of his life in the shadow of the drug, but the more he was exposed to the glare of publicity, the more the rumours proliferated about a morphine addict in the highest reaches of political power. But many years still stood between him and the power for which he yearned. It was the lowest point in Göring's life when in 1927 he returned to Germany under an amnesty for those accused of political offences; he got by with a job as a salesman and tried once again to gain a toe-hold in politcs.

For the 'Führer' who had been released from prison in Landsberg some time ago, the arrival of a man like Göring was certainly opportune. This imperious, authoritative figure was just what he needed to fill the gap in his innermost circle of confidants. He was not from the lower middle class, as Hitler was; he wasn't a footsoldier like Röhm, nor a hustler like Goebbels; he had what the roughnecks of the 'Movement' lacked: a good pedigree, polished manners and a talent for getting people on his side. With his *Pour le Mérite* he also possessed something that would open doors in the corridors of power and unlock the vaults of the financial aristocracy.

> Bad-tempered scene with Göring, who is becoming more and more of a liability to the Party. Added to which he is as thick as two planks and bone idle. He has always treated the others like rabble and yesterday he even tried it with me.
>
> *Goebbels (Diary) 1929*

As his political representative in Berlin Göring would have to win over the capital's high society to Hitler's cause, and in the event he succeeded not only in securing an audience for his Führer with the head of state, President von Hindenburg, but also in filling the empty Party coffers – with donations from Krupp, Thyssen, the Deutsche Bank, BMW, Lufthansa, Heinkel, Messerschmitt . . .

As a member of the Reichstag, he was soon swanning into the most influential circles of the aristocracy, high finance and industry, where his amusing small-talk and calculated charm won many victories for Hitler in the best Berlin drawing-rooms. Despite taking slimming-pills, Göring grew ever fatter, suffered from insomnia and had to cope with the death of Carin on 17 October 1931. Yet he did not lack the energy to apply all his skill, wiles and unscrupulous subterfuge to helping Hitler across the threshold of power. As the elected Speaker of the Reichstag he bribed Oscar von Hindenburg, the President's son, with gifts and promises, brought the Army over to Hitler's side and in gruelling negotiations talked the aged President himself into appointing Hitler as Chancellor. As the diarist Joseph Goebbels noted, it was probably Göring's 'happiest moment', when 'this upright soldier with the heart of a child' brought the news to Hitler on 29 January 1933, that nothing more stood in the way of his assumption of power. Göring took a considerable share in this triumph, and Hitler rewarded the services rendered by his henchman with a series of official posts: Reich Minister, initially without portfolio, Reich Commissioner for Aviation and acting Minister of the Interior for Prussia. This meant not only that Göring was empowered to act with full authority in Hitler's name, with the task of building up an Air Force in secret. He also commanded the strongest police force in the Reich – a weapon of power which the outwardly affable Göring wielded with unexpected brutality.

The lion of the drawing-rooms bared his claws and, under the cloak of spurious legitimacy, terrorized political opponents, Social Democrats as well as communists. With emergency decrees, signed by President Hindenburg, he introduced a reign of terror in Germany. Now there was no longer any pretence: 'Fellow Germans, my intentions will not be sapped by any judicial scruples. My measures will not be hampered by any bureaucracy. I am not here to dispense justice, I am here only to eliminate and eradicate, nothing else!'

Göring had no difficulty in keeping these promises. In Prussia he made 50,000 SA and *Stahlhelm* troops into 'auxiliary policemen', purged the administrative and police authorities, and before the last – and no longer free – Reichstag elections on 5 March 1933, gave the signal for an unprecedented hunting down of political opponents. The police were to 'combat with the severest measures the activities of organizations inimical to the state,' and 'if necessary make unhesitating use of firearms.' Pistols replaced rubber truncheons and Göring was enthusiastically true to his motto: 'Every bullet from a police pistol is my bullet.' There was no holding the brown-shirted mobsters now. Squads of hit-men did their worst, unhindered by the civil police. Joseph Goebbels noted approvingly in his diary: 'Göring is clearing up in Prussia with a refreshing forcefulness. He's got what it takes to do really radical things, and also the nerves to survive a tough battle.'

Göring, too, believed that this battle first had to be fought out with the German Communist Party. But in truth the left was weak and divided. The persecuted opponents of Nazism relied on slogans rather than force. Nevertheless Hitler, Goebbels and Göring clung obsessively to the idea, which was effective as propaganda, that at the last minute the 'Commune' might challenge them for power. It almost seemed as though this vision was being realized when, on the night of 27 February 1933, flames leapt from the dome of the Reichstag building. Who had started the fire? Was it the man caught at the scene of the crime and later condemned to death, a communist named Martinus von der Lubbe? Was it the Communist Party? Or could it have been the Nazis themselves, on orders from Göring? The Reichstag building and the official residence of the Speaker of the Reichstag, Hermann Göring no less, were connected by an underground passage. Did Göring get someone to start the blaze, even though several of his most precious heirlooms were destroyed in the flames? To this day there is no conclusive evidence as to who was responsible.

But what mattered was that Göring seized on the burning of the Reichstag, symbol of the Republic, as a pretext to intensify his persecution of communists and other opponents. He was the first official to arrive at the scene, the first to announce to the world that this was a *coup d'état* by the left, in order to legitimize the Nazis' seizure of power. 'This is the start of the communist uprising,' Göring shouted above the wail of sirens at the scene of the fire, to Rudolf Diels, who later became Head of the Gestapo. 'They'll launch their attack now! There isn't a moment to lose.' The same night orders went out for the arrest of over 4,000 officials, mainly in the Communist Party, for their offices and newspapers to be closed down and for undesirable writers like Carl von Ossietzky to be placed in 'protective custody'. Even before word of the blaze had spread across the nation, Göring's blacklist of named victims had been drawn up.

When I was appointed head of the Prussian Ministry of the Interior, I knew that I must be taking on the hardest office, for in it lies the key to the whole position of power. I will sweep clean with an iron broom and get rid of all those post-holders and dignitaries who are only there because of their Communist or Catholic leanings and who are suppressing all national aspirations.

Göring, 1934

From 28 February onward, when the 'Reichstag Fire Decree' introduced a permanent state of emergency, basic rights like the freedom of the individual were suspended. State terrorism was now 'legal'. Göring had a free hand. On his orders, not only political opponents but also homosexuals and Jehovah's Witnesses were rounded up into concentration-camps. Göring had these places of imprisonment and torture, which he called 're-education camps', built at Oranienburg and Papenburg.

At the end of July 1933, six months after Hitler's seizure of power, these camps were already bursting at the seams with 27,000 political prisoners. The arrests, as Göring would bluster on the Nuremberg witness-stand, were 'a political act of state, carried out in defence of the state'. Admittedly in the camps there had been cruelty, beatings and 'acts of brutality', but 'you can't make an omelette without breaking eggs'. However, he insisted: 'I naturally gave instructions that such things had to stop.' Nevertheless, conditions remained almost unchanged. In conversation with prisoners such as Ernst Thälmann, the chairman of the Communist Party, he regretted the use of violence in interrogations, but after all, he said, he could not be everywhere at once. Thälmann returned to concentration-camp and on 18 August 1944 was shot in Buchenwald – at a time when the camps were no longer run by Göring but by the *Reichsführer-SS*, Heinrich Himmler, who, at Hitler's request took over another of Göring's creations, the secret state police, or Gestapo. In July 1934, Göring, a keen huntsman, was given two new posts as a consolation: Reich Master of Forests and Reich Master of Hunting. To this day, a hunting-law passed by Göring, which bans vivisection, is still in force. Clearly the well-being of wild animals meant more to him than the lives of political opponents. A wooden sign in his office bore the words: 'Anyone who tortures animals offends German national sentiment.'

He wanted to know what people in general and his rivals in particular were thinking and feeling. Very soon after the Nazi Party came to power he therefore set up the 'Research Office of the Reich Air Ministry', which proved to be an endlessly bubbling wellspring of information. From it he collected reports which he could use to keep the upper hand in all the intrigues and power-games. At peak times as many as 3,000 staff listened in on telephone lines to the Reich Chancellery, ministries, Party offices and embassies. Around the clock bugging experts deciphered coded messages and copied them down, in order to satisfy their boss's thirst for information about people's political and private activities.

> Fat Göring ought to try giving up some of his caviare. He makes me puke.
>
> *Goebbels (Diary), 1933*

Whether it was the sweet nothings that passed between Joseph Goebbels and Lida Baarova or political discussions among foreign correspondents – Göring's eavesdroppers dutifully noted them down, word for word, no matter how banal. 'Guess what this is!' giggled the wife of the former Chancellor Kurt von Schleicher on the phone. 'Without the letter "i" it's something nobody wants to be. *With* an "i" it's what everybody wants to be! Well, d'you give up? The answer's "*Arisch*!" ('Aryan': with the 'i' removed the word means 'asshole'.) With much smirking and thigh-slapping Göring would repeat 'information' like this to his staff. By contrast, other 'research findings' collected in the 'brown pages' were kept in the strictest secrecy. On several occasions they contained political dynamite which would cost Ernst Röhm, the SA Chief-of-Staff, his life.

From the 'research reports' Göring knew that Röhm, the dissatisfied revolutionary, was taking an increasingly critical stand against Hitler. For some time Göring had been pressing for the Party and the SA to be 'cleaned up'. Now here was a chance for him to get even with Hitler's closest friend, the only man he addressed with the familiar *Du*, and who was *de facto* what Göring wanted to be: Number Two in the Party. It was Hitler himself who organized the killings in southern Germany; Göring and Heinrich Himmler pulled the strings in Berlin and the north. For Göring this was another opportunity to present himself to Hitler as an eager executioner. In his old cadet school in Lichterfelde he had forty-three alleged insurgents shot. It was the first of the regime's mass-murders. But even at Nuremberg Göring showed no remorse: 'The SA was nothing but a mob of gangsters and perverts! It's a damned good thing I got rid of them, otherwise they would have done for us.'

> This man could be very friendly and engaging. But at any moment he could ram a dagger in someone's back, if he thought it necessary.
>
> *Egon Hanfstaengl, son of Hitler's press chief*

Hitler liked the way his 'most loyal champion' acted 'as cold as ice' in moments of crisis. Göring, the old warhorse, had proved his worth. The fact that he was ideologically rather 'unsound' hardly mattered. Göring enjoyed Hitler's trust, the trust of a man he slavishly served, to the point of self-denial. Hitler's mere presence was enough to rob him of his critical faculty. 'I try so hard,' he once told the Economics Minister, Hjalmar Schacht, 'but every time I face him, my heart drops into my boots.' Most of all it was his awe of Hitler's power that made Göring his willing executioner, inwardly falling on his knees before the idol he worshipped, and writing in his 1934 book *Aufbau einer Nation* (*The Building of a Nation*):

Anyone who knows anything about Germany knows that each of us possesses only as much power as the Führer wishes to give us. And only with the Führer standing at one's back is one truly powerful, holding the reins of state power in one's hands. But acting against his will, or merely against his wishes, one becomes in that moment totally powerless. One word from the Führer and anyone can fall . . .

Göring's devotion paid off. On the death of President Hindenburg, Hitler rose in December 1934 to become 'Führer and Reich Chancellor', and Göring made his Luftwaffe officers swear an oath of allegiance to his leader. It was the fulfilment of his deepest desire. In a secret document Hitler named him as his successor. Now he was recognized as the second in command, the next in line for the tyrant's throne. The dream of exercising sole and absolute power became the driving force of his life.

The fight for Hitler's favour was like being among the Borgias. This was doubly odd, since the chief protagonists, Himmler, Bormann and Lammers, really had none of the qualities – in inverted commas – which in history one associates with such figures. How shall I put it? The three men were – 'bourgeois' is not the right word – they were really very coarse individuals. Goebbels and Göring, who intrigued as well of course, weren't coarse; they were very intelligent. Göring was corrupt, but perhaps his corruption was a consequence of his illness, of his morphine addiction. How will we ever know? Goebbels was never corrupt, just terribly dangerous.

Albert Speer, 1979

Everyone was meant to see how far Göring had come. He acquired a luxurious house on Berlin's Kaiserdamm, with furniture as massive as his waistline. He hired numerous staff and had the official residence of the Minister-President of Prussia lavishly redesigned at the tax-payers' expense. Money was no longer a problem. The tobacco company, Reemstma, alone provided him with an annual income of one million Reichsmarks, and the German motor industry bribed him with a motor-yacht – the *Carin II* – worth one-and-a-half million marks, in return for anticipated defence contracts. 'Fat Hermann', as he was popularly known, enjoyed his success to the full. He gave himself up to the pleasures of the flesh without inhibition.

In the evenings his butler Robert Kropp would keep him well supplied with beer, sandwiches and cakes with whipped cream. By the end of 1933 Göring weighed in at 280 pounds. 'He has the typical proportions of a German tenor,' mocked the American Ambassador, William C. Bullet. 'His backside is at least a yard in diameter. And since he is squeezed into a skin-tight uniform the effect is unique.' Without embarrassment Göring grabbed whatever took his fancy: jewelry, pictures, uniforms, decorations. The cabaret-singer Claire Waldorff summed up his passion for resplendence: '*Links Lametta, rechts Lametta, und der Bauch wird immer fetta*' ("Gongs" on his left breast, "gongs" on his right, and his belly gets fatter and fatter').

The way I saw it, Göring was different from the other big nobs, especially from Hitler and Goebbels. He seemed more harmless, more naïve, somehow more human, because he was so incredibly vain and pleasure-seeking. Those are fairly harmless qualities, after all – the kind which Goebbels, for example, did not share. That's why to begin with he was less feared than the others. He was just a bit shadier than Goebbels or Hitler, who were definitely looked on negatively.

Isa Vermehren, cabaret-artiste in the 1930s

He was the Sun-King of the Third Reich: in the Schorfheide, an idyllic landscape of forest and lakes north of Berlin, he spent millions from the budgets of the Aviation and Prussian ministries on having a magnificent residence built with a sauna, cinema, gymnasium and a reception room as high as a church nave. Where Prussian kings and dukes once stalked game, Göring, the new lord of the manor, invited industrialists and diplomats to hunting-parties or indulged in nostalgia for the medieval fantasy-world of his childhood. He could be seen in a leather hunting outfit, with bow and arrow, on lengthy journeys by horse-drawn coach and in the evenings at the control-panel of an enormous model railway, a gift from the Prussian State Theatre, which he demonstrated as proudly as any child to ambassadors like France's François-Poncet.

> It is surely not too great a sacrifice to give up certain comforts, in order to achieve the freedom of the people and to ensure the strength of the nation. The more strongly we are armed, the more secure we stand, and the less easily can anyone attack us. The Führer and all of us here, all we leaders, ask nothing of you that we are not ourselves prepared to do or give at any time. Too much fat – stomachs too big? I myself have been eating less butter and have lost twenty pounds.
>
> *Göring, 1935*

For the diplomat the scene revealed something about the ideas running round in Göring's mind, and he recalled:

> When he showed me the toy, one of his nephews shouted: 'Uncle Hermann, run the French train now!' The train left its shed. Then the nephew made a little aircraft glide along one of the wires that was stretched across the garden, and out of the plane fell bombs fitted with detonators, with which the boy tried to hit the French train.

Göring named his estate 'Carinhall' after his first wife. Just for her, the woman he worshipped like a saint all their life together, he had a granite crypt dug into the ground beside a lake. In the summer of 1934 Carin's coffin was brought from Sweden to Schorfheide, where another woman was at Göring's side enjoying the pleasant aspects of power. The blond actress Emmy Sonnemann had achieved modest fame in provincial theatres as Gretchen in Goethe's *Faust*. On 10 April 1935 she married a man who, as rumour had it, was unable to father children, but who appeared outwardly

unperturbed when, after the ceremony, some 'friends' released two
storks into the air.

Though Göring refused to allow any chaplains in the Luftwaffe,
contrary to custom in the Nazi Party he insisted on a wedding
ceremony in church, provided it did not go on too long. No more
than five minutes were allotted to Reich Bishop Ludwig Müller for
his sermon in Berlin Cathedral. For Göring was less concerned
with pious words than with the external trappings. Ten Luftwaffe
Generals, 30,000 troops, eight bands and the most up-to-date
aircraft in the sky over Berlin, all lent the ceremony the air of a
great state occasion. The British Ambassador, Sir Eric Phipps,
noted acidly: 'There's only one thing left for him now – either the
throne or the scaffold.' Göring was quite brazenly using his
wedding to display Germany's military strength. Only a month
previously he had made public what he and the Permanent
Secretary of the Air Ministry, Erhard Milch, had been secretly
working on since 1933: Germany once again possessed an Air
Force of its own, which was no longer an appendage of the Army,
but had been elevated to an independent element of the armed
forces. As Commander-in-Chief of the Luftwaffe, Göring had
increased his political prestige. He was now a member of the
military elite, running an Air Ministry of 2,800 rooms and
claiming to have 1,600 aircraft ready for combat. In fact there
were initially no more than 200 outmoded machines.

Even before the Nazis seized power Göring had shown himself
to be a ruthless advocate of rapid re-armament. Now, as
Commander-in-Chief of the Luftwaffe, it was in his power to drive
forward the costly equipping of the Air Force, with its heavy
demand on valuable raw materials, and to provide Hitler with a
powerful weapon of aggression. 'I dream of having an Air Force,'
he told a group of young pilot-officers at their oath-taking
ceremony, 'which, if ever the hour should strike, will descend on
the enemy like an avenging host. Our opponent must feel he is
beaten even before he has crossed swords with you.' In the summer
of 1935, when general conscription had just been announced,
Göring pressed Hitler for an immediate doubling of the strength of
the Luftwaffe, which, in view of the shortage of raw materials, was
a delusion. In April 1936, in order to improve the supply situation

and to 'further assure our defensive capability', Hitler placed the new Office of Raw Materials and Foreign Exchange in the hands of his all-purpose minister, Göring. In four years' time, Hitler demanded in a secret memorandum, the German Army must be 'combat-ready' and the German economy placed on a 'war footing'. He brooked no objections. Economic problems were for Hitler 'problems of will-power', and Göring was the only man he credited with a strong enough will.

> If you really want to do something new, then the great and the good won't help you. They are self-satisfied, lazy, they have a God of their own and they want to do things their way – you can't get anywhere with them. 'Let me have men about me that are fat' – is something an anointed king can say, but not a Führer who has created himself. Let me have villainous rogues about me. The bad guys with a bit of a record, they're useful people; men who are alert to dangers, because they know what to expect, and are on the lookout for loot. You can offer them something, because they are takers. Because they have no compunction. You can hang them if they step out of line. Let me have villainous scoundrels about me – provided that I have the power, the complete power over life and death. I am the one and only boss and no one can meddle with me. What do you know about the possibilities of evil! Why do you write your books and philosophize, if all you know anything about is virtue and how to achieve it, whereas the world is fundamentally driven by something different.
>
> *Göring to his Defence Counsel at Nuremberg, 1946*

'He is the best man I have . . . a man of determination, who knows what's required and gets it done.' Although this man had no experience of economic matters, in 1936 while out walking at his mountain retreat on the Obersalzberg, Hitler entrusted him with a post which made him the second most powerful figure in the state: as 'Commissioner for the Four-Year Plan' he had orders from the Führer to accelerate German re-armament, to 'fight for the right of the German people to feed themselves', but above all to acquire raw materials and foreign currency, in order to prepare for what Hitler termed the 'war in peacetime'. Like Hitler, Göring dreamed of an economically self-sufficient Germany – and fobbed the population off with artificial products like *ersatz* honey or manmade fabrics, while he had his suits and Ruritanian uniforms tailored from the finest cloth. 'Göring is as ridiculous as he is dangerous,' opined the French diplomat Robert Coulondre. 'One can laugh about him being upset that his collection does not include Napoleon's baton; but one trembles when he talks of his aircraft and guns, whose production he pushes forward with a ferocious energy.'

Guns instead of butter: aircraft, tanks and ships were now more important than private consumption or solid state finances. Warnings from experts like Hjalmar Schacht, the respected Reich Minister of Economics and Chairman of the Reichsbank, were brushed aside by Göring. As he had at the beginning of the dictatorship, he now devoted himself entirely to forcing Hitler's policies through against all opposition. Anyone who put two and two together must have realized that, if it did not bankrupt the state, this headlong re-armament was bound to lead to a decision to go to war.

Göring insisted to a group of leading industrialists in 1936:

There is no foreseeable end to re-armament. If we are victorious, the economy will be adequately compensated. . . . We must not calculate what the cost will be. . . . We are now playing for the highest stakes. What could be more profitable than armaments contracts?

He spoke in even plainer terms to senior Luftwaffe officers on 2 December 1936:

The general situation is very serious. We would like to be left to ourselves until 1941. But we can't be sure we won't get caught up in something before then. We are already at war, only the shooting hasn't started yet.

That was not strictly true. At that moment Germany's 'Condor Legion' was giving support to the Fascist leader General Francisco Franco in the Spanish Civil War – for the Luftwaffe this was an opportunity, as Göring put it, 'to find out whether our equipment is up to requirements when the bullets are flying'.

This war in peacetime soon began to take its toll on daily life. The dizzying levels of military expenditure could only be maintained at the cost of house-building and food supplies. Soon, not only was there a shortage of raw materials and foreign exchange, but also of labour. Even before the outbreak of war the supposed 'people without territory' lacked the manpower to implement the military plans of the regime. But Göring's biggest headache was the problem of iron ore. In July 1937, when supplies of iron and steel suddenly dwindled and the private sector seemed about to lose control of the situation, Göring made a surprise move to push forward the Nazification of heavy industry. Under the name *Reichswerke Hermann Göring* he had the largest steelworks in Europe constructed on a greenfield site at Salzgitter, near Hanover, and had plans laid out for a new town for the workers, modestly named 'Hermann-Göring-Stadt' – the worst example so far of his pathological need for self-promotion. This strutting dilettante with his ruinous craze for armaments proved too much for Hjalmar Schacht. In November 1937, the Minister handed in his resignation – a triumph which Göring, who briefly succeeded him, savoured to the full. Derisively he told his erstwhile rival on the telephone: 'I'm sitting in *your* chair now!'

Already Göring's greedy eyes were on the next and even more influential post. As the Finance Minister, Count Schwerin von Krosigk, observed: 'He wanted to crown his array of honours with the office of Minister of War.' The incumbent of that post was *Generalfeldmarschall* Werner von Blomberg, who had just married for the second time. But his bride was, as the police file put it, 'a lady with a past', a former prostitute who had also posed for nude photographs. The wedding deteriorated into a moral and political scandal, putting an unexpected trump-card into Göring's hand. He calculated his chances of stepping into the shoes of the now unacceptable Blomberg. Like a spider he wove a web of smutty intrigue in which to trap his most likely rival for the job, the

Göring himself lay on an ottoman in a white uniform; he was already very corpulent by then. His left leg, with the trouser-leg rolled above the knee, was raised and supported on a cushion. He wore red silk stockings, like a cardinal. In profile he resembled a *Heldentenor* in a Wagner opera, and yet there was something powerful in the self-assured, almost brutal set of his jaw. Göring's mouth, on the other hand, was sunken and puckered like an old woman's.

Carl Jacob Burckhardt, Swiss diplomat and historian, League of Nations High Commissioner in Danzig 1937–9

Commander-in-Chief of the Army, *Generaloberst* Baron Werner von Fritsch. Another police dossier, hastily organized by Göring, accused Fritsch of homosexuality – the accusations were unfounded but sufficient to force Fritsch to resign. The man pulling the strings seemed to have emerged the winner, but the disgusting farce ended with a resounding slap in the face for Göring.

Hitler appointed himself Supreme Commander of the Armed Forces and fobbed off the over-ambitious contender with yet another title, that of '*Feldmarschall*'. On 1 March 1938 the German-Jewish novelist Victor Klemperer noted in his diary: 'Today, on Shrove Tuesday, as part of Berlin's Carnival celebrations, Hitler solemnly presented Göring with his field-marshall's baton. They have no sense of their own absurdity.'

With Blomberg and Fritsch out of the way, thanks to Göring, Hitler had bloodlessly rid himself of two influential sceptics who doubted the wisdom of taking Germany into a war. Göring knew what Hitler wanted, ever since a secret conference on 5 November 1937, when Hitler had revealed to him and the highest ranking military officers that he intended to resolve the 'territory question' at the latest by 1943–5, or earlier if possible. Hitler did not want to go to war – yet. He was still warning Göring to 'tread a political line that avoids resorting to force'. This applied above all to the 'Austrian Question'. Hitler wanted to bring his native country 'home to the Reich' without the use of force and found in Göring a fiercely resolute helper, who promoted the *Anschluss*, or annexation of Austria, regardless of the interests of allies like Italy and even urged Hitler to bring Vienna to heel by armed intervention if necessary. Like a trainer whispering in a boxer's ear, Göring forced a wavering Hitler on to the offensive, and finally climbed into the ring himself, when the Austrian Chancellor, Kurt von Schuschnigg, set the date of 13 March 1938 for a referendum on the independence of his country.

In fact it was Göring who, in the last turbulent days of Austria's freedom, took command and controlled everything by telephone from the Reich Chancellery in Berlin. On 11 March, in twenty-seven telephone calls between the German and Austrian capitals, Göring set the seal on the *Anschluss*. His ultimatum demanded the resignation of Chancellor Schuschnigg and presented as his successor the pro-Nazi Minister of the Interior, Dr Arthur Seyss-Inquart. However, the Austrian President, Wilhelm Miklas, refused to appoint Hitler's front-man. Shortly after 8 p.m. that night, when it was clear that Italy and Britain would stand aside and do nothing, Göring issued the order 'in the name of the Führer', for the Army to march into Austria. Not until an hour-and-a-half later did he dictate the cynical telegram which purported to be from Seyss-Inquart, asking Berlin 'in the name of the provisional Austrian government' for the 'earliest possible dispatch of German troops'.

By this point Göring had long since fulfilled his own desire. 'It was less the Führer than I myself,' he truthfully told the Nuremberg tribunal in evidence, 'who set the pace and by overriding the Führer's anxieties brought matters to a conclusion.' This was the first hint that Hitler and Göring were in less than perfect harmony. The swift triumph drew attention away from the first hairline cracks appearing in their alliance. Never again would Hitler allow Göring to seize the reins.

Neither Hitler nor Göring were willing to miss the obligatory walkabout among the jubilant Austrian crowds. In Linz Göring seized the opportunity to make it clear that, with the German troops, a regime of systematic terror had arrived: 'The city of Vienna can no longer be described as German. Where there are 300,000 Jews, one cannot speak of a "German" city. But Vienna must become a German city once again.' In the very moment of euphoria over unification Göring ordered the immediate and thorough 'Aryanization' of commerce, forcing Jews to flee abroad. The 'Commissioner of the Four-Year Plan' now accelerated the Jewish exodus throughout the Reich. By law Jews had already become second-class citizens, ever since 1935, when Göring as Speaker of the Reichstag promulgated the Nuremberg Race Laws and took the opportunity to declare the swastika the 'sacred symbol' of the struggle against 'the Jews as destroyers of our race'.

He was completely his Führer's henchman and acted in accordance with Hitler's view of the world. He was also extreme in his anti-Semitism. During the *Kristallnacht* in 1938 he took the view that too much valuable Jewish property had been destroyed. He would have been happier if more Jews had been killed. That would have been of greater service to the Reich. This was his attitude at the time.

William Jackson, son and assistant of the Chief Prosecutor at Nuremberg

In public utterances Göring presented himself as a fanatical Jew-hater and yet his relationship to Jews remained unclear to the end of his life and, for a man who belonged to Hitler's closest circle, untypically complex and undogmatic. When it came to bureaucracy, he was open to persuasion. True to his wilful motto: '*I* decide who is a Jew', Göring, whose godfather was half-Jewish, would issue letters of safe-conduct for Jews, such as art-dealers for example, who were useful to him. He supported Erhard Milch, later *Generalfeldmarschall* and Second-in-Command of the Luftwaffe, who was also half-Jewish, and helped his own wife Emmy to keep Jewish fellow-actors and actresses out of the hands of the SS and the Gestapo. In 1936 the actress Käthe Dorsch, for whom Göring had a soft spot, told the playwright Carl Zuckmayer reassuringly: 'If they haul you in, I'll run straight to Göring and cry my eyes out until you're released again.'

Käthe Dorsch's tears opened the camp gates for many lucky

inmates. The fact was that Göring's anti-Semitism was a matter of mood and inclination. His hatred of Jews was part of his 'sense of duty' as a leading National Socialist and influenced by his eagerness to obey Hitler, whose racial beliefs he espoused for reasons of opportunism. He claimed to have had a moderating influence on Hitler's Jewish policy and is believed to have told his nephew Klaus Rigele that he wanted to remove the Jews from political and economic life, but to do no harm to any of them.

Even though Göring's anti-Semitism was less single-mindedly aimed at annihilation than that of someone like Joseph Goebbels, he still concealed behind a tolerant façade a deeply rooted hatred of Jews, which was remarked on as early as 1925 in the Swedish mental home and which he allowed to become the driving force of Jewish persecution in the Third Reich. He made no effort to conceal this hatred even from old comrades. When a Jewish jeweller, who had been a pilot under his command, came to him and anxiously reported receiving anti-Jewish hate-mail, Göring at first appeared benevolent: 'Don't worry. I'll see to it.' But when the petitioner stressed that he was a German too, Göring barked at him: 'I'll do anything for an old comrade. But I deny you the right to call yourself German. You've *never* been German. You are a Jew.'

In Göring's view Jews had to be removed from the economy 'by every possible means'. True, he criticized the *Reichskristallnacht* pogroms of 9 November 1938, which Goebbels had incited, not, however, out of sympathy for the Jewish population, but simply for economic reasons: 'I would have preferred it if you and your boys had killed a couple of hundred Jews and not destroyed such valuable assets.' Two days after the night of the burning synagogues, as a cynical conclusion to the violent episode, Göring invited all the departments concerned to a 'decision-making' session in the Reich Air Ministry, where he at once addressed one of Hitler's wishes: the 'Jewish Question' must be approached in a systematic manner and dealt with 'one way or another': 'In a telephone-call yesterday from the Führer I was once again instructed to co-ordinate centrally all decisive steps.' Thus Göring acted as the first overlord for the 'solution of the Jewish Question', this was, in his words, 'a far-reaching economic problem', which he wanted to get rid of through a 'root-and-branch Aryanization' of the economy.

Under Göring's chairmanship the meeting decided to set up a 'clearing-house for Jewish emigration' and to impose a levy of one billion marks on the Jews of Germany – as an 'expiation' for the devastation wrought by the SA and SS.

In this period it was not only the 'Jewish problem' which was keeping Göring occupied. Immediately after the *Anschluss* of Austria Hitler's next foreign policy objective came into Göring's sights: the Sudeten Question. From archives plundered from the Austrian embassies in Berlin, Prague, Paris and London, and from the phone-tapped transcripts of his 'Research Office', he knew how much Britain and France feared a war; this certainty confirmed him in the view that the Sudeten Question could be resolved with the same blackmailing tactics as had been applied to Austria in March 1938. But his plan did not get off the ground. This time Hitler made the running and Göring found himself back in the role of spectator. He wanted, without the use of force, to 'cut up' Czechoslovakia, 'the appendix of Europe', and 'divide it between Poland, Hungary and Germany'. He feared that the 'grab for Prague' might bring the western powers into the picture and provoke a world war. Meanwhile, however, Hitler had told his senior officers and civil servants of his 'irreversible decision' in the foreseeable future to 'destroy Czechoslovakia by military action'. Only one cautious reservation was voiced by Göring: would it not be better to bring the Reich up to a high level of preparedness in order to reduce the risk of an attack against Germany? Hitler turned a deaf ear to his henchman's objections. He wanted to attack. The peace was now just a prelude to war.

Göring was cool towards Hitler's war plans, but took pains to avoid contradicting them. He knew from long experience that stubborn opposition would simply strengthen Hitler in his purpose. Rather than making a stand against Hitler, Göring tried to find alternative courses of action which might yet prevent the 'big war' from breaking out. He indicated to London and Paris that Germany was willing to negotiate, and with a mixture of threats and cajoling sought to persuade the western powers to stay their hand. Göring was certainly no dove, but compared to Hitler he was a rather small hawk, who clung to the notion of an Anglo-German domination of Europe. Unfortunately Hitler was no longer interested in the vows of peace which he had made Göring profess to British diplomats at his Schorfheide hunting-parties. The Wehrmacht was given orders to be ready to move on 1 October 1938. The smell of war was in the air. Feverishly, but with growing pessimism, Göring searched for a way out.

On the fringe of the Nuremberg Party rally the Reich Master of Hunting promised the British Ambassador, Sir Neville Henderson, he could have the four best stags in Germany, provided Britain ceased to act as protector to Prague. Several times Göring stressed to the envoy that Hitler and the British premier, Neville Chamberlain, must meet for face-to-face talks. Although Chamberlain, who was anxious to preserve peace, took Göring's wishes to heart, the situation continued to deteriorate. Hitler issued an ultimatum demanding that Czechoslovakia hand over its mainly German-speaking Sudetenland region. This finally put an end to Britain's policy of appeasement and Göring's nightmare threatened to become reality. On 28 September 1938, shortly before the ultimatum was to expire, he barked at the German Foreign Minister, Joachim von Ribbentrop: 'If war breaks out now, then it'll be me who tells the German people that you drove us into it.' Ribbentrop retorted furiously that he refused to accept such a charge. In the presence of Hitler, two of the most senior members of the government were hurling insults at each other, as an eye-witness put it, 'like two primadonnas before a dress-rehearsal'. Later Göring claimed he had told the Führer that he did not want a war, because he knew what war was like. But he went on to say that once the Führer gave the order to march, 'then I will be in the first plane that goes into battle'. Göring did indeed say this, though not on this occasion at the Reich Chancellery and not in Hitler's presence. Göring never had the courage to put his views strongly to Hitler face to face. Confronted by his Führer, the veteran bruiser acted with obsequious and undignified humility. Göring's dilemma was simply Hitler himself. There was no escaping him. As the French Ambassador, François-Poncet, observed, Göring was 'sensitive and easily wounded. He would then withdraw to his tent like Achilles.

But Hitler would call him back, slap him on the shoulder and say, "Good old Göring!" And Göring would blush and all would be forgotten . . .'

However, Hitler was now far less well disposed towards his designated successor than he had been even a year before. Ever since the 'wretched Munich conference', at which Mussolini submitted a compromise document drafted by Göring, granting Czechoslovakia a final brief grace period, Hitler visibly distanced himself from his Second-in-Command. It is true that the fate of the Czech state was sealed by the signing of the Munich Agreement, and Göring was pleased with this 'success'. But Hitler was disgruntled and even accused his henchman of cowardice.

He was forced to postpone his war and he rightly held Göring responsible. The suspicion began to grow in Hitler's mind that his disciple no longer stood so unquestioningly behind his ruthless territorial and racial programme as did his compliant Foreign Minister, Ribbentrop. In the coming months Ribbentrop slipped into the role which Göring had played in the *Anschluss* of Austria. Officially Göring remained 'Number Two' in Germany, but in those fateful spring and summer months his position of power began to crumble, even though for the sake of appearances the 'friendship' between the Führer and his 'most loyal champion' was preserved.

The spirit of Munich rapidly evaporated. Storm-signals were hoisted. Hitler set about crushing Czechoslovakia. On 11 March 1939, a Saturday, *Generaloberst* Wilhelm Keitel received instructions to draw up an ultimatum: Prague was simply to accede to the occupation of its provinces of Bohemia and Moravia. Göring was excluded from all this. His health had suffered and he was recuperating in San Remo. His walks and games of tennis contrasted bizarrely with the dire crisis which overshadowed Europe. Hitler had himself ordered Göring to take a holiday, so that he could prepare the fatal strike against Czechoslovakia without interference. 'His stay will contribute to the calming of feelings in Italy,' the Führer announced. Thus it was only on the day of the invasion, on 15 March 1939, that Göring learned what Hitler had planned behind his back. At Nuremberg he recalled:

I was furious because the whole thing had been decided over my head. I had advised patience and had stressed that to breach the Munich Agreement would mean a loss of prestige for Chamberlain, and would probably put Churchill in power. Hitler didn't listen to me.

It seems clear that Hitler wanted to prevent Göring from making a plea for peace, as he had done at Munich.

By now things had become even worse for Czechoslovakia. Hungary demanded the cession of the Carpatho–Ukraine region, and Slovakia declared its independence. Nazis shouting 'Sieg Heil' swept across Prague's Wenceslas Square. In this precarious situation the Czech President, Emil Hácha, headed for Berlin in a desperate state of mind. The ageing politician, who suffered from a weak heart, intended to plead with Hitler for the continuing existence of Czechoslovakia as an independent nation. His mission ended in a humiliating and degrading charade, in which a re-invigorated Göring took the leading part. Hitler presented the supplicant Hácha with the death-sentence on his country and ordered him to ensure that the 'entry of German troops takes place in an acceptable manner'.

Hácha, despite suffering from fainting fits, was forced to sign away the freedom of his multi-racial nation. No doubt to please Hitler, Göring and Ribbentrop outbid each other in their hair-raising descriptions of what would 'certainly' happen if Hácha did not sign: 'Within two hours Prague will be a heap of ash and rubble.' – 'Hundreds of bombers are waiting for the take-off order, which is effective from 6 a.m should you fail to sign.' Broken down by Göring's psychological scare-tactics, Hácha put his name to the document. The so-called Rump Republic of Czechoslovakia would henceforth be referred to as the 'Reich Protectorate of Bohemia and Moravia'.

Once again Göring had been obliged to bow to the 'Führer's will'. Open criticism, let alone active resistance, would in his mind have been tantamount to treason against the man to whom he owed his entire political career. Göring was caught in the loyalty trap. Once the undisputed Number Two, he had been reduced, by the rise of Ribbentrop, to the position of Hitler's gofer. After many years as his closest confidant he now had to accept the fact that Hitler and his Foreign Minister were putting together important plans without him. However, nothing hurt this vain and egocentric mogul more than the feeling that he had lost his political clout and was being sidelined. Even so, he did not hold Hitler responsible for this; his devotion to the Führer was undiminished. His resentment was against his rival at the Foreign Ministry, Joachim von Ribbentrop – the man who supported Hitler's aggressive war-plans and thus outpointed Göring in influence and prestige – whom he described as 'Germany's Principal Parrot', a 'criminal idiot' and 'conceited peacock'. When the 'Pact of Steel', the military alliance between Germany and Italy, was negotiated without Göring on 22 May 1939, Ribbentrop nevertheless asked him to pose behind him for the signature photograph. Göring's reply was an admission of his powerlessness: 'I'm not a fool; I don't even know what's being signed here.'

Outwardly, however, Hitler stuck by the man who had been his colleague since 1922. The dictator once assured Prince Paul of Yugoslavia: 'I'm not lonely. I have the best friend in the world. I have Göring.' And when Emmy Göring, who thanks to Hitler's bachelor status was the 'First Lady' of the Reich, to everyone's amazement gave birth to a baby girl, Hitler was godfather when the infant was christened Edda, after Mussolini's daughter. This admittedly failed to prevent satirical comment about the new addition to the Göring family. A joke went round: 'What do the letters E.D.D.A. stand for? Answer: *'Ewiger Dank Dem Adjutanten'* ['Eternal thanks to the Adjutant'].

The cabaret comedian Werner Finck quipped that the child should really be called Hamlet: *'sein oder nicht sein'*. (The German words can mean either 'To be or not to be', or 'his or not his'.) Göring took this amiss and Finck was sent to a concentration-camp. The jovial heavyweight might like to present himself as a man of the people with a good sense of humour – but anyone who made fun of him soon found they themselves had little to laugh about. On board a warship in 1936 the seasick Göring vomited over the side, and two rather brash lieutenants awarded him the title of *'Reichsfischfüttermeister'* (Reich Master of Fish-food) along with the appropriate string vest. This prank also ended in arrests.

Hitler's 'best friend' was playing a double game; on the one hand he boasted having the strongest Air Force in the world, both in numbers of planes and their technical capability, though in truth it was far from being equipped for a war of any great length – while on the other hand he worked intensively for an understanding with London, in the deluded hope that peace could be rescued with a 'second Munich', so that he could go on enjoying his life of luxury undisturbed. From his home at Carinhall he was continually establishing new contacts. On several occasions he played host to the super-rich Swedish head of the Electrolux company, Axel Wenner-Gren, who had a direct line to Chamberlain. Four times Göring sent his special envoy, a department head named Helmut Wohltat, to London. He asked German aristocrats to open channels through their English kinsmen. Yet Anglo–German relations worsened still further when, in late August 1939, Hitler and Stalin signed a Non-Aggression Pact, and the British Ambassador in Berlin, Henderson, announced that his government would stand by Poland. When Hitler scheduled *Fall Weiss* ('Plan White', the invasion of Poland) for the end of August, the Secretary for Air, Erhard Milch, noted in his diary: 'At eleven o'clock G. tells me the plan! He is nervous.'

Time was pressing; the chances of defusing the powder-keg at the last minute were minimal. Göring knew that once Hitler had set his mind on something, there was no way of persuading him otherwise, particularly as his own opinion had lost most of its weight. Nevertheless, he risked making one final attempt to keep Britain out of a war between Germany and Poland. He had two hopes left: first that Hitler was only playing a high-risk game of bluff; and second that the feelers he had put out in London through another Swedish intermediary, Birger Dahlerus, would bear fruit.

Göring had known this industrialist, who had excellent contacts both in Britain and Germany, since 1934. Like Göring, Dahlerus was convinced that Britain would enter the war and for economic reasons, if nothing else, was interested in 'a last attempt to save the peace'. Several times during these fateful summer days Dahlerus shuttled as a peacebroker between London and Berlin. Göring did manage to arrange for his emissary to talk to Hitler who, for his part, hoped Britain would remain neutral but who was pressing for action rather than negotiation. Göring's half-hearted intention of preventing war through Dahlerus failed. He knew by now from his 'Research Office' eavesdroppers that Britain and France would stand by Poland and that Italy was refusing to fight on Germany's side. Once again he tried to dissuade Hitler from his decision.

GÖRING: We've got to stop going for broke!
HITLER: All my life I've gone for broke.

The struggle to prevent war seemed finally to have been lost. Nonetheless Göring made one last effort through Dahlerus to set up mediation talks in London. Göring was like a cat on hot bricks. The engines of two Junkers Ju 52s were warming up on the tarmac, the valet was ironing his dinner-jacket and his bodyguards had been instructed to wear their best suits. But the naïve hope that the United Kingdom could be held back at this late hour from going to war was shattered. Britain and France declared war. As the Luftwaffe struck deep into Polish territory, Göring complained to his friend and State Secretary, Paul 'Pilli' Körner: 'It's terrible – Hitler has gone mad.'

His gloom did not last long. A new demonstration of Hitler's favour made him forget how much he had fallen by the wayside. On 1 September 1939, the first day of the war, Hitler announced in the Reichstag: 'Should anything befall me in this struggle, then my immediate successor is Party Comrade Göring.' This consolation prize was enough to corrupt Göring once and for all; his dependence on Hitler was sealed. As long as Hitler lived, Göring would have to remain loyal to him, if he did not want to be disinherited. The decree – confirmed in writing on 29 June 1941 – made him Hitler's compliant tool. As far as Hitler was concerned, the succession arrangement was no more than a formality. But to Göring it indicated that he once again belonged to Hitler's innermost circle. It was only the prospect of one day stepping into the Führer's shoes that compensated for the humiliating loss of authority during the war, and the disastrous performance of 'his' Luftwaffe.

Dazzled by unreal statistics on air strength and deceived by imaginary 'design successes' which engineers at the Luftwaffe's

Rechlin test-centre exaggerated for his benefit, Göring placed hopes in his squadrons which could never be fulfillled. The truth was that his Air Force lacked the long-range bombers it needed if it was to meet the strategic demands of a protracted war in the air. The Luftwaffe was equipped for short, sharp *blitzkrieg* assaults against Poland or France, but not for the duel against Britain's Royal Air Force. No more than four Junkers Ju 88 bombers were ready for action. Long-range bombers only existed on the drawing-boards of the Heinkel designers in the Baltic city of Rostock. Göring himself had put the building of long-range bombers on ice, on 29 April 1937. This meant one thing was certain: strategic bombing missions could not be flown with any chance of conclusive success. The outbreak of war had caught the Luftwaffe totally unprepared.

The swift victory over the Polish Air Force, outnumbered twenty to one, disguised Germany's real weaknesses and boosted Göring's unfounded confidence with an ecstatic triumphalism. In the first mass air-attack on any city, 400 German aircraft reduced the fortified western side of Warsaw to rubble, after which Göring boasted that the Reich had the Luftwaffe to thank for its defeat of Poland. The destruction of Warsaw was followed on 14 May 1940 by the bombing of Rotterdam at the very moment when surrender negotiations were in progress.

On one hand, the war which Göring still wanted to stop offered him undreamed-of opportunities to raise his profile with Hitler. But on the other hand he knew that the economy was also unprepared for war. Not least for this reason he continued to make efforts, by means of private channels to London and Washington, to reach a 'respectable peace settlement'. Through the American oil-millionaire William Rhodes Davis, President Roosevelt received peace-signals from Göring. His offer sounded nothing short of sensational: as the new German Chancellor, Göring would immediately withdraw from Poland and put an end to the persecution of Jews. The US President reacted positively with a guarantee to reinstate Germany's 1914 frontiers and to restore its former colonies. Simultaneously Birger Dahlerus took soundings – with Hitler's consent – in London. Once again, however, all attempts came to nothing. The last illusion of peace was gone.

Hitler summed matters up: 'Any hope of compromise is childish. Now it's victory or defeat.'

On 3 September Göring was stricken with doubt: 'If we lose this war, may heaven have mercy on us.' Göring anticipated a long war fought on several fronts. Traumatic memories of November 1918 were revived, but from the start, in spite of all his reservations, he supported Hitler's war of annihilation. He had tried very hard to prevent it; now he would do all he could to win it. He was co-signatory with Hitler of the 'Germanization Decree' and thus shared responsibility for the ethnic cleansing of the occupied regions; and he issued instructions for the economic plundering of Poland. If he could not impose moderation on Hitler, then he would obey him like a true soldier. Admittedly, Hitler was not greatly impressed by Göring's efforts. He was already planning the war in the west, the *Fall Gelb* (Plan Yellow). On 17 January 1940 France was about to be attacked, when an incident in Belgium halted the military machine. A German dispatch aircraft of the Luftwaffe was carrying secret operational orders when it made a forced landing near Malines. Now Germany's plans for the west were out in the open and Göring was in the firing-line. Hitler blamed him, and demanded a scapegoat – the Luftwaffe Chief had to dismiss one of his most able Commanders, *General der Flieger* Helmuth Felmy. Meanwhile, Hitler postponed the invasion until the spring.

Göring sought refuge in a world of unreality. For a fee of several million marks he ordered a rainmaker to favour the attack with good weather. Not long before that he had required a fortune-teller to find out why Britain had not intervened in Poland. When 'Yellow' finally started, Göring, wishing to travel to the Front, ordered a massive headquarters-train called '*Kurfürst*' (Prince-Elector) to be assembled, complete with a special coach carrying eight motor-cars, a photographic laboratory and a sickbay. With naïve enthusiasm he boasted that the British and French troops encircled at Dunkirk could be knocked out by the Luftwaffe unaided. Hitler enjoyed hearing words like that. 'When I hear Göring talk,' he told Albert Speer, around this time, 'it's like a steam-bath. After it I feel refreshed. He has an exciting way of putting things.'

Yet these grand words were not always followed by action. At Dunkirk the Luftwaffe suffered its first débâcle. For the first time control of the air over a battle-zone had been lost. It was now plain to see how ill-informed he had been about the capability of his bomber- and fighter-squadrons. The mistakes in his staffing policy, the appointment of old comrades to senior positions, came home to roost with fatal results. On 31 January 1939, out of the obligations of friendship with an old wartime chum, he appointed the former flying-ace Ernst Udet to the post of *Generalluftzeugmeister* (Air-Armourer-General) – a decision which had dire consequences, since Udet was not up to the demanding job of controlling air armaments production. Under Udet's aegis there began a fatal series of technical mishaps and misguided staff appointments. Coupled with Göring's ignorance of technology and his irresponsible turning of a blind eye to the strength of the opposition, Udet's incompetence sealed the Luftwaffe's fate. Too comfortable, too credulous when listening to misleading advice and occupied with too many other tasks, Göring failed to control the equipping and training of the Air Force with a firm hand. Udet was certainly part of the problem, but Göring's weakness as head of the Luftwaffe was decisive.

> How do you know when the war is over? When Goebbels' trousers fit Göring!
>
> *Underground joke*

However, the first warning signs went unnoticed in the general jubilation over the rapid succession of victories over France, Holland and Belgium. Göring's egocentric nature seldom allowed room for self-criticism. What mattered more to him was to heap exaggerated praise on the genius of the Führer and to extol him as the 'greatest military leader of all time'. The German phrase *grösster Feldherr aller Zeiten* was soon abbreviated to the rather less flattering '*Gröfaz*', which Göring's brother Albert amended to '*Grövaz*', for *grösster Verbrecher aller Zeiten* ('greatest criminal of all time').

Albert's impertinence very nearly landed him in concentration-camp, while Göring earned new honours for his loyalty to Hitler.

After the successful campaign in the west Göring's idol decorated him with the 'Grand Cross of the Iron Cross' – a medal especially created for him. At the same time Hitler awarded his status-hungry squire the title of *Reichsmarschall*. This guaranteed that he would still outrank the *Generaloberste*, or full generals, who had been promoted to *Feldmarschall*, after the French campaign. Once again Göring could look to the future with confidence.

After the British retreat from Dunkirk on 4 June 1940 Hitler expected that his opponent would knuckle under and prepare the ground for a 'sensible peace agreement'. But Britain's new Prime Minister, Winston Churchill, had no intention of making peace with Hitler, even when the dictator publicly assured him that the British Empire would be left intact under a negotiated peace. Hitler had not expected this resistance. In fact, after France's capitulation on 25 June 1940, there seemed every prospect of achieving what had long been the central objective of his foreign policy: 'We are putting out feelers to England, on the basis of a division of the world between us.' Hitler hoped, as Göring did, that London would soon compromise and come round to Germany's view. When nothing of the kind occurred, Hitler resorted to the only thing left: Britain must be forcibly compelled to the negotiating table. On 21 July 1940, Göring revealed to his Luftwaffe chiefs at Carinhall that air attacks on England would have to be systematically intensified and the Royal Air Force destroyed. On 13 August 1940, designated *Adlertag* (Eagle Day), one of the decisive air battles of the war began, with 1,485 missions flown by *Luftflotten* (air fleets) 2, 3 and 5. It was a baptism of fire for the Luftwaffe, which to date had had an easy run against weak opposition.

After only a few days it became clear that, as regards fighting capability and number of fighters, the Royal Air Force was fully a match for them. Göring's prediction of victory within five weeks was an unachievable fantasy. Britain's modern air defence was well able to stand up to the often amateurishly led Luftwaffe – and what is more the RAF were even able, on 25 August, to launch their first attack on Berlin. The damage inflicted was slight, but the surprise raid gave a foretaste of the devastating saturation-bombing in the last two years of the war.

At the very climax of the battle, Göring's rapacious greed for art treasures grew to an almost pathological hunger. On his orders a whole army of agents combed the occupied countries of Europe for works of art to grace his private museum at Carinhall. Throughout the conquered regions, in Paris, Amsterdam or Brussels, the 'king of the black-market' (as Himmler dubbed him) ecstatically seized anything of high value whose ownership was unclear. As a regular visitor to the Jeu de Paume museum in Paris he was delighted to see the property confiscated from French Jews. Göring particularly loved the masterpieces by Rembrandt, van Dyck and Rubens. The fact that quite a few of his paintings were officially condemned as 'decadent' did not worry him, as long he could exchange them abroad for other artworks. Renaissance tapestries, marble statues, alabaster vases and sundials, and oriental weapons – Göring 'bought' them all. The more valuable and exotic, the better. His appetite seemed insatiable. His castles at Mautendorf and Veldenstein brimmed with looted treasures, and at Carinhall, where priceless paintings hung in four rows above one another, the lack of wall-space meant that some of the pictures had to be attached to the ceiling. The attics looked like a warehouse full of loot, which Göring flogged off to senior Party officials at horrendous prices. The best pieces, however, remained in Carinhall, where the art-thief planned to put them on public display in a 'Hermann Göring Gallery'.

> Corrupted by power and the temptations of the good life, he visibly fell victim to the habits of ageing tyrants, to lethargy and megalomania, and in the end was no longer capable of any initiative; no military catastrophe could distract him from his fashionable preoccupations; a 'perfumed Nero' who played his lyre in a reverie while Rome went up in flames.
>
> *Joachim Fest, author and journalist*

In order to lend this art-grab an aura of legality, Göring drew up a decree dated 1 May 1941, which gave him *carte blanche* to plunder the museums of Europe. It was, after all, 'the urgent task

of National Socialism to secure all research material and cultural
assets of the designated areas and transport them to Germany'. By
this sleight-of-hand he made sure he could help himself, before
any other art-lovers in the Nazi hierarchy. By 1944 Göring had
assembled an art collection worth several hundred million marks.
While he played out his fantasies at the control panel of his model
railway, real trains laden with stolen art treasures left every corner
of Europe, and headed for Germany.

Meanwhile, Hitler was planning his invasion of the Soviet
Union. When he disclosed his intentions on 4 November 1940 to
the chiefs of the three armed services, they reacted with
astonishment. Once again, Göring bombarded Hitler with
arguments as to why there should be no war with the Soviet
Union, at least not at this point in time. He stated in his evidence
at Nuremberg:

> That evening I put the matter to the Führer in this way: I urged
> and beseeched him not to start a war with Russia at this moment
> or in the foreseeable future. Not that I was guided by any
> considerations of international law or other such motives; my view
> was based exclusively on political and military reasoning.

Göring warned against a war on two fronts, warned of war with
the United States, of the endless spaces of the Russian steppe and
of a Britain which, while Germany was preoccupied in the east,
might gather new strength. Given the poor state of Russia's
military machine, he advised, there was no need for haste. First of
all, the war in the west had to be won. Otherwise it might be the
case 'that we are giving up a secure situation here, in exchange for
an insecure one'. Göring's warnings went unheeded. Five weeks
later, on 18 December 1940, Hitler signed directive No. 21 for
'Operation Barbarossa', the invasion of the Soviet Union. At that
moment Göring was out hunting on the Rominten Heath – still
firmly believing that Hitler would abandon his suicidal war-plans.
Once again he was overruled. Once again he could tell how slight
his influence over the dictator had become, and it was this anger at
his own powerlessness that drove Hitler's vassal to treason. On 9
June 1941, Göring informed his intermediary, Birger Dahlerus,

that Germany would attack the Soviet Union 'around June 15th'. Dahlerus grabbed the telephone and passed the word on to the British and American Ambassadors in Stockholm. On 15 June, Göring and his Swedish messenger were facing each other across a table. Göring went into more detail: the invasion would begin in seven days, on Sunday 22 June.

Once the decision had been taken, Göring no longer dared to pester Hitler with warnings. In any case, the relationship between him and Hitler, once so close, was now much more casual, a fact for which a new and dangerous rival to Göring was largely responsible. In painstaking detail the devious deputy leader of the Nazi Party, Martin Bormann, who had direct access to Hitler, noted down every one of Göring's wrong decisions in a bid to foil his most heartfelt ambition – to succeed Hitler.

In the days that followed, Göring was noticeably anxious to prove his willingness to carry out Hitler's orders. He unhesitatingly slipped into the role of a ruthless advocate of Hitler's race war against the 'Bolshevist peril'. He instructed that Russian prisoners were 'to be shot without any judicial process'. As Head of the 'Economic Staff East' he ordered the merciless plundering of the occupied regions of Russia and the Ukraine. While Russian civilians were dragged off for forced labour in Germany, Göring ordered 100 villages in the Bieloviecz Forest to be razed to the ground – to make way for a private hunting reserve. Göring presented himself to Hitler as a man of rabid brutality – prepared to sign any document which would further aggravate the situation of Jews in Germany and the rest of Europe.

On 31 July 1941, at the height of Germany's deceptive certainty of victory, Göring, as 'Commissioner of the Four-Year Plan' and on Hitler's instructions, authorized Reinhard Heydrich to 'make all necessary preparations, as regards organization, for a comprehensive resolution of the Jewish question in the German sphere of influence in Europe.' The Holocaust, which had begun in the east with the murders by the *Einsatzgruppen* ('action squads'), was now to spread across western Europe and even as far as French North Africa. Göring used the powers vested in him to appoint Heydrich to be 'supremo' for dealing with Jews throughout Europe – responsible for accomplishing Hitler's central purpose: the annihilation of European Jewry. Two weeks after issuing this blank cheque to Heydrich, Göring announced that Jews no longer had 'any business to be in the territories under German domination'.

How much did Göring know about the mass-killings in the extermination-camps? 'We were never shown figures or anything of that kind,' was his excuse on 21 March, at Nuremberg. It has been proved that Göring knew about the shootings behind the German lines in Byelorus (White Russia), and the entry made by Joseph Goebbels in his diary for 2 March 1943 after a four-hour conversation with Göring, speaks for itself: 'Göring knows exactly what danger we would be in if we were to weaken in this war. He has absolutely no illusions about it. In the Jewish question especially, we have committed ourselves to such an extent that there is no running away from it now.' But in Nuremberg the defendant claimed to have known nothing of the 'terrible incidents' in the camps and never to have done more than 'stress the differences between races'. He stubbornly denied that the genocide had taken place. With a look of innocence he asked Gustave Gilbert in April 1946: 'How could it be possible in practice to murder two-and-a-half million people?' The psychologist repeated to him what the camp Commandant at Auschwitz, Rudolf Höss, had reported to him about the gas-chambers, and the fact that Hitler had ordered the genocide. 'Would it not have been better,' Gilbert wanted to know, 'if someone had killed the man who ordered the mass-killings?'

'Oh, it's easy to say that,' retorted Göring, 'but you can't *do* that kind of thing. What sort of system would it be if anyone could kill the commander-in-chief when they didn't like the orders he gave? In a military system there has to be obedience.'

At the start of the Russian campaign the obedient Göring was able to report to Hitler a rise in the number of aircraft shot down by 'his' Luftwaffe. By the end of 1941, 8,000 Soviet warplanes had been destroyed. But beyond the range of German bombers, east of the Ural mountains, Stalin was successfully re-equipping the Red Air Force. As early as November 1941, Hitler's attitude towards Göring's squadrons became much more sharply critical. The problems of the Luftwaffe increased and, when it proved impossible to capture Moscow and Leningrad in simultaneous attacks, Hitler directed all his anger against the Air Force commanders for the first time. The onset of winter cut a swathe through strategic planning, but the chief problem was that the chaotically disorganized aircraft production could not keep pace with the losses. While Udet was *Generalluftzeugmeister*, the number of fighters rolling out of the construction hangars never exceeded 375 a month; in the autumn of 1944, when Albert Speer was armaments minister, the number of new aircraft reached 2,500 in peak months.

Hitler now relied principally on the Army. Respect for the Luftwaffe had significantly declined. In this crisis-laden scenario Göring was shattered by a series of fateful blows. First of all, on 27 November 1941, Ernst Udet took his own life, after Göring had laid the sole blame with him for the wretched equipment situation. Immediately before shooting himself with a revolver, Udet had written on a blackboard: '*Eisener* ['ironsides'], you betrayed me.' *Eisener* was Göring's nickname. Shortly afterwards Werner Mölders, *Inspekteur* of Fighter Pilots, died in an accident on the way to Udet's memorial service. A few days later, in December, Hitler declared war on the United States without consulting Göring, and in February 1942, the man Hitler appointed as Armaments Minister was not Göring, the 'Commissioner for the Four-Year Plan', but the young architect Albert Speer. Speer was now responsible for large areas of the war economy and thus *de facto* in charge of the Four-Year Plan. Göring's descent from power proceeded relentlessly. Following the British bombing-raid on the fine old Hanseatic city of Lübeck, on 28 March 1942, Hitler gave orders for the 'retaliatory' bombing of historic British cities, like Bath, Exeter and Canterbury. These attempts at revenge were derisively nicknamed 'Baedeker raids' by the island race, in an allusion to the famous guidebooks. The British had long ago ceased to take the bombing very seriously. Göring was forced to stand idly by while 'his' Luftwaffe flew its missions against England. Hitler's word was law.

Given the cold shoulder, his responsibilities curtailed, and with drug abuse leaving its mark, he retreated more and more into a private existence. He often sent a representative to speak for him

The attributes that led to his personal rise to power were at the same time those of his failure, since both rise and failure were based on an entirely uninhibited egocentricity, devoid of any control-mechanisms, which was aware of no norms of obligation beyond those of satisfying his own needs and which gave him, in all his naïve cravings, the character of a large and dangerous child.

Joachim Fest, contemporary German author and journalist, biographer of Hitler

in discussions at the Führer's headquarters. Göring escaped into a dreamworld of art, at Carinhall he took an intoxicated delight in a canvas by Cézanne or Van Gogh, he went on art-buying sprees to Paris and made a grotesque impression in Rome. The Italian Foreign Minister, Count Galeazzo Ciano, described him as 'puffed up and arrogant', as a political clown in a vast sable coat, which looked like 'a cross between a motorist's outfit circa 1906 and the fur worn by an expensive courtesan going to the opera'. Göring succumbed increasingly to the attractions of idleness. 'In 1942,' Albert Speer recalled, 'he was generally thought of as lethargic and not at all keen on working.' Hitler's once impulsive vassal, who had tackled the expansion of the Luftwaffe and the Four-Year Plan with such energy, now looked sleepy. His glassy gaze betrayed his addiction. As Speer put it: 'He gave a visible impression of instability. He took up too many ideas indiscriminately, he was erratic and generally lacked a grasp of reality.' In all seriousness he proposed building locomotives out of concrete, because of the steel shortage. Albert Kesselring, Commander-in-Chief South, came to the conclusion:

The Göring of 1934–5 and the man of 1942–3 are very different phenomena. In the 1930s he was an energetic, self-confident and pugnacious personality, in the 1940s a tired and irascible man who distanced himself from the patriotic cause and was no longer able to assert his authority.

Yet although the *Reichsmarschall* with 'be-ringed and sausage-like fingers' (as the Chief of the General Staff Franz Halder noticed) could no longer keep his promises and left German cities unprotected against the bombs dropped by American Flying Fortresses and British Lancasters, Göring astonishingly continued to enjoy popularity among ordinary Germans, thanks to his facile warmth and 'sincerity', even when they were faced with the fact that air-raids on the Reich were intensifying dramatically. Between 1940 and 1942, the city of Cologne alone suffered 104 nights of bombing. But it was not until the 'thousand bomber raid' on the night of 31 May 1942, that it became clear how defenceless the Luftwaffe was against these massive attacks.

No less than 1,500 tons of bombs turned the cathedral city into a wasteland of rubble. Up to that date this was the greatest air-raid in the history of warfare and brought annihilating catastrophe on Cologne. But the Luftwaffe refused to admit that this deadly destruction had taken place. It actually boasted a 'great victory' and even considered covering itself with glory in a special announcement. 'With the number of enemy bombers shot down so far confirmed at 37,' this would have read, 'approximately half the enemy aircraft flying over Reich territory were destroyed. In the course of this action one night-fighter formation scored its 600th night kill.' Here were too many lies in one sentence, even for Hitler. We read in the war-journal of the Commander-in-Chief of the Army: 'In view of the losses, the Führer firmly rejected a victory report of this kind on psychological grounds and went on to express the view that the report could not possibly be correct.' Enough was enough. 'When Göring tried to put his hand out to Hitler,' Göring's adjutant Karl Bodenschatz recalled, 'Hitler ignored him. In the presence of young officers he cut the *Reichsmarschall* dead.' Private conversations between the two of them – once a daily occurrence – became much rarer. For a long time, important discussions had taken place without him. Nevertheless he was perhaps the only realist in Hitler's inner circle. He had a pretty good idea of what lay in store for the Reich. Allied superiority gave them much to fear. 'We ought to be happy,' he said in late 1942, 'if after this war Germany has kept its 1933 frontiers.'

What irritated Hitler most was the over-staffed bureaucracy of the Air Ministry. In addition to countless departments, Göring's

> If Catholics are so convinced that the Pope is infallible in all religious and moral matters, then we National Socialists declare with the same deep conviction that for us too the Führer is quite simply infallible. It is a blessing for Germany that in Hitler we find the rare combination of the most acutely logical thinker with the truly profound philosopher and the iron man of action, tough in the extreme.
>
> *Göring, 1942*

private office consisted of no less than 104 people, occupying an entire floor of the Ministry. Two million men served in the Luftwaffe and for this reason alone it had an obligation to perform. In the battle for Stalingrad Göring wanted to prove finally what his forces were really capable of achieving. The tide was to be turned on the Volga by an airlift, like the one mounted in the previous winter at Demyansk. In the hope of polishing up his tarnished image Göring pompously promised Hitler: '*Mein Führer*! The supplying of the Sixth Army in Stalingrad from the air is personally guaranteed by me. You can rely on it.' Vacillating between apathy and euphoria, the head of the Luftwaffe hoped to bring 500 tons of provisions, ammunition and fuel daily into the encircled 'cauldron' – which, in view of his air-cargo capacity and the weather conditions, was an illusory project.

Influenced by Göring's reassurances that the supply situation of the encircled Army was 'not at all bad', Hitler gave orders that they should hold out at all costs. For the exhausted troops in the ice and snow the Luftwaffe was the last remaining hope. Yet its Commander-in-Chief preferred to travel to Paris in his luxurious special train, *Asia*, returning with chests full of paintings, tapestries, silver plate and marble statues. Stalingrad seemed a long way away. To Göring, Gobelins were more important. The Luftwaffe only managed to bring in a daily average of 160 tons of supplies to the Stalingrad pocket – too little for survival. When the situation was already beyond hope, Hitler transferred the command of Stalingrad's air-lift to *Feldmarschall* Milch, whose organizational talent he valued. Hitler knew that the big-talking

Göring had failed. Stalingrad was to be the greatest disaster of his career. On the day the remnants of the Sixth Army surrendered he wrote in his personal appointment-book: 'Rested in bed all day.'

Even Joseph Goebbels now noted with surprise that Göring's standing with Hitler had 'suffered enormously'. On 9 March 1943, he wrote in his diary that Hitler expressed 'extraordinarily sharp criticism', since Göring had 'let himself be lulled into false security by his staff officers . . . Göring only likes to hear what is pleasant; that is why the people around him tell him nothing unpleasant . . . The Führer explodes in rage at the *Reichmarschall*'s irresponsible entourage.'

Hitler's anger with Göring was to increase, when in March the Royal Air Force dropped a carpet of bombs on the Ruhr and, in five massive raids on Hamburg within eight days from 24 to 30 June 1943, released such a firestorm with its incendiaries that even the tarmac road surfaces were ablaze. Hamburg endured the catastrophic fate that Göring had intended for London. The RAF had crippled German radar defences by dropping clouds of tinfoil strips, ironically codenamed 'Windows'. This meant that all the night-fighters were working blind; after dark the Reich was without protection. Göring was neither capable of warding off the Anglo-American attacks, nor did he succeed in mounting effective counter-offensives.

My friends and I were so naïve. We simply didn't think it possible that anyone could lie the way he did. Göring claimed he could get the troops out of Stalingrad. We only found out later that it was quite impossible. Göring must have known that. It was a dirty trick and that's when we began to have doubts about the man's character. Then his weaknesses became more and more obvious. He made himself ridiculous with his fancy dress. I thought, how can he strut about like a cockatoo, in a snow-white uniform with red stripes down his trousers and all those medals – and in the middle of the war, when we didn't know where the next meal was coming from.

Walter Wittkampf, victim of the bombing

By night, almost without interruption, British formations flew in ever more precise strategic raids on German cities. Mannheim, Nuremberg, Darmstadt, Heilbronn – every city of any size became a potential target. The 'roof' of 'Fortress Europe' was open to the skies. At this stage in the war all hopes were pinned on the 'V-weapons' (V for *Vergeltung*, 'reprisal' or 'vengeance') which were being worked on feverishly at Peenemünde.

In August 1943, the RAF launched a large-scale attack, apparently aimed at Berlin, but then the bombers swung north and bombed the secret rocket installations at Peenemünde, which the British had been tipped off about by Polish intelligence sources. Hitler's wrath was uncontainable. He demanded a scapegoat. His anger should actually have been directed at Göring, but Hitler did not want to impugn the *Reichsmarschall*'s authority. Instead he placed the blame on the Chief of the General Staff, *Generaloberst* Hans Jeschonnek, who was already in a state of despair over Göring's moods, his lack of interest and knowledge and his megalomania. Crushed by the accusations heaped on him, Jeschonnek took the same way out as Udet and put a pistol to his head. A note was found on the dead man's desk. It read: 'I can no longer work with the *Reichsmarschall*. Long live the Führer!'

Hitler also wanted less to do with Göring. Insults and abuse, in public as well as private, became more frequent. 'Your pigsty of a Luftwaffe,' Hitler bawled at Göring, not willing to admit how overstretched his Air Force was by all the assignments it was given. 'Göring! The Luftwaffe is useless. And that's your fault. You're lazy!' For some time now Hitler had been observing with growing displeasure Göring's Byzantine lifestyle in Carinhall, Rominten or Veldenstein Castle. While the Luftwaffe was fighting for its life, Göring invited Germany's new Ambassador to Sweden, Hans Thomsen, to some hunting at Carinhall, followed by a fashion-show.

Göring's grotesque appearance was described by the German diplomat and anti-Nazi, Ulrich von Hassell:

In the mornings he wore a sort of doublet with billowing white sleeves, then he changed costume several times during the day and in the evening appeared at table in a blue or violet kimono and fur-lined bedroom-slippers . . . Even in the mornings he carried a gold dagger at his side, wore a cravat-pin mounted with precious stones and around his fat girth a broad belt studded with more precious stones, to say nothing of the number and magnificence of his rings.

And still Hitler hung on to Göring as the Luftwaffe's Commander-in-Chief 'for reasons of state policy', as he put it to *Generaloberst* Heinz Guderian. This was because his designated successor still enjoyed undiminished popularity with the nation as a whole, something the regime could exploit. Above all, however, Göring remained a factor whose power was not to be underestimated; this was because Hitler could still not quite break away from the image of Göring as the 'old campaigner', that he had built up in the 'fighting days'.

As though hypnotized he enthused repeatedly during a situation-review following the fall of Mussolini on 25 July 1943:

The *Reichsmarschall* has come through a great many crises with me. In a crisis he stays completely cool. One cannot have a better adviser in times of crisis than the *Reichsmarschall*. In times of crisis the *Reichsmarschall* is both brutal and ice-cool. When it's make or break, I've always seen how he's the ruthless one, as hard as iron. So, you won't find a better man, there isn't a better man around. He's been with me through every crisis, the most difficult crises, and has always been ice-cool. Whenever things got really bad, he became ice-cool. . . .

In spite of disappointments and failures, the bond between the Führer and his 'first champion' seemed unbreakable. He would never be free of Hitler, Göring once confided to Albert Speer, and he explained to the psychologist Gilbert:

If I take an oath of allegiance, I cannot break it. Even for me it was hellishly hard to keep, I can tell you! Just try playing the crown prince for twelve whole years, always devoted to the king, even though disagreeing with many of his political actions, but incapable of doing anything about it and having to make the best of the situation.

After the war, in one of his rare moments of self-criticism, he defined his relationship with Hitler as 'prostitution of the soul'.

'From a political point of view, Göring might just as well have been dead,' wrote Rudolf Semler, Goebbels' adjutant, in his diary for 10 August 1943. 'In fact, rumours of his death were circulating. That is why Hitler, who still, remarkably, held Göring in high regard, suggested that the *Reichsmarschall* should show himself in public again, in order to regain his popularity.' It might be thought that for a man like Göring to mix with ordinary people would not be without its risks. But when seen walking around Berlin, it was clear that thanks to his overt *bonhomie* and informal charm, he could astonishingly still count on people's sympathy. The

I have to say that I too – like Hitler – had a soft spot for Göring. I had found him to be a charming and highly intelligent man, and continued to see him more as an individualist, an eccentric, and less as a sick man, or even an evil one.

Speer, 1979

worst he had to put up with was being greeted occasionally by a passer-by as 'Herr Meier', in a mocking allusion to the claim he once made, that 'if a single enemy bomber reaches Reich territory, then my name's Meier'. Apparently the blame for the bombing and for his failure as Chief of the Luftwaffe was laid at the feet of others: usually the 'leadership', but not the 'Fat Man'. He was more a figure of fun than a lightning-conductor for the desperate victims of the bombing. In a joke that went the rounds, Göring was compared to 'Tengelmann', a large grocery chain which claimed 'a branch (*Niederlage*) in every town'. (*Niederlage* is also German for 'defeat'.) About the Luftwaffe people used to say: 'Göring's fighters are up there now. The air-raid must be over.'

This black humour had a basis in truth. Every day in May 1944 2,000 Allied aircraft flew over German territory. Day after day bombs fell on hydrogenation plants, refineries and armaments factories. By the winter of 1944 the situation looked utterly hopeless. The Luftwaffe was falling apart, and Germany's cities

> After Stalingrad we heard little or nothing from the
> Commander-in-Chief of the Luftwaffe. When we talked
> about Göring amongst ourselves, all we said was: Fatso had
> better just keep his trap shut.
>
> *Joachim Matthies, member of the Luftwaffe*

were sinking in ash and rubble. Göring accused his fighter-pilots
of cowardice and cursed Udet for the chaos in the aircraft
industry. When Adolf Galland, one of the Luftwaffe's most
successful pilots, urged that the Messerschmitt 262, the world's
first production-line jet aircraft, should be immediately put into
service as an interceptor-fighter, Göring refused, in order to
preserve his fragile peace with Hitler, who illogically wanted to use
the Me 262 as a bomber.

For months the wrangling over the deployment of the Me 262
dragged on. Not until the late summer of 1944 was it delivered to
the Luftwaffe as a 'lightning-bomber', along with the Arado 234,
a twin-jet bomber capable of 480 mph – too late to clear the skies
over Germany of Allied aircraft. Even the record level of aircraft
production was rendered almost ineffectual by the hail of Allied
bombs. In 1944, 38,000 aircraft (compared to 11,000 in 1941)
left the workshops, but the fighters were paralysed by a lack of fuel
due to the bombing of the hydrogenation plants. As they rolled
out from the hangars on to the aprons, they were exposed and
unprotected against the bombs. On 6 June 1944, Goebbels
confided to his diary:

> Our inferiority in the air is downright catastrophic. The Führer
> is very hard hit by it, particularly in view of the fact that Göring
> is of course directly and indirectly to blame. But he can take no
> action against Göring, because if he did it would deal a severe
> blow to the authority of the Reich and the Party.

Even within the Luftwaffe confidence in the Commander-in-Chief
was waning. Göring, as a highly decorated First World War hero,

had once been the idol of younger pilots, but now he kept himself far removed from the worries and difficulties of airmen. How much the relationship between the Commander and his officers had suffered became clear when, at a conference at Wannsee, outside Berlin, on 7 November 1944, he once again branded the combat-weary airmen present as 'cowards' and had a gramophone-record of his insulting speech sent to every fighter unit – an open affront which almost provoked a mutiny. And the atmosphere got no better when Göring tried to rectify the unpleasant situation by calling a 'Luftwaffe Parliament' of thirty senior officers, but then told the delegates they could 'criticize anything and anyone in the Luftwaffe – with the exception of myself'.

> In the current war situation Göring shows himself to be completely passive.
>
> *Goebbels (Diary), 1944*

Göring had his back to the wall: he had no support either from Hitler or from his troops. 'At some point between the middle and end of January 1945,' he said at Nuremberg, 'all hope was gone.' In January 1945, when Soviet troops were getting close to the holy soil of Schorfheide, he arranged for his wife Emmy and daughter Edda to be moved to Bavaria. While the city of Dresden was being consumed by an inferno, he was making sure that the first shipments of his art treasures were hidden in a tunnel in the mountains near Berchtesgaden. One last time, in the dying days of the Reich, he nurtured hopes of a peace settlement. He wanted to negotiate with the Allies and, completely misreading the situation, believed the 'match could end in a draw'. Yet secretly he feared the worst – and wrote his will.

It was time for him to say farewell: on 20 April 1945, Hitler's final birthday, Göring made his way for the last time to the Reich Chancellery, to stand once more before the man he had followed, in all his crimes, with blind devotion. More than twenty years earlier he had vowed to remain loyal to Hitler – unto death. Now he had made up his mind to abandon his Führer and the encircled capital as quickly as possible. As Albert Speer described the scene: 'Göring announced that he had some very urgent matters to attend to in southern Germany. Hitler looked at him absently, and with a few apathetic words proffered his hand.'

Then Göring drove to Carinhall, personally demolished the country manor with explosives and headed south to the Obersalzberg. He was raddled by drug abuse, as lethargic and bloated as a jellyfish, like Hitler a physical wreck, but hoping at last to achieve the great goal of his life: to step out from Hitler's shadow and succeed him. Finally to be the sole ruler of Germany! The news of Hitler's apparent nervous breakdown drove him once more into frantic activity. Was Hitler really dead? At 10 p.m. on the same day, 23 April 1945, Göring sent a fateful radio-telegram to Hitler's bunker in Berlin. Merely reading the first lines brought a flush of fury to the dictator's cheeks. '*Mein Führer*, are you in agreement that . . . in accordance with your decree of 29.6.1941 I immediately assume overall leadership of the Reich as your deputy with full freedom of action at home and abroad?' As if this question alone was not enough of an affront to Hitler, the following sentence guaranteed the ultimate break with Göring. 'If no reply is received by 22.30 hours, I will assume that you have been deprived of your freedom of action. I will then regard the conditions of your decree as fulfilled and will act for the good of people and Fatherland.'

Towards the end of the war Göring was no longer discussed in Hitler's entourage. He was so again only after his telegram of 22 April 1945, in which Göring offered to deputize for Hitler, since Berlin was now encircled and Hitler deprived of his capacity to act. Bormann had apparently been very meticulous in passing on the full contents of the telegram, probably more meticulous than Göring had intended. This was a result of the strained relations between Göring and Bormann. Then came the explosion: Hitler burst into a seething rage. He felt it was a betrayal, that Göring wanted to take over the function of Führer.

Traudl Junge, Hitler's Secretary

It did not take Martin Bormann long to make up his mind. He saw this as the chance for a final plot against his personal enemy. 'Göring is committing treason!' he assured Hitler. 'I've known that for a long time,' shouted the latter, scarlet in the face. 'I know Göring is lazy. He let the Luftwaffe go to the dogs. He was corrupt. His example made corruption possible in our government. On top of all that he's been a morphine addict for years. I've known for a long time.'

> It is a pity that a man like Dönitz does not represent the Party, but that the Party is represented by Göring, who has as much to do with the Party as the cow has with research into radiation.
>
> *Goebbels (diary), 1945*

A short time later, in Berchtesgaden, *SS-Obersturmbannführer* Bernhard Frank was holding in his hand an order which Bormann had hastily scribbled on paper: 'Surround Göring house immediately, overcome any resistance and immediately arrest former *Reichsmarschall* Hermann Göring. Signed, Adolf Hitler.' Later that night in Göring's palatial country house on the Obersalzberg, Frank clicked his heels smartly and announced to the presumed traitor: '*Herr Reichsmarschall*, you are under arrest!' Six days later Hitler decreed in his 'Political Testament': 'Prior to my death I expel the former *Reichsmarschall* Hermann Göring from the Party.' His accusation that Göring had negotiated with the Allies behind his back was groundless. But Bormann had achieved his objective.

Göring felt he had been misunderstood by Hitler and that he was the victim of a plot. Although it was not he, but *Grossadmiral* (Grand Admiral) Karl Dönitz who stepped into Hitler's shoes, he still saw himself as the only person entitled to decide Germany's fate. On 6 May 1945 he over-rated himself to such a degree as to propose to Dönitz that he, Göring, should negotiate an 'honourable peace' in talks with Eisenhower as 'marshall to marshall'. When Dönitz did not even reply, Göring, as 'ranking officer of the German armed forces' made a direct

> He's dead, Emmy. Now I'll never be able to tell him that I remained loyal to him right to the end.
>
> *Göring to his wife, about Hitler's death, 1945*

appeal to Eisenhower to 'receive me in person' in order 'to prevent further bloodshed in a hopeless situation'. On 7 May 1945, the *Reichsmarschall*, travelling with his wife and daughter, was taken prisoner by the Americans on a mountain road near Radstadt, on his way to the rendezvous with the US Army. It was the last time that Hermann Göring would see his family at liberty. His comment spoke volumes: 'At least for twelve years I lived decently.'

> I remember well that my relationship with Göring, for whom I always had a soft spot, changed in Mondorf. He was arrogant and full of self-pity in a really repugnant way. One day at lunch Brandt was talking about the mountains and about how sad he was that they had lost their house there. 'Oh, come on,' Göring retorted, 'You have no reason at all to complain, when you had so little anyway. But what about me, with all *I* had. Just think what that means to me.' I was sitting with my back to Dönitz and heard him mutter to his neighbour: 'Yes, and all of it stolen.' He was right, of course – and men like that had been ruling the Reich!
>
> *Speer on his period of imprisonment in Mondorf before the Nuremberg Trial*

'He looked down and out,' recalled Leon Thanson, an interpreter at the Mondorf prison-camp in Luxembourg, 'and demanded pills. "I can't live without pills," he said. Not until he had been given some pills three days later, did he come out of himself and then he was the most affable of all the prisoners.' What the Swedish nursing-home had failed to do in 1925, US Army doctors now managed. The victors put 'Mister Göring', as they called him, on a diet and administered daily reducing doses of paracodeine tablets. It was during this period that Göring encountered Gustave Gilbert for the first time. In the remaining seventeen months of his life, no one was closer to the notorious prisoner than this psychologist serving with the US Army. Gilbert examined Göring under a magnifying glass. In an IQ test his score was an above-average 138. Less flattering to the man who had lost none of his vanity, were the results of the personality tests. Gilbert told Göring:

To be frank, you have shown that despite your active, aggressive character, you lack the courage to take real responsibility. In that ink-blot test you gave yourself away with a small gesture. Remember the card with the red stain? You tried to flick it away with your fingers, as though you thought you could wipe away the blood with one little movement. You did the same thing all through the trial. You took the headphones off, when the evidence of your guilt became intolerable.

Göring used the Nazi period as his stage. He was always an actor, a performer, who tried to put himself in the best light. His banana-republic uniforms always reinforced the theatrical impression. Even in his gestures, in his whole behaviour he always tried to place himself in the public eye. His productions at Carinhall, his parties, his parades and his speeches all revealed a talent for theatre. And in the courtroom he simply continued in a different role. There he tried to convey the impression that the 'noble figure of Hermann Göring' would never even have considered committing war-crimes and crimes against humanity.

Arno Hamburger, observer at the Nuremberg trials

Of Göring's intolerable guilt there could be no doubt in the eyes of the international military tribunal at Nuremberg. The verdict stated:

There are no mitigating circumstances to be adduced, since Göring was often, indeed nearly always, the driving force and was second only to Hitler. He was the leading personality in the wars of aggression, both as a political and a military leader; he was in charge of slave-labour and the originator of the programme of suppression against Jews and other races in Germany and abroad. All these crimes were openly admitted by him . . . The monstrous nature of his guilt is unique. For this man there is no excuse to be found in the entire evidence presented at the trial.

As the psychologist Gilbert observed after the verdict on the war criminals had been pronounced:

Göring was the first to leave the court and walked to his cell with long strides, a fixed expression and eyes bulging with horror. 'Death!' he said, as he fell on to his bunk. Although he tried to appear casual, his hands were trembling. His eyes were moist and he was breathing heavily as though fighting to hold back a mental collapse. That evening the German prison doctor, Dr Ludwig Pflücker, had to treat him for a racing heartbeat. As the doctor remarked: 'The verdict has certainly upset him very much.'

Göring had told one of the interpreters: 'Everyone has to die, but dying as a martyr makes you immortal. One day you will lay our bones in marble coffins.'

> I recall Göring being questioned about the art-theft. He was embarrassed that it had been noticed. He really wanted to be seen as a military leader and not as an art-thief and someone who had enriched himself.
> *Susanne von Paczensky, observer at the Nuremberg Trials*

Against his wishes the defence counsel entered a plea for clemency. Göring himself did not want to plead with the victors for mercy. Instead he wrote three letters: to the prison chaplain, to his wife Emmy and to the Allied Control Commission. In the last of these he emphasized: 'I would have had myself shot without delay! It is, however, not possible to execute the *Reichsmarschall* of Germany by the noose! For the sake of Germany I cannot permit this. I therefore choose the same manner of death as that of the great Hannibal.'

At 10.45 p.m. on 15 October 1946, in cell number 5 of the Nuremberg gaol, Hermann Göring bit through the thin glass of a cyanide capsule. Who had slipped the poison to him is a matter of dispute to this day. Suspicion fell at first upon Emmy Göring, who had been allowed to visit her husband in prison, but nothing could be proved. It may be presumed that the deadly capsule was smuggled into the cell by Jack G. Wheelis, a young American officer of the guard and a hunting enthusiast, to whom Göring had even presented his gold ring and a gold watch. Wheelis has since died, taking the secret with him to the grave.

Göring could be very charming when he wanted to be. That is how he succeeded in building a relationship with a young American officer, one of his guards in Nuremberg. Göring even gave him presents, one of his watches and a gold ring. As we later found out, this guard officer actually obtained for Göring the cyanide capsule with which he committed suicide. Apparently he had previously taken it from Göring's luggage which was stowed in a room to which the officer had a key.

William Jackson, son and assistant of the Chief Prosecutor at Nuremberg

On the day after the suicide, in the Munich suburb of Solln, American soldiers scattered the ashes of several corpses in the Conwentz Brook, a tributary of the River Isar. One of the dead men bore the name 'George Munger'. The GIs believed they were interring one of their comrades who had died in an accident. They had no idea that 'Munger' was in fact Hermann Göring.

No one was told where the ashes had been scattered. 'In a river somewhere in Germany,' was the official version. It was essential, at all costs, to prevent a shrine being created. For, to the very last, Göring was convinced that one day a memorial would be erected to him. On the last night before his suicide he prophesied: 'In 50 or 60 years time there will be statues of Hermann Göring to be seen all over Germany.' He paused, hesitated for a moment and then added: 'Well, perhaps not statues, but a portrait in every home.'

CHAPTER THREE

THE ENFORCER:
HEINRICH HIMMLER

KNOPP/GÜLTNER

We are obliged, whenever we meet together, to remind ourselves of our principles: blood, quality, toughness.

We have to behave with honesty, decency, loyalty and comradeship towards those who are of our own blood and to no one else.

We intend to eradicate homosexuality root and branch.

Lawyers are legally sanctioned thieves, frauds and exploiters.

Whether other nations live in prosperity or die of starvation interests me only to the extent that we need them as slaves for our civilization.

Whatever good stock of our sort is available in other nations, we will take away for ourselves, if necessary by seizing their children and raising them here in Germany.

We had the moral right, we had the duty towards our own people, to destroy that nation that wanted to destroy us.

For myself, my ideal would be eventually to die a poor man.

Himmler

He appears to be a very keen pupil whose tireless application, burning ambition and active participation in class have produced excellent results.

Himmler's class-teacher, 1914

He has always been well-behaved and has shown conscientious diligence.

Himmler's school-leaving report, 1919

Himmler is not overly clever, but industrious and honest.

Goebbels, 1930

Oddly enough, I gained the immediate impression from this man of something far more unnerving than I did from 'his' Führer, in whom, during the two very different meetings I had with him, I always sensed a streak of weakness, an obsessive trait. In Himmler there was none of the latter. What was unnerving about him was the degree of concentrated servility, his narrow-minded conscientiousness. He was almost inhumanly methodical, with something of the automaton about him.

Carl Jacob Burckhardt, 1938

He was half schoolmaster, half crackpot.

Albert Speer, 1953

I hear there is a great deal of annoyance on the Alb about the Grafeneck establishment. The local population recognize the grey SS cars and think they know what goes on in the continuously smoking crematorium. What happens there is meant to be secret but that is no longer so. This has created an extremely bad atmosphere there, and in my view the only thing to be done is to cease operations in this establishment, and in a shrewd and sensible way appear informative by having films about people with mental and hereditary illnesses shown in that particular locality.

Himmler, 1940

The concentration-camp is certainly a severe and stringent measure. Hard, re-educative labour, a regulated daily life, an unaccustomed cleanliness in accommodation and personal hygiene, an excellent diet, strict but fair treatment, the opportunity to learn how to work again and to acquire manual skills – these are our educational methods. The motto written above these camps is:

There is one road to freedom – its milestones are: obedience, industry, honesty, order, cleanliness, sobriety, truthfulness, self-sacrifice and love of the Fatherland.

Himmler, 1939

Of course, I didn't want to liquidate the Jews at all. I had quite different plans. It's that man Goebbels who has the whole thing on his conscience.

Himmler, 1942

Anti-Semitism is exactly the same sort of thing as delousing. The removal of lice is not a great philosophical question. It is a public health matter. We will soon be free of lice.

Himmler, 1943

The Russians do everything *en masse* and so this mass must be trampled down and slaughtered to the last man. To use a very brutal metaphor, it is like cutting a pig's throat and letting it gradually bleed to death.

Himmler, 1942

Among ourselves this must now be discussed quite openly, though we will never speak about it in public. I am referring to the evacuation of the Jews, the eradication of the Jewish people. It is one of those things which is easy to put into words – 'Eradicating the Jewish people,' any Party member can say, 'fine, it's in our programme; removal of the Jews, eradication – we'll do it.' Then along come all the eighty million good German souls, and every one of them knows a decent Jew. Of course, the rest are dreadful, but this one is a

really splendid Jew. Of all the people who talk like that, none
have watched, none have been through it.

Himmler addressing SS Gruppenführer, 1943

If National Socialist Germany is really about to be destroyed,
then its enemies and the whole gang of criminals now sitting
on concentration-camps must not live to experience the
triumph of emerging as victors. They must share in our
downfall. That is a clear order from the Führer, and it is my
task to ensure that it is carried out thoroughly and precisely.

Himmler, 1945

* * *

As a schoolboy he was considered hard-working. His class-teacher
praised him as 'a very keen pupil whose tireless application,
burning ambition and active participation in class have achieved
excellent results'. His zeal and intelligence, his thoughtfulness and
pleasant nature were singled out in many reports. The lad was
never attributed with any tendency to violence. His schoolfriend,
the German-American historian George Hallgarten, later
remembered his mild-mannered fellow-pupil; he was 'the gentlest
lamb you could imagine. A boy who couldn't hurt a fly.' The
model pupil came from a good family, had benefited from an
education in the humanities, obtained the best marks and
graduated successfully from university. Even if severe short-
sightedness robbed him of a hoped-for military career and if the
inconspicuous young man left little impression behind him, he was
nevertheless able to carve a career for himself, albeit a modest one.

As a student he could pursue his passion for plants and
agriculture. He sought advancement and recognition, joined a
whole raft of societies. He was certainly not remarkable for any
radical views, tub-thumping speeches or revolutionary ideas. But
after passing his examinations he quickly found a good job –
something that was not so easy to achieve in the slump that
followed the First World War. He could have been a civil servant
and would certainly have become a valuable cog in the machinery
of Germany's fiscal bureaucracy: painstaking, incorruptible, always

meticulously law-abiding. A brilliant high-flyer he was not. Wilhelm Höttl, one of his closest colleagues, allowed him 'at best the appearance of a minor tax official'. 'A fairly insignificant bureaucrat'. was the crushing verdict of the Swedish diplomat, Count Folke Bernadotte.

As a teacher he might perhaps have been able to develop his talents. Had he become one, he would have educated his pupils to exemplify the 'minor virtues' in the traditional sense: order and obedience, a sense of duty and respect for authority, hard work and thrift. He was described as 'a schoolmaster with a pronounced sense of frugality' by an SS functionary, Oswald Pohl, singling out the most prominent traits in his character. The man who later held a multitude of posts, even at the height of his career only drew a salary of 24,000 Reichsmarks a year. This was mere pocket-money compared with the corrupt excesses to which other top functionaries and members of the ruling clique treated themselves. He was caricatured by those of his contemporaries who knew him well, as the embodiment of a headmaster. Albert Speer characterized him, admittedly in retrospect, as 'half schoolmaster, half crackpot'.

> As an estate-manager, as mayor of a small town, or possibly even in the higher reaches of the cultural civil service, with his interest in academic research, Himmler might have achieved something worthwhile. But fate placed him in a position which he was unable to handle. There was a kind of effortful strain in everything he did. Though he was by nature soft, he preached toughness. Acts which were totally foreign to his nature he carried out like an automaton and, when the Führer ordered it, this even meant the physical annihilation of human beings.
>
> *Felix Kersten, Himmler's doctor and masseur, 1952*

His odd-seeming fascination with the occult, his superstition, his passion for herbal remedies, would not have extended beyond his own backyard, had there been no Third Reich. His neighbours would have called him kindly, eccentric perhaps, at worst a screwball – but dangerous? His would have been a humdrum life, almost a banal one – if the times he lived in had not pushed him in a quite different direction. Hannah Arendt's phrase, 'the banality of evil', was coined to describe Adolf Eichmann, Himmler's henchman, but it applies equally well to the master himself. Heinrich Himmler was one thing above all: Hitler's willing executioner, who put millions to death without ever laying a finger on them himself. He was a man with qualities which even today are thought of as 'typically German': efficient and exact, conscientious and deferential, neat and tidy. Was Heinrich Himmler's a German career or a German sickness?

As indescribable as were the crimes which we associate with the name of Himmler, the man who committed them was merely nondescript. There was nothing magnificent or even great in his nature. Even his contemporaries described Himmler as 'a completely insignificant personality who rose in an inexplicable manner to a prominent position' (Albert Speer), as a man who had 'nothing outstanding or special' about him (*Generalmajor* Walter Dornberger, in charge of V-weapons) and whose only distinctive feature was his lack of distinction. There was 'nothing terrifying or demonic' in his character, writes the British historian Hugh Trevor-Roper. But Himmler certainly became demonic in his efficiency. Just as a tax-inspector signs off hundreds of tax-declarations, so did Himmler discharge his task. Genocide was a matter of organization. Ultimately he cared nothing for the suffering of the victims, but worried a great deal about the mental trauma of those doing the hideous work.

> There was nothing terrifying or demonic in Himmler's character. His coldness was not icy but bloodless. He took no pleasure in atrocities, he was indifferent to them. The scruples of others did not seem contemptible to him, only unwise.
>
> *Hugh Trevor-Roper*

Heinrich Himmler was born on 7 October 1900 at Wittelsbacherstrasse 2, in Munich, the second of three sons. His father, Gebhardt Himmler, was a respected high-school teacher. Compared to most top Nazi functionaries, Himmler came from a privileged and secure background. The family were Catholic and royalist, respectable and cultivated, solid and Bavarian. As late as 1941 the man who in his official capacity ordered the persecution of Catholic clergy, attended the strictly Catholic burial of the mother he revered to the end of her days. His father, the Deputy Headmaster of the Landshut High School, was a pious man, humorous within certain limits but excessively pedantic. He was a German nationalist, but not anti-Semitic. This highly educated man brought up his sons in the spirit of humanism. Did Himmler misread his Plato?

Although Heinrich's parents were not rich, they could be considered well-off. This was thanks to an eminent godfather, HRH Prince Heinrich of Bavaria. Himmler's father had been a tutor to the royal Wittelsbach Princes, and his uncle was a chaplain to the court. The Himmler family counted for something at the Bavarian court. This family now had the honour 'to be permitted to offer a glass of champagne' to the Prince, as the invitation to the royal family read, in order to drink the health of the baby Heinrich at his christening. It was regarded as a great favour for a member of the royal family to agree to be godfather to a schoolmaster's son. The connection between Prince Heinrich and the Himmler family lasted beyond the death of the Prince, who fell at the Front in 1916. As a parting gift Heinrich received from his godfather's estate war-bonds to the value of 1,000 Reichsmarks. It was not poverty that drove him into the claws of National Socialism.

'Heinrich was often ill. 160 absences, but by taking extra lessons with Fräulein Rudet, caught up completely and passed with a grade of II.' So noted his father about Heinrich's primary-school years. Throughout his life Himmler suffered from poor health. Just as the schoolboy had done, the *Reichsführer-SS* compensated for these physical shortcomings by hard work. The Landshut high school aimed 'to instil moral probity on a religious foundation, to provide a general higher education in the spirit of patriotism and to foster the ability to think independently' – and in Heinrich Himmler's case they seem at first glance to have succeeded: 'He has always been well-behaved and has shown conscientious diligence,' his final report stated on 15 July 1919.

With top grades in history, Classical languages and religion, he began a course in agricultural science at Munich's Technical University. Just as he had been at school, Himmler the under-graduate was rather inconspicuous, and his fellow-students described him as 'gauche'. In his search for acquaintanceship, he became a club-freak: from the 'German Society for Genetic Science', through the 'Society of Friends of the Humanist High School', to the 'Old Bavarian Rifle Club', he was a member of about a dozen associations – and of course the Catholic Church: 'I will always love God, and remain true to the Church!' he wrote in his diary.

In his younger days he had performed the obligatory duties of altar-boy. In December 1919 he joined the Catholic-orientated Bavarian People's Party and only left it after four years, in August 1923, in order to join a wholly insignificant party, but one with big ambitions.

At the fancy-dress balls for the *Fasching* Carnival in Munich, the diligent Heinrich was to be seen in the costume of a Turkish sultan. But when it came to drinking he could not keep up. At this point the otherwise conformist student had to depart from the Bavarian norm. The 'Apollo' duelling club even declared him 'unable to give satisfaction'. Only when medical opinion confirmed an irritable stomach condition and thus excused him from beer-drinking, was he initiated into this exclusive student fraternity.

No failure at school, no dropping out of university; a not unsuccessful education – hardly the career of a future mass-murderer. Only his military service was, as he saw it, a stain on his record. At the age of only seventeen he had 'taken part in fighting in the Great War as an ensign with the 11th Bavarian Infantry Regiment'. At least that was the bombastic description in his official *curriculum vitae* reproduced in the 1943 Handbook of the Greater German Reich. At that point in time he had not seen the Front, let alone been in action in the west (the war in the east was already over), although he sometimes claimed that, as a sergeant in the Bavarian Guards Regiment aged only sixteen, he had led his men 'into battle'. This was the beginning of Heinrich Himmler's lifetime of lying. The truth is much less impressive.

What is true is that in the final days of the 1914–18 war, Gebhardt Himmler had tried to make use of old contacts to smooth his son's path into a military career. He did this under pressure from young Heinrich who wanted at all costs to become an officer, although his father had at first insisted that he complete his schooling. 'I look forward to the fighting, when I will wear the King's tunic,' was what the model pupil, whose only bad mark was in gymnastics, wrote in his diary.

When young Himmler finally obtained permission to leave high school, the Imperial Navy would not accept the very short-sighted recruit, despite his royal patronage, since 'as a rule spectacle-wearers are not permitted to serve at sea'. So the schoolboy, not yet seventeen, applied to join the Army. 'My son has a fervent wish to make his career as an infantry officer,' his father wrote in support of the application. But the German empire needed ordinary soldiers, cannon-fodder for the Front, to replace the appalling losses in the trenches of France. Heinrich, however, was intent on higher things. From the training-camp in Regensburg, he signed a letter to his parents: '*miles* Heinrich' (the Latin for 'soldier'). All that swotting of Latin vocabulary had to have *some* use, after all. The overprotected youth with ambitions to better himself shared in the general excitement about the war, seeing it as a way of breaking out of the social constraints of that era. In his enthusiasm for all things military Heinrich was a child of his time. He wanted to be part of the 'just war', the 'sacred struggle' of the German Fatherland, and to pass his 'greatest test of maturity'. 'In my heart of hearts I am a soldier,' he confided to his diary. In the next war of liberation, 'I'll play my part, as long as I can move a muscle.' The would-be warrior was certain of this, even though he knew war only through writings that glorified it, and not through painful first-hand experience.

Hitler had experienced the horror of war. He was a product of it. His state was a prolongation of the hell that he had seen in the trenches – a modern apocalypse. Himmler, on the other hand, who organized this apocalypse, would dream all his life of an archaic world, a world of flaming torches and burnished swords, of ploughshares and good German earth.

Active service was denied to the aspiring warrior. Before he had finished his military training, peace had broken out. Himmler had completed his course as an officer-cadet but it was too late for him to be deployed at the Front. While Hitler could often cite his personal experiences in the trenches, these were not available to the man who, in the final phase of the next war, found himself at the head of Army Group Vistula, with orders to hold off an attack by the Red Army. The officer-cadet who dreamed of winning brilliant victories in a handsome uniform, never had to live through the bloody carnage of industrialized warfare. The silent horror of an invisible gas-attack, the death-dealing assaults from the air, the sudden onslaught of tanks – he had been spared all that. Nothing disturbed his idealized image of heroic combat.

In April 1919 Himmler joined one of the many *Freikorps*, in order to crush Bavaria's short-lived communist regime, the *Räterepublik*. He served in various paramilitary organizations that were on the march against democracy, against the 'Versailles Treaty of Shame', and, naturally, against the 'Marxist dictatorship'. These units included the 'Landshut' and 'Oberland' *Freikorps*, the '21st Rifle Brigade' and the 'Home Defence Force'. Like many others at the time, frustrated in his desire to fight in the war and lacking any direction, he sought confirmation, an explanation, something to hold on to – and above all he sought an idol.

At that time Himmler, in his search for a new orientation, read the anti-Semitic pamphlets which were circulating in Munich student circles. He became familiar with the book *Race and Nation*, by the Anglo-German writer Houston Stewart Chamberlain, and he encountered the 'Protocols of the Elders of Zion', a spurious document purporting to contain proof of an attempted 'Jewish world conspiracy'. Pedantically precise as he was, Himmler left behind for posterity a reading-list with his comments on each book. From this we find that the pallid youth had a preference for books on ancient Teutonic history and works about supposed international conspiracies by a variety of groups: Freemasons, Jesuits, Jews.

But this reading is insufficient in itself to explain the process that Himmler went through in the early 1920s. Himmler was not stupid but his critical faculty was rather limited. He looked for simple explanations for the complexities of a rapidly changing world. The turmoil of social and political upheaval created insecurity and stirred up fear and anxiety. The old order would have allotted a secure place in society for the son of a royal tutor. But instead the young Heinrich was forced to scrap the plans he had laid for his life. He found the answer he was seeking in simplistic theories, which identified a scapegoat on which blame for the whole wretched situation could be heaped: that Jewish world conspiracy which would deprive the Germanic heroes of the fruits of their labours. Himmler was one of those who saw the solution in a revival of arcane traditions.

The schoolmaster Gebhardt Himmler had instilled in his son an enthusiasm for ancient German history, a particular passion of his own. In *Germania* by the Roman historian Tacitus, Heinrich Himmler found 'the splendid image of how superior and morally pure our ancestors were'. How different from this ideal, which had so inspired his father, was the reality of the situation in which the son now found himself. The German people, or so it seemed to him, was sliding into decadence and amorality. He dreamed rather of the good old Germanic days. His greatest wish was 'to be again as we once were'. If later the National Socialist utopia of the noble Germanic warrior found its most fervent advocate in the person of the *Reichsführer-SS*, then these fantasies can be traced back to the early 1920s. In 1924 he wrote in his diary that 'racially pure' Teutons would have to be bred from the 'racially mixed' German people. At the same time he imagined a kind of *Kshatriya* caste, like the aristocratic, landowning warriors of the ancient Indian caste system; this was how his 'new' Teuton should be – a higher being, bound to the soil, superior to all others. The substance of his romanticized vision of a future 'paradise of the Germanic race' was an extensive network of new model towns in the east, with cult temples, fortified villages and mausoleums – a 'rampart of Germanic blood'.

The inhuman consequences of these early delusions would become clear when Himmler, who unlike many clung on to such fantasies, was presented with the opportunity of turning them into reality. In his diary he described the necessary conditions for his 'Germanic paradise': between the dwellings of those of 'Nordic blood' there would be camps of 'labour-slaves who, with no regard to human cost, will build our towns, our villages and our farms'. That is exactly how things were intended to be in Hitler's *Ostland*, the newly conquered territories of eastern Europe and Russia.

The amateur historian's son distorted historical facts to suit his purpose. Consequently 'the Teutons', according to Himmler, 'were a people who possessed a high culture even in prehistoric times' and lived according to unwritten laws. 'What would our forefathers have done in this situation?' was one of Himmler's commonplaces when faced with a decision.

Another of his father's hobbyhorses, medieval German history, was also to inspire Himmler later. He considered Heinrich der Vogler (Henry the Fowler) and Heinrich der Löwe (Henry the Lion) to be the founding fathers of the Greater German Reich. Henry the Fowler had himself crowned Emperor without the blessing of the Church and waged war against the Slavs and the Hungarians. In a speech on the 1,000th anniversary of the death of Heinrich I (The Fowler) on 2 July 1936, the *Reichsführer-SS* evoked the monarch's 'unfinished task': to tear eastern Europe out of Slav hands and colonize it with 'German blood'.

If Himmler's political vision, even in the 1920s, was the forcible conquest of a 'great Germanic empire', his goals in private life at that time were comparatively modest. He had studied agriculture because he hoped he might 'live peacefully with a German *Mädel*', as the manager of a large country estate – an idyll on German acres. Thus, even for Heinrich Himmler things could have taken a different course. History is never a one-way street.

In the early 1920s the young student was making plans to emigrate. On 23 November 1921 he wrote in his diary: 'Today I cut an article out of the newspaper about emigration to Peru. Where will I end up: Spain, Turkey, the Baltic countries, Russia, Peru? I often think about it. In two years time I will no longer be in Germany.' No destination seemed far enough away for him. In 1924 he enquired at the Soviet embassy if he might go to the Ukraine as an estate manager. This man, who twenty years later ordered his units in the Ukraine to destroy the harvest and gun down the Jewish inhabitants, wanted to carry out development aid work as a peace-loving agriculturalist. Had the Soviets agreed, Heinrich Himmler on his

Ukrainian farm would have been able to observe the German invasion in 1941 from a quite different perspective.

Thus he dreamed of the east, while his actual horizons were still restricted to Bavaria. On 1 August 1922 he completed his studies in agriculture with an average mark of 1.7. No sooner had he collected his degree than he found a job as agricultural assistant in a fertilizer company. Himmler became a salesman for Stickstoff-Land GmbH in Schleissheim.

From now on life could in fact have taken its comfortable, middle-class course. The shy Heinrich even found his 'German *Mädel*': a nurse from Bromberg called Marga, who was a few years older than him. This Protestant daughter of a well-to-do West Prussian landowner matched Himmler's ideal image of German womanhood. Any director of a Wagner opera would have seen her as perfect for the role of a Valkyrie: she was tall, blond, blue-eyed and rather well-built. When Himmler married her – against her parents' wishes – on 3 July 1928, the dowry she brought with her enabled him to realize his dream of owning a farm. The young couple bought a chicken farm at Waldtrudering near Munich. The man who later planned to breed 'human material' into a race of heroes, began as a breeder of poultry – if only a moderately successful one.

Himmler was married to a woman who had been his hospital nurse. She was older than him. The marriage appears not to have been particularly happy, though he always spoke of his wife in the most chivalrous terms. Himmler always showed marked chivalry towards women; he hated double-entendres or smutty jokes, seeing in them an insult to his own mother.
Felix Kersten, Himmler's doctor and masseur, 1952

He was more adept at working on his career in the Nazi Party. He had, after all, been an 'old campaigner' and party member since 1923. Himmler the hanger-on had taken part in the march on the Feldherrnhalle. As standard-bearer of the *Reichflagge* unit under the command of Ernst Röhm, he and his brother Gebhardt, together with about 400 armed men, had occupied the Bavarian war ministry.

While Röhm and Hitler were imprisoned (Hitler in Landsberg, where he wrote *Mein Kampf*, Röhm in Stadelheim), the inconspicuous Himmler remained untroubled by the state authorities. He was considered small fry and that hurt him: 'I am a sloganizer, a prattler, I have no energy, I fail in everything,' he wrote in his diary.

Having been fired by Stickstoff-Land he was unemployed and in the spring of 1925 he devoted all his time and energy initially to the 'National Socialist Freedom Movement', which was politically active under the leadership of the Great War hero, General Erich von Ludendorff. At this time he made the acquaintance of Gregor Strasser, a pharmacist from Landshut who was standing as a candidate for the Reichstag. Himmler took on the job of Strasser's secretary in the election campaign. In return for a monthly salary of 120 Reichsmarks he worked full-time, tearing around Lower Bavaria on a motor-cycle and making inflammatory speeches against Jews and capitalists. At that time Strasser was holding the remains of the National Socialist Party together, but was seen as more of a socialist. Heading the left wing of the Party he was later defeated by Hitler in the internal power-struggle. But for the moment Himmler committed himself to Strasser and his political beliefs as uncompromisingly as he later did to Hitler.

The confused situation which followed the ban on the refounded Nazi Party on 27 February 1925 made it possible for Himmler to advance rapidly in the Party. As manager of the Nazi *Gau* of Lower Bavaria, from a headquarters in Landshut, Himmler administered the regional Party branches and in the same year rose to the position of Deputy *Gauleiter* of Lower Bavaria with Upper Palatinate. Then came the next rungs on his career ladder: in 1926 Deputy *Gauleiter* of Upper Bavaria with Swabia, *Deputy Head* of Reich propaganda and finally Deputy *Reichsführer-SS*. It looked as if he were predestined to be a Number Two, owing his rise to his unquestioning loyalty to the top man, to whom he blindly subordinated himself. Hitler needed men like that.

Meanwhile the man from Braunau had been released from prison and his book, *Mein Kampf* (*My Struggle*), had been published. Himmler had read it. His verdict: 'There are an extraordinary number of truths in it.' Himmler had found his God-substitute. It was not long before party colleagues in Lower Bavaria were amazed to see Strasser's former secretary in the Landshut head-office now in conversation with his new idol.

In the mid-1920s Hitler's *Schutzstaffel* (Protection Squad), later to become so feared, was a forlorn bunch, scarcely 200 strong. Hitler was aware of the weakness of his one-time bodyguard. In one of his dinner-table conversations in 1942, he recalled its modest beginnings: 'When I came out of Landsberg, it had broken up into a number of feuding gangs. I said to myself then that I needed a bodyguard which, no matter how small, would be unquestioningly devoted to me and would even march against their own brothers.'

Hitler the demagogue knew that he needed special protection, not only to keep political opponents at bay, but even to protect himself from members of his own Party. Hitler need a force totally loyal and dedicated to him. And he needed a man at its head who would be equally unwavering in his loyalty: Heinrich Himmler.

When Hitler appointed SS member No. 156 to be *Reichsführer-SS*, on 6 January 1929, the SS was a small division of the large *Sturmabteilung*. The SA had risen under Röhm's power-conscious leadership to be the Party's private army. Unlike the SA, which always relied on numbers, the Schutzstaffel saw itself from the beginning as more of an elite force. With their black peaked caps adorned with a skull and their black-bordered swastika armbands, the SS deliberately created an aura for itself reminiscent of the Nibelungs, the legendary sixth-century Burgundian knights around whom Wagner wove his operas: 'When all are faithless, yet do we stay true. Let there always be a doughty troop on earth for you.' Hitler liked to promote this self-image: at the Nazi Party rally in Weimar on 4 July 1926 he presented to Joseph Berchtold, the leader of the Schutzstaffel, for safe keeping, the 'Banner of Blood' which had been carried on the march to the Feldherrnhalle.

However, the final breakthrough for the SS only came with Heinrich Himmler. Even as a boy he had always been fascinated by the Praetorian Guard that protected the Roman emperors. He wanted to create just such a guard, sworn to defend the great leader. This troop would put Hitler's will into action – efficiently and without asking questions. The most visible symbols of this unconditional subordination to the Führer were the belt-buckles of the later SS uniform, on which were engraved the words: 'SS man, loyalty is thy honour'. The same motto was to be found on the blade of the SS ceremonial dagger. It was with this weapon that, in April 1931, Adolf Hitler honoured the achievement of the Berlin SS units who, led by Kurt Daluege, succeeded in nipping in the bud an attempted coup by the radical Berlin SA. This was not the first intra-Party quarrel and it would not be the last. But even in the early 1930s it was becoming clear how Hitler intended to solve such problems – and with whom.

> He could be a loving father to his family, correct as a superior officer and congenial as a man. But at the same time he was an obsessed fanatic, an eccentric dreamer and a will-less tool in the hands of Hitler, to whom he was bound in a love-hate relationship which grew ever stronger.
>
> *Karl Wolff, Himmler's Adjutant*

Himmler, too, coined a formula for himself and his guard. It sounded considerably more modest and exuded the air of his Catholic upbringing, although it was in fact stolen from the old Prussians: 'Be more than you seem'. Himmler was certainly not just a servile '*Anhimmler*' (idolizer), as Röhm derided him. He was also a shrewd tactician, who unerringly and unobtrusively made all the right moves on his path to power – and at the right moment.

After Himmler took up the post of *Reichsführer-SS* it was clear what role had been assigned to the SS in the quarrel with Hitler's opponents. In his New Year's message for 1934, Himmler admitted openly that his one great objective was to eliminate all those who resisted Hitler: 'One of the most urgent tasks facing us is to track down all overt and covert enemies of the Führer, to combat them and to annihilate them.'

By this time the Schutzstaffel and its leader had long since

Himmler was not a person with any arresting or attractive qualities, and that made him quite different from Hitler and Goebbels, who could, if occasion demanded, be thoroughly likeable and charming. Himmler, on the other hand, behaved in a deliberately coarse and unsubtle way, put on the manners of a common trooper and adopted anti-bourgeois attitudes, although it was obvious he only did so to cover up his innate insecurity and gaucheness.

Yet one could have put up with all that. What made him into someone almost intolerable to be with, was the stupid and basically vacuous chatter he forced on me without interruption.

Albert Krebs, Gauleiter of Hamburg until 1932

emerged from the shadow of the once all-powerful SA. From 200 men at the end of 1928, the membership had grown fivefold to 1,000 the following year. Then followed an annual doubling until it had reached a strength of 50,000 SS-men in June 1934. As early as 1931 the notorious Ic service had been created under the leadership of Reinhard Heydrich. This was the kernel of what later became the Security Service, an effective surveillance organ initially watching the Party and its constituent elements. The acid-test came in June 1934.

Without Hitler, Göring and Himmler would never have struck against Röhm. Without Himmler and Heydrich, Hitler would not have been *able* to strike. Hitler knew that now he had wormed his way into political power the SA was in fact superfluous. The new Chancellor of Germany was no longer dependent on troops of street-fighting ruffians. They would only detract from his image as a man who was there to maintain calm and order. The SA stood in the way of his plans for expanding his power. Blomberg, the Minister of Defence, had made it clear to Hitler that he could only count on the support of the regular Army, the Reichswehr, if it remained the only body in the Reich entitled to bear arms. Among the forces of conservatism in business, politics and the military there was great mistrust, even fear, of a 'proletarian People's Army'.

Two of Hitler's 'champions' had a strong interest, as Hitler had, in breaking the power of the SA: Hermann Göring and Heinrich Himmler. Röhm was Göring's arch-enemy. With the help of his SA Röhm wanted to become the military *Führer* of Germany, on an equal footing with the political *Führer*, Adolf Hitler. Röhm was convinced of his indispensability and raised ever more strident claims on a place at Hitler's side. But Göring had his eye on that spot for himself.

Himmler, too, was Röhm's enemy. Admittedly he did not shout it from the rooftops. After all, the SS was nominally subordinate to the SA and thus under Röhm's command; the Praetorian Guard was by force of circumstance a part of the undisciplined 'brown' rabble, which talked of permanent revolution and mouthed socialist slogans. If the SA's wings could not be clipped there was no future for the SS. Röhm had to be dealt with.

In the preparations for the operation which would go down in the annals of the Nazi Party as 'the Night of the Long Knives', Himmler's SS played an essential role. Spying, denunciation and finally murder were its weapons in the struggle for power. Behind the scenes of this St Bartholomew's Night for the brown-shirts the strings were being pulled by Reinhard Heydrich, the man who had the documents forged supposedly proving that an SA *putsch* was imminent. It was Himmler who personally brought to Hitler the news of this fictitious attempt by Röhm to overthrow the regime. That was on 28 June 1934, when the Führer was in the Rhineland attending the funeral of the *Gauleiter* of Essen, Josef Terboven. Himmler's spurious report claimed that the life and authority of the Führer were threatened by a widespread conspiracy.

This alleged planning of a coup provided the pretext and justification for what happened next. Death-lists were drawn up containing the names of leading figures in the SA, as well as individuals who had nothing to do with the SA nor with the fictitious revolt. The opportunity was just too tempting to have not only Röhm murdered, but also old adversaries of Hitler such as the former Chancellor, Kurt von Schleicher, and the Bavarian royalist leader, Gustav von Kahr, or supposed 'traitors' like Gregor Strasser. With the murderous assignment of 30 June 1934 the deadly star of the SS was finally in the ascendant.

In the lakeside resort of Bad Wiessee the unsuspecting Röhm was called to account by Hitler himself. 'You're under arrest,' Hitler shouted at the astonished companion of his old campaigning days, as Röhm opened the bedroom door in his pyjamas in the early hours of the morning. A few hours later a number of senior SA officers, whose names were on the so-called 'Reich List', were arrested in Berlin. The victims of 'Operation Humming-bird' were shot without much delay in the Lichterfelde Army Cadet College. In Munich things were different. There Röhm was taken to the Stadelheim gaol where he had already been imprisoned eleven years earlier. Hitler scanned the list of over 100 names of those threatened with the death penalty and crossed off all but twenty. Röhm's name was not among them. Hitler was reluctant to sign the death-sentence on his old campaign colleague. Many historians of the Nazi period see this as evidence that Hitler was actually a 'weak dictator', who was manipulated by his henchmen and by those with special interests – in this case by Himmler and Göring – and could be steered in different directions. It is true that the practical plans for this murder operation originated with Heydrich and Himmler. And it is true that at first Hitler even wanted to show mercy to Röhm, but

Himmler had a certain sober capacity for weighing things up. He was completely without inhibitions, without scruples. But by talking to Himmler my father managed to get one or two people out of concentration-camp, for example a socialist who was locked up in Oranienburg. So my father went to Himmler and said: 'The British Quakers are taking up this man's case. A very active lady has come over here and is campaigning on his behalf. If he were released, it would be a great publicity plus for us abroad, if not it would be a very harmful minus.' Himmler listened to this and said: 'Yes, all right. I see that.' And so the man was freed and even allowed to go abroad: his name was Ernst Reuter and after the war he became Governing Mayor of Berlin.

Egon Hanfstaengl, son of Hitler's press chief

Himmler and Göring browbeat him into having the SA Chief killed. However, it is also true that Hitler was the chief beneficiary of this deadly exercise. One of his most dangerous, most popular and most powerful rivals could now no longer be a threat to his leadership. When Hitler sacrificed Röhm and the SA he was also assured of the approval of the conservative elite. 'The Führer protects the law' was the title of a celebratory article by a leading journalist in Goebbels' compliant press. It reflected prevailing public opinion: this meant at last an end to street terrorism.

Hitler's hesitation in this as in many other cases cannot be explained as weakness in the dictator, but by his personal tendency to wait patiently until a dramatic opportunity arose for the problem to be resolved satisfactorily in his favour. Thus it is also the case that Hitler did not punish the unauthorized enlargement of the death-lists after the event. Röhm, who refused to commit suicide, was finally murdered anyway. It was Himmler's SS that took on the odious task. Theodor Eicke, Commandant of the first concentration-camp at Dachau, shot Ernst Röhm, the man whose gunmen had softened up the Weimar Republic ready for Hitler's final assault. Hitler's deputy, Rudolf Hess, delivered the telling justification: 'Since it was a question of whether the German people should continue or cease to exist, the degree of guilt of any individual could not be adjudged.'

The cynical question 'Who gained from it?' yields another answer, for beside Hitler there was a second beneficiary from the 'Night of the Long Knives': Heinrich Himmler. It is possible that neither Göring nor Röhm himself knew how calculating Himmler was. He was often seen with Röhm and both men agreed to be godfathers to Heydrich's first son. Now Himmler had whetted the knife against Röhm and had demanded a high price for participating in his removal: he took over command of the Gestapo from Göring. Throughout the Reich the secret police was in Himmler's hands. Heydrich assumed the management of the *GEheime STAatsPOlizei* (Secret State Police), whose headquarters in the former School of Arts and Crafts, at Prinz-Albrecht-Strasse 8, would henceforward be the most feared address in Germany. In return Himmler had ordered the killing of the man he had once followed into the NSDAP, and who had been a kind of foster-father to him. It was on this occasion that the *Reichsführer-SS* had Gregor Strasser shot – the man he had served as Deputy in Landshut. First Röhm then Strasser – the one-time Deputy had no qualms about murdering his first two mentors. In 1929 Goebbels had noted that Himmler was good-natured, perhaps even vacillating: 'a Strasser product'. In his murder of Röhm and Strasser Himmler displayed neither good nature nor vacillation. It was his first great betrayal.

> Himmler was cleverer than his manner and actions made him appear, and perhaps that was the reason for his marked fickleness.
> *Carl Jacob Burckhardt, Swiss diplomat and historian, 1938*

The 'thirty pieces of silver' he received took the form of a decree issued by Hitler on 20 July 1934: 'In view of the great service rendered by the SS, especially in connection with the events of 30 June 1934, I elevate it to be an independent organization within the framework of the NSDAP.'

With this Himmler was awarded a special position, which provided him permanent and direct access to the man who was the sole source of all power in the Third Reich: Adolf Hitler. And he exploited this to the full: in 1939 a code of law applicable only to the SS was introduced. It was comparable to the martial jurisdiction of the Wehrmacht and was valid for all civil and military offences. Thus the SS became a state within the state.

In addition to this leap up the Party career ladder, Himmler also pursued his upward path in the state hierarchy. When the NSDAP seized power Himmler took over the post of acting Chief of Police in the Bavarian capital, Munich, on 9 March 1933. Reinhard Heydrich, Himmler's right-hand man, was also considered and appointed to the political department of Munich's criminal police. In the official announcement of these personnel changes, it was clear what lay behind each appointment: they were intended to 'guarantee that in Bavaria, too, the Reich government finds true allegiance to the elevation of the nation under the leadership of Adolf Hitler'. This already anticipated the Führer-state, which was not to be fully realized until after the death of Hindenburg, when the Army swore an oath of personal allegiance to Hitler. The duty of the police was no longer the maintenance of state order, but the enforcement of Hitler's personal will.

> Himmler was of course the son of a schoolmaster and was, I believe, very much influenced by his upbringing. There was something pedantic and schoolmasterish about him; he was cold, distant, disparaging. He had absolutely no kindness and his only – or his most important – means of educating people was always through punishment.
>
> *Ernst-Günther Schenck, nutrition officer of the*
> *Wehrmacht and SS*

Having started with Bavaria, Himmler proceeded to occupy the top position in the political police of every German province. By January 1934 he was in command of the entire political police other than in Prussia. On the Führer's birthday. 20 April, the *Reichsführer-SS* became Deputy Head and *Inspekteur* of the Prussian Gestapo, the most important political police force in the Reich. Nominally he was still subordinate to Göring, the Minister-President of Prussia, but on 20 November 1934 the latter transferred full discretionary powers to Himmler. Although Göring had needed a good deal of persuading before yielding his authority to Himmler, the solving of the Röhm problem had put him under an obligation to his ally. Göring now had to accept Himmler's rise to be head of the German police and face the fact that on 1 October 1936 the Gestapo law became applicable at Reich level. The political police, up till then the responsibility of the provincial governments, was thus centralized. As the Nazi jurist Hans Frank described the situation in 1937: 'The direction of all political-police activity in the German Reich lies in the hands of *Reichsführer-SS* Himmler.'

In his new capacity Himmler was able to take part in cabinet meetings, since he had the rights and status of a minister. Frick, the Reich Minister of the Interior, tried very hard to retain the police within his sphere, by claiming that Himmler, as 'Inspector of Police', was subordinate to his Ministry, but his efforts were in vain.

The police was no longer an arm of the state but an instrument of power for the Führer under the command of a man who would henceforth be nicknamed 'Reichsheini'. Only the name could never be spoken out loud; that could be fatal. In his new function Himmler issued his decree of 26 June 1936, which imposed a fundamental re-organization on the German police: *Polizeigeneral* Kurt Daluege became Chief of the *Ordnungspolizei* (civil police), which in turn was responsible for the *Gendarmerie*, the *Schutzpolizei* (constabulary) and local police forces. *SS-Gruppenführer* Reinhard Heydrich, as Chief of the security police, took over the political and criminal police divisions. This twin command of the policing function concealed the upgrading of the political police to an autonomous branch. Furthermore, the criminal police was integrated into the sphere of influence of the political police. The establishing of two separate *Hauptämter* (headquarters) for the civil and security police forces further made it clear that the police was *de facto* being incorporated into the SS, since the organizational term *Hauptamt* was unknown in the civil administration and was part of SS terminology.

> Go to see Himmler. I settle with him the basis of our future co-operation in the propaganda field. He is a small, cultured man. Good-natured, but probably also vacillating.
>
> *Goebbels (Diary) 1929*

What manner of man the new police chief was, was impressively demonstrated in a speech given by Himmler on 11 October 1936 in, of all places, the Academy of German Law. He made clear his basic aversion to any action by the state being governed by law or statute. In his best saloon-bar style, he harangued his audience about the impotence of the democratically controlled police force, which, he claimed, was chiefly concerned not to walk into a trap, when a criminal was bent on putting the guardians of the law into the wrong. Himmler propounded his own version of justice:

Whether or not our actions conflict with a particular article or sub-section is a matter of complete indifference to me. In the fulfilment of my duty I do precisely what I can answer for in my work for Führer and nation, and what equates with healthy common-sense. Whether or not the others whined about a breach of the law was. . . of no concern to me. In truth, through our work we were laying the foundations for a new code of rights, the rights of existence of the German people.

It was this attitude that made Himmler the Führer's most effective henchman. Whereas Hitler had intended the SS to be no more than an instrument of his personal power, Himmler had planned a second task for it: it was to be the germ of a future Nordic master-race.

Back in the spring of 1933 the SS was still a kind of 'superior SA'. In the eyes of many ordinary Germans, the vulgar brown-shirts were no more than louts who went about the streets beating people up. Those who believed that, with the Nazis now in power, it was necessary to join one of the NS organizations without committing themselves too much, rushed into the SS or its 'sponsoring organization', which accepted members who paid a subscription but were otherwise passive. Although Himmler was anxious to develop the Schutzstaffel as soon as possible into effective and necessarily larger units, recruitment into the SS was slow at first. Himmler believed that merely increasing numbers was less important than assembling the 'right human material' in the SS. In the years 1933 to 1935 60,000 men signed the SS membership register. Compared with the 200 men in 1929 this was a huge rise. But if one compares it with the 3 million men in the *Sturmabteilung* at the end of 1933, the SS strength appears at first relatively modest. Hitler's restraint in recruiting SS men had a reason: 'Of every 100 applicants we can on average only use 10 or 15, not more,' the *Reichsführer* explained. Opportunities to join the SS were handled restrictively, because Himmler had got it into his head to turn the SS into a racial elite. 'I haven't taken any men under 1.7 metres [5ft 7in].' Ironically this was an entry criterion that he himself would certainly not have fulfilled. Yet Himmler based all his abstruse notions on the assumption that a racially valuable individual must be of a certain physical size. The facial features also had to be proof of 'Aryan blood'. Himmler had photos of all applicants shown to him. These he personally scanned through to see if he might find 'any distinguishing features that appear somehow odd to our German eye', features of the kind he would have looked for in 'soldiers' council types' during the revolutionary years of 1919–20. Broad cheekbones suggested Mongol or at least Slavic blood – Himmler was sure about that. He himself suffered from the fact that with 'his wide cheekbones and round face, he was more reminiscent of someone from the Baltic region', as his personal doctor and masseur, Felix Kersten, noted.

The qualified agriculturalist applied his knowledge of Mendel's laws of plant genetics to human beings: 'We went about it like the plantsman who takes a good, old strain, but one which has become intermixed and exhausted, and has to re-breed it. He goes out in the field and proceeds to select the best specimens. So we initially weeded out people on external appearance.' Through special marriage regulations Himmler attempted to guarantee that those with 'first-class heredity' should marry one another. A procreation order was issued to the entire SS on 28 October 1939. It was the highest duty of German women and girls of 'good blood' to conceive children by the soldiers before they went off to battle. A particularly important point was that the reproductive act should be the result of a deep sense of moral responsibility and not of frivolous passion. Himmler dreamed of tall, blond, blue-eyed heroes and wanted to create the ideal Germanic type: a hardened member of the master-race, proud of his blood and consistent in belief and action.

A smallish man, and with his wide cheekbones and round face reminiscent more of the Baltic type, he looked at me sharply from behind his pince-nez. He was not athletic; instead of being relaxed and springy he was stiff and tense in himself.

Felix Kersten, Himmler's doctor and masseur, 1952

These obsessions with breeding found their most inhuman expression in 'Operation Lebensborn' (Fount of Life). It should be possible for any woman, Himmler believed, to experience the joy of motherhood, as long as she could demonstrate 'racially unexceptionable blood'. For this purpose marriage was not necessary. Single women were provided by Himmler with 'procreation assistants'. The SS chief wove great plans for after the war: it was to be the legal duty of every woman to present the state with at least one child. Even during the war an order went out to the SS, that every healthy SS-man, whether married or not, had to father at least one child – to make up for losses in the fighting, which hit the 'valuable SS blood' particularly severely. Despite his Catholic upbringing, Himmler held monogamy to be a sin. The Church's ban on divorce and insistence on the exclusivity of marriage were immoral, and childlessness and infidelity resulted from misleading Church teachings. In contrast to this, the procreation supervisor of the SS praised Islam and its prophet Mohammed:

> He promised every warrior, who fights courageously and falls in battle, two beautiful women as his reward. That's a language that a soldier understands. If he believes he will have that kind of reception in the hereafter, he willingly risks his life, goes into battle with enthusiasm and does not fear death.

Men were to be allowed to have several wives, so they could father many heroes. The abolition of monogamous marriage would have an additional advantage, as Himmler explained to his doctor, Kersten: 'In bigamous marriage one wife will spur the other on to match the ideal image in every respect; the viragoes and the plump ones will disappear.' Thus a husband's disinclination after years of monogamy would no longer be a problem, and there would be an end to childlessness. Behaviour so comprehensively supported by philosophy was something Himmler allowed himself to indulge in as well: while married to Margarete he kept a mistress. She bore him two children who are both still living in Germany.

> In the Führer's headquarters my father had a mistress, with my mother's consent. Himmler also had an extra-marital relationship, and his mistress bore him two children. My father arranged for this woman and her children to be given a farmhouse near Königssee, where they could live.
>
> *Martin Bormann Jr, son of Martin Bormann and*
> *godchild of Hitler*

In the summer of 1936, in Quedlinburg, a small town in the Harz mountains, Himmler staged a celebration of the 1,000th anniversary of the death of the German king Heinrich I, and used the occasion to present a vision of the SS as guarantors of Germany's future:

> Thus have we formed ranks and are marching according to immutable laws, as a National-Socialist and soldierly order of exclusively Nordic men and as a sworn clan brotherhood, along the path into a distant future, and we wish and believe that we may not only be the grandsons, who put up a better fight, but beyond that the forefathers of those remote future generations necessary for the eternal life of the Teutonic German people.

Exit into the Nordic mists. These were the kind of woolly notions that the Nazi ideologues came up with whenever they talked of the earthly paradise that was to be created. And Himmler was no exception. Like the others, his visions of the future were based on a misunderstanding of the past. For National Socialism the future always had something anti-modern about it – a nostalgia for the ancestral idols. In this sense the Germans of the future would be nothing but rocket-borne Nibelungs.

In Himmler's case this nostalgia brought forth the most absurd blooms. Many of its roots reached back into his childhood. The young Heinrich grew up near an old apothecary's shop which fascinated him with all its powders and herbs, pills and salves, crucibles and pots. This passion would stay with him for the rest of his life. Later, he would recommend a breakfast of leeks and mineral water for the SS men and prescribed raw garlic for women on war service, so that they could stand the strain of work for as long as possible. He was deeply concerned with the question of whether potatoes should be boiled in their skins, and personally insisted that this should 'be settled quite clearly'. Later, when the SS was building up a vast business empire, the *Reichsführer*'s fads were paramount in that as well. Thus in 1944 three-quarters of Germany's consumption of mineral-water was supplied from SS-owned sources including the famous Apollinaris in Bad Neuenahr. As a student Himmler had had problems with beer-drinking, and as *Reichsführer-SS* he would have preferred to wean the Germans off the beverage altogether. Instead he sang the praises of mead, the 'highly nutritious biological drink' of the ancient Teutons.

> It was his hope, after the war if not sooner, to turn his entire force into vegetarians, non-drinkers and non-smokers. That was his vision of the future, and he believed this was the best way to breed the German race to a pitch of perfection. Later on, in order to keep his men off the alcohol, he used his business operations to buy up all the mineral-water springs in Germany. These ideas of Himmler's were of course the butt of plenty of jokes among the troops.
>
> *Ersnt-Günther Schenck, nutrition officer for the Wehrmacht and SS*

Another of his hobby-horses was homoeopathy. He was as familiar with oat-straw baths as with the herbal cures of the Middle Ages. Later he even had herb gardens laid out in the concentration-camps. This was such an important matter to him that he arranged for his mother's doctor, Dr Fahrenkamp, to supervise the herb garden in the Dachau camp. Surrounded by misery and death the herbs were meant to thrive and grow up to provide a little green paradise in the midst of a dark world of infernal anguish. Himmler valued the teachings of the great Paracelsus as much as the hydrotherapy of Pastor Kneipp. In hypothermia tests, which the chief medical officer of the Luftwaffe, Dr Sigmund Rascher, carried out on the inmates of

Dachau, the SS chief suggested that the subjects frozen half to death in icy water should be resuscitated with 'animal warmth'. For the purposes of the experiment four women from the Ravensburg concentration-camp were handed over to Rascher. The result he found was that this method of re-warming people suffering from hypothermia was only to be recommended if other means were not available. Rascher was known for experiments intended to end in the subjects' death. When a number of his scientific colleagues refused to take part in these experiments, Himmler wrote a furious letter to *General der Luftwaffe* Erhard Milch: 'In those "Christian" medical circles the view is held that a young German pilot should naturally risk his life, but that the life of a criminal is too sacred for the doctors to stain their hands with his blood.' For Himmler humanity was never an argument, only utility.

Today we may smile at Himmler's ancient Germanic symbols like runes and yule-lights, or mock the cult rituals he staged by the light of flaming torches. Himmler's fantasies, such as his idea of turning the Westphalian village of Wewelsburg into 'the centre of the Aryan world', may seem quaint to us now and we may be tempted to dismiss it all as evidence of the chimeras of a distorted mind. Yet we should not forget that with just such symbolism Himmler the ideologue succeeded in creating a sense of community within the

---

In honour of his memory and in this sacred place we should stand in quiet reflection. We must live up to his virtues as a man and as a leader, virtues with which he brought happiness to our people a thousand years ago. We must again and again resolve and make clear that we can best honour him by honouring the man who, after a thousand years took up King Heinrich's political legacy in unprecedented greatness, and that we serve our Führer Adolf Hitler, for Germany, for Germania, in thought, word and deed, with the old loyalty and with the old spirit.

Himmler at the Reich celebrations of the 1,000th anniversary, in 1936, of the death of Heinrich I.

SS, replacing all former attachments. '*Wer auf die Hakenkreuzfahne schwört, hat nichts mehr, was ihm selbst gehört*' ('He who swears on the swastika banner, has nothing more to call his own') ran one of the shibboleths of the SS. Himmler gave the members of his order the feeling of being an elect group. For many the SS became a kind of substitute family.

Hitler himself had little interest in Himmler's theatricals and kept his distance from the goings-on of the SS at Quedlinburg. In fact the Führer liked to make fun of Himmler's cultism, his quack remedies, his romanticizing of history and fostering of pseudo-Germanic lore. Even in *Mein Kampf* he criticized the 'pseudo-academia of nationalistic occultism'. In 1938 he was more scathing in his rejection of his henchman's folkloric concepts – admittedly without singling out the 'faithful Heinrich' by name:

> At the forefront of our programme there is no mystic speculation but a clear recognition of the facts. And woe betide us if, through the infiltration of confused mystical elements, the Movement or the State starts issuing unclear instructions. There is a danger even in proposing a so-called cult site, because from that will come the necessity for subsequent consideration of so-called cult games and cult activities. Our cult has but one aim: to foster that which is natural.

But Hitler did accept that Himmler was incredibly efficient. Despite his irrational tendencies the *Reichsführer-SS* always acted in a purposeful manner. For Hitler results were all that mattered – and Himmler guaranteed those results. In return he was allowed to pursue his obsessions and live out his fantasies undisturbed. He could hold an annual mystic celebration with his men in the crypt of Quedlinburg Cathedral, or plant a grove in honour of the dead in the Sachsenhain at Verden, where '4500 Saxons were done to death' by Charlemagne, a figure whom Himmler despised. There, at every summer solstice, to the sound of Teutonic lurs, Himmler commemorated the ancestors who could no longer defend themselves.

Behind the scenes of Himmler's dreamworld there was always a hard realism. The castle of Wewelsburg, 'centre of the Aryan world', only functioned because it had its own concentration-camp attached. Thus Himmler combined his organizational skills with his racial and eugenic visions in a single dangerous brew.

> Himmler actually seemed diffident, not at all self-assured or militaristic, and certainly not brutal. He had more the manner of a shy, middle-class man.
>
> He did not have the aura of a mass-murderer. But that is probably just what makes mass-murderers so successful.
>
> *Traudl Junge, Hitler's Secretary*

Himmler's power was founded chiefly on his personal relationship with Hitler and the direct line of authority from him. The fact that he could exploit at all the opportunities which his position gave him, he owed to Reinhard Heydrich, the head of the security service. The intelligent and calculating Heydrich was hungry enough for power to use the unobtrusive Himmler, so that at the appropriate moment he could step into his place. Heydrich had made Himmler realize what a very prominent post he held as *Reichsführer-SS*; he was the driving force which enabled the SS to become the mighty executive arm of the Third Reich. His contemporaries were well aware of Heydrich's influence. A joke that was whispered around ran: '*H.H.H.H – Himmler's Hirn heisst Heydrich*' ('Himmler's brain is called Heydrich', in German the four H's are pronounced 'ha ha ha ha').

There was only one reason why Himmler never dropped back into the role of deputy within the SS organization, and why Heydrich did not emerge as the real strong-man: in June 1942, Heydrich was shot dead by Czech partisans in Prague. With his criminal energy no longer available to it, the SS remained what it was at the time of his death. Himmler himself did not know how to exploit fully the potential power at his disposal. On the contrary, he allowed himself to be tied into the old hierarchy, and on being appointed Reich Minister of the Interior became part of the very organizational structure which, with the SS, he had downgraded to insignificance. He made no use of the advantages which he, as *Reichsführer-SS*, had over the lower-ranking SS officers. We do not know whether Himmler, as their superior officer, ever gave orders to men like Martin Bormann or Joachim von Ribbentrop.

From his appearance Himmler was, as has often been said, a rather insignificant little pedant. In reality, however, he was anything but 'little', and he had remarkable abilities: the ability to listen, the ability to think things over for a long time before making a decision, the knack of picking people for his staff, who in general proved to be very efficient. As you see, that ultimately does not denote an insignificant personality. Of course, he had this other side, which made him appear grotesque in the eyes of intellectually more sophisticated people.

Speer, 1979

Why Himmler succeeded in combining his personal advancement with the expansion of the SS may well be explained by the SS motto, 'Loyalty is thy Honour'. In fact, 'loyalty' meant absolute obedience and unquestioning allegiance. Just as Hitler needed a politically reliable force that took on every task assigned to it and attempted to carry it out to his satisfaction, without asking too many questions about rights and law, he also needed someone at the head of this force who was totally loyal, and showed no ambitions to challenge his role as Führer. Unlike Röhm who, as leader of the SA, had clearly pursued his own agenda, Hitler could rely on Himmler, his 'faithful Heinrich', year in and year out.

Thus, although Himmler's rise was not a matter of chance, the central role of the SS in the Third Reich can only be explained in the light of Hitler's own intellectual framework. Nevertheless, even here there was an inevitable breaking-point: Himmler saw the SS not only as a potent and dependable force but as an elitist core of Nazi ideology. The SS was to be more than an executive organ of Nazi policy. In the all-male order of the SS. Himmler saw the foundation of the future single-race national state. Problems could have arisen from this divergent set of objectives, since at the heart of all elitist philosophy lies the idea that those who see themselves as superior to the rest are determined to occupy the very top positions, or at least to consider themselves on an equal footing with the supreme authority. Elitism conceals an oligarchic principle which aims at autonomy and stands in direct opposition to absolute dictatorship by an individual who, furthermore, is not a member of this elite.

The fact that, before the collapse of Hitler's rule, this explosive potential was never discharged in a coup against him, is explained by Himmler's character. Someone like Heydrich might have possessed the ambition to push through his own programme with the support of the SS. But Himmler was of a different stripe. As *Reichsführer-SS* and chief of the German police, he held a wealth of other offices from Reich Commissioner for the Conservation of German National Heritage to his military posts in the final phase of the Second World War – yet for all that he remained what he had been from the beginning: the perennial Deputy, the Number Two man who never wanted to be Number One. That is why the SS remained what Hitler intended it to be: an absolutely reliable weapon of power, which guaranteed his sole domination of Germany, and which was effectively organized to put his plans into effect without being concerned about moral principles. The SS

My father was not at all political and therefore posed no threat. But people like Heydrich and Kaltenbrunner were afraid of everyone around them. Kaltenbrunner went as far as mounting an ambush against my father: a barrier was set up on the road and my father and his driver were to be shot. An SS-man advised my father to take a different route, so he reached Himmler in Berlin on time that day. Later Himmler carpeted Kaltenbrunner and told him: 'If anything happens to Kersten, within twenty-four hours you will be dead yourself.'

Andreas Kersten, son of Himmler's doctor and masseur

was the instrument of power in Hitler's government by decree, which recognized only one norm: the will of the Führer. And Himmler was the right man to build up this organ. Count Schwerin von Krosigk, Hitler's Finance Minister, identified the secret of Himmler's success: 'Hitler could not have handed his political dirty work over to a more suitable man than [Himmler], who pedantically built up an organization of terror and who knew neither mercy nor remorse.'

If the name of Heinrich Himmler is forever linked with the darkest chapter of German history, it is not because he constructed an edifice of abstruse ideology or built up a new organization as a 'technician of power'. Even Himmler's network of spies, built up by his confidant Heydrich, and his successor as Police and Security Chief, Ernst Kaltenbrunner, was nothing unique – there were many no less effective organizations before and after it, operating in Germany and abroad. We should certainly not restrict our view to the military achievements of the SS. If today the SS has a daredevil image, then that is thanks to the *Waffen-SS* which was just one arm of the *Schutzstaffel*, along with the *Totenkopf* ('Death's Head') units, which supervised the concentration-camps, and the 'General SS'. The *Waffen-SS* developed out of the *Verfügungstruppe* ('Rapid Response Force') and became a second regular Army beside the *Reichswehr*.

Yet there were other parts of the SS which under Himmler's overall command carried out a racially based programme of

The most inscrutable of all Hitler's entourage was the *Reichsführer-SS* Heinrich Himmler. This nondescript man, afflicted with all the signs of racial inferiority, showed a simple nature to the world. He took care to be courteous. His lifestyle, unlike Göring's, could almost be described as spartan in its simplicity. But his fantasies were all the more extravagant. He lived on another planet. His racial theory was misguided and led him into serious crimes.

Generaloberst Heinz Guderian

annihilation. Their task was not to defeat another army in the field but to extirpate entire civilian communities. Heinrich Himmler created the organization which was used to discharge this task with deadly effectiveness.

Those who stood in the way of 'returning the nation to health' had been identified long ago. 'You should no longer be in any doubt,' Himmler said in a speech in 1935, 'that we are engaged in a struggle with the most ancient opponents that our people have had for thousands of years, namely Jews, Freemasons and Jesuits.' It was not long before he extended his definition of opponent to include anyone he considered 'un-German'. These included ethnic groups such as the 'subhuman Slavs' or 'gypsies', non-conformists such as 'communists and Bolshevists', invalids, Christians, social misfits and homosexuals. The theory of the *Untermensch* (subhuman species) gave Himmler 'legitimacy' for the elimination of all those who stood in the way of Hitler's plans. The war against Russia, the 'war within a war', created the necessary conditions for the real campaign of annihilation.

To wage this campaign Hitler could not deploy regular German soldiers and officers, but required some extra-governmental body. It is true that the *Wehrmacht* was also involved in war crimes and the tunic of the German soldier did not remain as stainless as many who served in the war have claimed in retrospect. But the actual operations of mass-murder were carried out by new units, specially created for this purpose.

From the ranks of the security police and SD Himmler had *Einsatzgruppen* ('action squads') formed, which undertook 'special duties' in the rear of the fighting. The tireless organizer was SD chief Heydrich who in May 1941 briefed the senior officers of this initially 3,000-strong force on their assignment: 'To take out all Jews, all low-grade Asiatics, all communist officials and gypsies'. The leaders of the *Einsatzgruppen* carried out their 'special duties' with inhuman exactitude. Otto Ohlendorf, one of four squad Commanders, put the number of shootings carried out by his unit up to the end of 1941 at about 90,000. Hitler's henchmen kept a punctilious record of the genocide, noting the date of each execution and the number of victims. Himmler's bookkeeping mentality set the tone. But one of the major problems with this appeared to be coping with the large numbers of victims in mass-shootings such as that at Babi Yar in the Ukraine.

How did those who perpetrated such slaughter live with themselves? Himmler's answer to this question revealed a vision of 'guiltless' murderers. In a speech to SS *Gruppenführer* at Poznan, in occupied Poland – a speech which leaves one gaping with disbelief – he said:

> I want to talk to you here today about a very difficult matter. Among ourselves this must now be discussed quite openly, though we will never speak about it in public. I am referring to the evacuation of the Jews, the eradication of the Jewish people. It is one of those things which is easy to put into words – 'Eradicating the Jewish people,' any Party member can say, 'fine, it's in our programme; removal of the Jews, eradication – we'll do it.' Then along come all the 80 million good German souls, and every one of them knows one decent Jew. Of course, the rest are dreadful, but this Jew is really splendid. Of all the people who talk like that, none have watched, none have been through it. Most of you, though, know what it means when a hundred corpses are lying side by side, or five hundred are lying there, or a thousand. To have gone through this and at the same time – apart from some exceptional cases of human weakness – to have remained decent people, has made us tough.

Remain decent people? The abandonment of all moral concepts went hand in hand with the destruction of human life. 'There are situations,' said Himmler,' in which normal civic values are inadequate and one person must be both judge and executioner, not because he is cruel and bloodthirsty', but because it is required by the 'honour of the higher community', for the sake of 'preserving of the soul and the life of the nation'. Himmler developed for his SS a morality of its own: 'The Führer is always right,' was its first maxim. 'The end justifies the means,' was its second.

On no account did Himmler want a force which murdered out of sadism or any other extraneous motives. Rather he attempted to present the horror of mass-extermination as some great secular

5. 'A certain remoteness . . .' Goebbels and his stepson, Harald Quandt. (National Archives)

6. 'Judah must be destroyed . . .' Two anti-Semites are agreed: Joseph Goebbels and Robert Ley, head of the German Labour Front. (National Archives)

7.   *'I'm a Renaissance man . . .' Göring on his yacht,* Carin II.
(Library of Congress)

8.   *'A corrupt morphine-addict . . .' Hitler visiting Göring's country estate,*
Carinhall. (Library of Congress)

9.   'Ironsides, you have betrayed me . . .' Göring with his Armourer-General of
     the Luftwaffe, Ernst Udet (1938). (Ullstein Bilderdienst)

10. 'To talk to Eisenhower man to man . . .' Göring at a press conference after
     his arrest (1945). (Keystone)

11. 'The godson of Prince Heinrich: Heinrich Himmler' (1901). (Süddeutscher Verlag)

12. 'Always well-behaved . . .' Heinrich Himmler (front row, second from right) with his fellow-pupils at the Landshut High School. (Archiv für Kunst und Geschichte)

13. 'The man to do the political dirty-work . . .' Himmler with Streicher (far left) and Ley. (National Archives)

14. *'The Führer is always right . . .' Himmler with Hitler and Göring.*
(National Archives)

15. *'Not comrades . . .' Himmler visiting a camp for Russian PoWs in the rear
of the Eastern Front (1941).* (Süddeutscher Verlag)

16. *'Time to bury the hatchet . . .' Survivors of Himmler's camps (1945).*
(Archiv für Kunst und Geschichte)

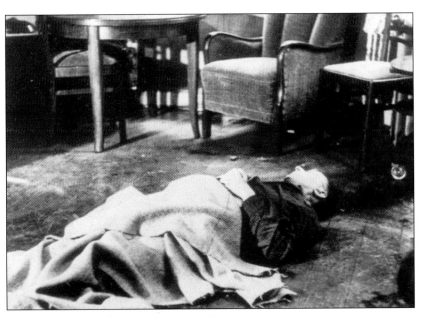

17. *'Then he bit on it . . .' Himmler after his suicide on 23 May 1945.*
(Archiv für Kunst und Geschichte)

18. 'More German than the Germans . . .' Rudolf Hess as a child with his mother Clara (1895). (Süddeutscher Verlag)

19. 'Hope for the day of vengeance . . .' Rudolf Hess as a student. (Bundesarchiv)

20. 'I hope he never has to replace me . . .' Hitler and his deputy Hess (with Goebbels) (1941). (Ullstein Bilderdienst)

21.   'I regret nothing . . .' Rudolf Hess in his prison cell at Nuremberg.
(Deutsche Presse-Agentur)

22. *'Why don't they let me die . . .?' The 'most expensive prisoner in the world' in the garden of Spandau gaol.* (copyright not known)

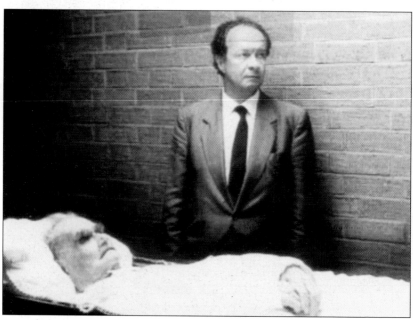

23. *'We cannot prove another hand was involved . . .' Hess' son Wolf-Rüdiger after his father's post-mortem (1987).* (NEXT EDIT)

24. The first commission: Speer (centre) with Goebbels and Nazi Party functionaries at the opening of the Berlin regional headquarters of the NSDAP (1932). (NEXT EDIT)

25. *'200 metres, mein Führer . . .' Speer and Hitler on the construction-site of the Reich Party assembly ground.* (Süddeutscher Verlag)

26. *'I like it . . .' The 'Palace of the Führer' on the 'Great Square' of the 'world capital Germania' (electronic simulation from Speer's drawing).* (NEXT EDIT)

27. 'It is to be completed by 1950 . . .' View of the 'Great Hall', looking down
the north–south axis to the 'Triumphal Arch' (electronic simulation
from Speer's drawing).

28.   Right: 'The
Führer shows us the
road and the
objective . . .' Dönitz
with staff officers
at his headquarters
(1943)
(Süddeutscher
Verlag)

29. 'Going the right way about making us ridiculous . . .' Dönitz as Hitler's executor (May 1945). (Keystone)

> We will never be rough or heartless, where we do not have to be. We Germans, who are the only people in the world with a decent attitude to animals, will also have a decent attitude towards these human animals.
>
> *Himmler*

mission which had to be fulfilled. 'It is the curse of the great man that he must step over corpses,' Himmler said after having asked to witness the execution of 200 Jews near Minsk, in the zone covered by *Einzatzgruppe Nebe*. At the very first salvo he almost fainted because the firing squad failed to kill two women immediately. His double standard of morality went so far as to assign to his men the right (even the duty) to commit mass-murder, yet he was harsh in condemning the theft of any valuables confiscated from Jews: 'We had the moral right, we had the duty towards our own people to kill those people who wanted to kill us. But we do not have the right to enrich ourselves even by one fur coat, one watch, one mark, one cigarette or anything else.' Himmler feared for the purity of his ideal and threatened draconian penalties: 'I will never allow even one small patch of rot to develop here. Wherever they may form, we will burn them out together. But in general we can say that we . . . have not been harmed by this in our inner selves, in our soul, in our character.'

In order for this to be achieved, the unfortunate victims had to be comprehensively denounced, and denied their very humanity.

That creation of nature, apparently quite indistinguishable biologically from a human being, with hands, feet, a sort of brain, with eyes and a mouth, is, however, something quite different, a fearful creature, a mere approximation to humanity, with humanoid facial features – yet mentally and spiritually of a lower order than any animal. In the depths of its nature lies a hideous confusion of wild and unbridled passions: a nameless urge to destroy, the most primitive desires, the most undisguised nastiness. Subhuman – there is no other word!

The words of the *Reichsführer* in 1942. Faced with such creatures there could be no question of forbearance – this was the message repeated by Himmler with the monotony of a prayer-wheel. Here lies the answer to the question why a man who, when out stalking, refused to 'shoot at poor animals browsing so innocently, defence-lessly and unsuspectingly at the edge of the forest', but could order the massacre of human beings without scruple. Because for him there were three categories of living creature – humans, animals and *Untermenschen*. At the same time Himmler reasoned that after the war German children should be 'indoctrinated with the love of animals', and that police powers should be granted to animal protection societies.

To Himmler humanity was no more than a sign of 'over-refined, civilized decadence'. The ethical values which were to weld his troops together, were different: loyalty, honesty, obedience, toughness, decency, frugality and courage. But the group who were to benefit from this ethos was a restricted one: 'One principle must apply to the SS man absolutely: we have to behave with honesty, decency, loyalty and comradeship to those who are of our own blood and to no one else.'

Disavowing the humanity of the victim, declaring the deed a

Frau Potthast, Himmler's mistress, said she wanted to show us something interesting, a special collection, which Himmler kept in a very special attic. She led us up into the loft. When she opened the door and we went in, at first we had no idea what we were looking at – until she explained it to us in a very knowledgeable manner. There were tables and chairs made from parts of human bodies. There was a chair whose seat was a human pelvis and the legs were human legs – on human feet. And then she took a copy of *Mein Kampf* from a pile. She showed us the binding – it was made from human skin, she said – and she explained to us that the prisoners in Dachau who had made it, had used the skin from someone's back.

Martin Bormann Jr, son of Martin Bormann and godson of Hitler necessary one and performing the tasks mechanically – can this explain the Janus-headed posture of Himmler and his accomplices? Can there in fact be any rational explanation for the irrational behaviour of a man who personally packs a basket of gifts for his parents' former parlour-maid and at the same time orders the shooting of more Jews?

In the notes of the Commandant of Auschwitz, Rudolf Höss, Himmler appears as the cold planner and executor of genocide. Even though Höss was trying to deflect some of his own guilt on to his superior, his accusations were not pure fabrication. In the summer of 1941, Höss tells us, Himmler summoned him to Berlin and told him: 'The Führer has ordered the final solution of the Jewish Question. We, the SS, have to carry out that order. The existing extermination sites in the east are not in a position to handle the large operations that are envisaged. I have therefore selected Auschwitz for this.' Sworn to total secrecy by Himmler, Höss was to organize the genocide, together with Adolf Eichmann, the head of the Jewish department in Office V of the Reich security headquarters. With great attention to detail Eichmann planned the transportation, and Höss, with no less zeal, the extermination of the victims. Both went about their appointed tasks with an unscrupulousness matched by their total lack of compassion. They

There was only one occasion when I remember Hitler bringing the conversation at dinner round to the subject of Himmler and concentration-camps. We got the impression that they were labour-camps. Hitler mentioned that in them Himmler used a very clever system. For example, a notorious arsonist was put in charge of fire-watching. Then, said Himmler, 'you can be sure, *mein Führer*, that no fires will break out.' We had the feeling that these were well-organized labour-camps, managed with skilful psychology. In Hitler's voice there was a note of respect and admiration for Himmler's organizational talent.

Traudl Junge, Hitler's Secretary

were organizing the murder of human beings as though it were a matter of destroying inanimate objects.

With Auschwitz there appeared an entirely new type of concentration-camp. 'The war has brought about a visible change in structure and the task with regard to deployment of inmates has fundamentally altered,' wrote Oswald Pohl, head of the industrial and commercial arm of the SS, in a letter to Himmler on 30 April 1942. 'The detention of inmates purely for security, re-educational and preventive reasons is no longer the prime consideration. The mobilization of able-bodied inmates initially for war work is becoming more and more important.' What Pohl euphemistically describes as 'educational tasks' was a mockery of the actual function performed by concentration-camps from the earliest years of the Third Reich. The camps, which initially came under the authority of the SA, were the spearheads of the whole apparatus of suppression. Political non-conformists – from communists and Social-Democrats, through clergy, Jews and Freemasons, to homosexuals and social 'misfits' – were 'concentrated' in these places. Theodor Eicke, whom Himmler appointed as 'Inspector of Concentration-camps and Commander of the SS guard units' brought the organization of the camps into line in 1934. As in Dachau, where he had been Commandant, Eicke now introduced general regulations for the guarding and punishment of prisoners; and the design and construction of the camps was standardized. Some 4,000 SS men provided teams of guards, organized into *Totenkopf* units. Publicly Himmler defined the role of the camps in this way:

Toughness, new values, creative work, a strict and fair treatment. The encouragement to learn how to work again and to acquire skills of a manual nature, are the methods of education. The motto written above these camps is: 'There is one road to freedom – its milestones are obedience, industry, honesty, order, cleanliness, sobriety, truthfulness, self-sacrifice and love of the Fatherland.'

In contrast to this idyllic picture, the reality of camp life was very different. For many inmates there was only one way out: as ashes, which were presented to their surviving relatives.

> People cheered Hitler and Göring and many others, but I never saw in a picture or personally heard anyone cheering Himmler.
>
> *Ernst-Günther Schenck, nutrition officer for the Wehrmacht and SS*

Remote from the public gaze, the prisoners were abused in cruel medical experiments. No profession sank so low in the Third Reich as the doctors in the service of the SS. Though obliged by the Hippocratic Oath to help mankind everywhere and with all available means, they exploited the opportunity in the unlegalized environment of the camps to torture defenceless human beings for 'research purposes'. In the 'interests of science' they were injected with deadly viruses in order to test the effectiveness of antibodies. Vivisection, experiments in low temperatures and low atmospheric pressures, sterilization by radiation, sulfonamide as a treatment for gangrene, 'terminal experiments', in other words, research methods intended from the outset to result in the subject's death – the list of horrors is long.

> The concentration-camp – like any form of imprisonment – is certainly a harsh and severe measure. Hard work that brings new values, a regulated pattern of life and an unprecedented cleanliness in living accommodation and personal hygiene, an impeccable diet, and strict but fair treatment.
>
> *Himmler*

Those passing through the gates of Auschwitz and other camps were 'weeded'. The ones selected for 'special treatment' had to go straight to the gas-chambers, in which the Nazi thugs killed their victims in less than 15 minutes with the highly poisonous gas, Zyklon B. For the ones considered fit for work, the suffering lasted longer. The inmates were treated – mistreated – as cheap labour in order to raise the output of armaments. The cynical motto over the gates of many concentration-camps was '*Arbeit macht frei*' (roughly 'Work is liberation'). In practice, work meant annihilation.

At the beginning of the war there were six large concentration-camps in Reich territory with about 21,000 prisoners. But the numbers grew rapidly thereafter. By 1940 as many as 800,000 people had vanished behind barbed wire. But the horror grew and took on a completely new character. The concentration-camps were joined by extermination-camps, in which only one objective was pursued: the putting to death of as many victims as possible at the lowest possible cost. These human abbattoirs – Auschwitz, Sobibor, Chelmno, Majdanek, Treblinka, Belzec – did not lie within Greater Germany, but in the territory of the *Generalgouvernement*, the German-administered part of Poland. The German people were not meant to get wind of what was going on.

> Yesterday we heard that Himmler has been given the Ministry of the Interior. In other words the most extreme, the most notorious bloodhound in the Party, the head of the police, opponent of Göring, and exponent of actual condemnation by blood. How bad things must be in Germany, when the hangman is made Minister of the Interior!
>
> *Victor Klemperer, Jewish novelist, 1943*

In 1942 Himmler visited Auschwitz, attended the selection of victims and watched the gassing through a spy-hole in the door of the gas-chamber. He made no comment on any of the procedures. Höss interpreted this correctly: the *Reichsführer* was satisfied. Himmler proceeded to an inspection of the entire camp, during which Höss drew his attention to the overcrowding, the consequent danger of epidemic which threatened the SS guards and the effect of starvation on the already low labour output of the inmates. According to Höss, Himmler saw the misery and squalor but refused to let himself be disturbed by it. 'I don't want to hear any more about your difficulties!' he retorted to Höss. 'For an SS officer there are no difficulties; his duty is always to remove difficulties himself, as soon as they arise. How you do it is for you to figure out, not me!'

How could extermination on such a huge scale be carried out without interruption? The Third Reich was an empire built on secrecy and Himmler was a past master at keeping and trading secrets. In 1945 Göring claimed he had had no insight into the affairs of the SS: 'No outsider knew anything about Himmler's organization.' Not in detail, perhaps, but can genocide remain a secret? Surely not. Camp-Commandant Höss himself makes us wonder:

> Even with the first open-air incineration, one could see that in the long run this was not going to be feasible. In bad weather or strong winds the smell of burning spread for many kilometers around and left the whole surrounding population talking about the burning of Jews, despite counter-propaganda from the Party. It is true that all members of the SS who took part in the extermination programme were under the strictest orders to say nothing about the whole process, yet even severe punishment could not prevent some tongues from wagging.

The murder of Jews was admittedly a matter of state secrecy, yet there were enough people who knew enough to know very well that they did not want to know any more.

What can be said first of all about those who actually handled the victims? Those involved mostly pleaded the necessity of obeying orders. The responsibility was passed on up to a higher level. Behind every murderer stood someone who had ordered the murder. Everyone wanted to unload the blame on the supreme commander, Hitler, even though they would go down with him.

Yet it is not as simple as that. Hitler himself had not, any more than Himmler had, personally committed a single murder. Himmler told his immediate colleagues that he had received the order from Hitler to resolve the 'Jewish Question' by murder. But no proof in the form of a written document exists. Himmler's masseur, Felix Kersten, reports that as early as September 1942, Himmler had told him: 'Of course, I didn't want to liquidate the Jews at all. I had quite different plans. It's that man Goebbels who has the whole thing on his conscience.' Apart from the fact that any number of other statements by Himmler exist, one thing

No one who had not seen it for himself, would believe that a man with the power and authority of Himmler was afraid whenever he was summoned to Hitler, and was as pleased as if he had passed an examination, when things happened to go well or if he had even received some praise. Then you realized how much he hated presenting anything unpalatable to Hitler and flinched at every frown. Himmler carried no weight when faced with Hitler's personality. Reliable witnesses told me that with a few words or gestures Hitler could simply sweep him aside or deal with him so effectively that Himmler dared not say another word. Himmler suffered personally in this situation.

Felix Kersten, Himmler's doctor and masseur, 1952

remains unarguable, that the *Reichsführer-SS* passed on orders for the extermination of the Jews. Who can invoke the need to obey orders? After Hitler, Himmler was the most powerful man in the Third Reich. If anyone had the opportunity to disregard the orders of the Führer then it was the man at the head of the SS. But he saw himself specifically as the right hand of a 'demi-god'. He once told his doctor, Felix Kersten:

He came to us in the hour of direst need, when the German people were finished; he was one of those great guiding lights who always emerge in Germanic history just when the nation has sunk to its lowest point, physically, mentally and emotionally. Goethe was such a figure in the intellectual sphere, Bismarck on the political front. The Führer is our leader in every field, political, cultural and military.

Himmler not only saw Hitler as being on a par with Goethe and Bismarck but also as the saviour of the nation. To Himmler the man from Braunau was one thing above all else: the Messiah. Against this background, his later attempts in the face of imminent defeat to lay all the blame on Hitler alone are just not credible.

At lower levels, was it a case of 'having to obey orders'? Was this true for Höss and Eichmann, for example, two of the key organizers of the mass-murders? Was it true for the SS man on guard-duty at a death-camp? Or for the doctor selecting the ones for the gas-chamber, wielding a godlike power of life and death? They all claimed that they were forced to obey orders. Yet how many cases do we know of, where a refusal to obey a specific order led to drastic consequences for the refuser?

> We have only one task and that is to stand firm and wage this race-war without pity. Let the world call us what it will; what matters is that we are the ever loyal, obedient, steadfast and invincible troops of the Germanic people and of the Führer, the Schutzstaffel of the Germanic Reich.
>
> *Himmler, 1943*

It is certainly true, at least, that there was no compulsion to aggravate the killings ordered by committing further atrocities. Himmler himself was concerned about the morale of the troops, who might become coarsened by the acts they had to commit. For this reason he demanded on more than one occasion that SS men should remain 'decent'. Extremes of violence were frequently rooted in the nature of the perpetrator. To justify these retrospectively as 'acting under orders' contradicts the historical truth. The men who performed their duties in the *Einsatzgruppen* or the 'Death's Head' units were not compelled to do so. Having made the decision to volunteer, could they then refuse to follow service regulations and thus refuse to carry out the killings? They certainly had the opportunity to evade orders of that kind and this evasion carried no particular risk. No one who declared himself unequal to these demands, or who withdrew without giving any specific reason, needed to fear for his own life or safety. It was not impossible to extricate oneself from the Nazis' killing mechanism. It might not have been altogether easy, and is certainly simpler today to claim in retrospect that one had to obey orders. But simple though it may be, it would be wrong. This excuse is not available to anyone involved in those terrible things. From Himmler, through Heydrich and Höss, down to the last SS man and camp doctor – without their active involvement the manic extermination policy of the Nazis would never have been possible at all. Hitler had many helpers.

Why did those who were not under the heel of the system not take any action against it? The Allies learned at a very early stage about the genocide that was beginning to take place. Why did they not bomb Auschwitz and destroy the annihilation-plant, just as they destroyed the Frauenkirche in Dresden? And the Germans who risked their lives listening to the so-called enemy radio-stations and learned from them of the mass-extermination – can we reproach them for doing nothing about it? Can we today demand from them the heroism that would have been needed then, threatened with imprisonment in a concentration-camp, to protest about Auschwitz, Sobibor and Majdanek?

The prisoners in Niedernhagen camp died from malnutrition and punishments which were reminiscent of the Middle Ages. Many of the prisoners had their hands tied behind their back and then pulled up until their shoulders were dislocated. Or else their hands were tied in front of them, both knees pulled up between their elbows and an iron rod wedged under them. Then they were left lying like that on the concrete floor.

In the camp young SS doctors performed their first operations. It was a requirement that by the ninth day after their operation the prisoners had to be fit for work again. My hernia operation was carried out without anaesthetic. Four men held me down while I was operated on and then sewn up. After nine days I was released for wood-chopping duties. Within half an hour the wound opened up again, and my intestines were hanging down to my knees. Then I lay on my back while the overseer wasn't looking and pushed my guts back into my stomach. After that I held one hand firmly on my stomach and chopped wood with the other.

Max Hollweg, concentration-camp inmate

Anyone who today rides a moral high horse and condemns those people who did not prevent the killing, might ask themselves another question: how healthy is the moral courage of today's society? How long were men like Pol Pot in Cambodia or Idi Amin in Uganda allowed to go on murdering before the civilized world intervened? For how long did the community of nations stand by and watch while the Hutus and Tutsis butchered each other in Rwanda? What differentiates the massacre of innocent Moslems in Srebenica from the murder of innocent Jews in Babi Yar? *Today* you do not need to be a hero to protest against it.

In the end the executioner turned traitor. Himmler knew the Berlin lawyer Dr Carl Langbehn and the former Prussian Minister of Finance, Dr Johannes Popitz, both of whom belonged to the group who were planning a coup against Hitler. We can be sure that neither revealed to Himmler the plans for an attempt on Hitler's life, made on 20 July 1944, even if they knew about it at all. However it is indisputable that long before 20 July Langbehn discussed with SS-General Karl Wolff, a confidant of Himmler, the possibility of seeking an alternative policy towards the west, aimed at negotiating an end to the war with the western Allies. For this purpose Langbehn was allowed to travel to a neutral foreign country in 1943. The fact that the men of 20 July were able to carry out their plans at all suggests that Himmler may have been aware of what was afoot but chose to ignore whatever the Gestapo had discovered about the plot. At Himmler's Hochwald quarters, near Hitler's 'Wolf's Lair' at Rastenburg, his masseur, Kersten, asked him: 'Can it really be true that with your far-reaching intelligence network you knew nothing about the plot to assassinate Hitler? Won't that count very heavily against you?' Kersten's question was justified. And Himmler himself feared that his masseur would not be the only one to ask it. He could refuse an answer to Kersten, but not to others. Himmler's Chief of Criminal Police, Arthur Nebe, and his Foreign Intelligence Chief, Walter Schellenberg, were themselves among the active conspirators. Schellenberg tells us in his memoirs that he had asked Himmler several times what ought to happen in Germany after Hitler, or 'in which drawer he kept his alternative plans', should the Russian campaign take an unfortunate turn. It is a fact that, on 17 July 1944, Himmler turned down a written Gestapo request for permission to arrest two of the principal plotters, Carl Goerdeler (who was to be appointed Chancellor after Hitler's death) and General Ludwig Beck. *Sturmbannführer* Willi Höttl, one of Himmler's intimates in the Foreign Department of the SD, spoke of an apparent delaying tactic by his boss. Whether, behind this, there lay an intention to let the plotters proceed with their deed, or whether Himmler simply wanted to await further developments, is something we will never know. Nonetheless, it can be regarded as certain that Himmler was informed about the resistance groups in the Wehrmacht and the aristocratic Kreisau Circle. It is also clear that Himmler's normally faultless persecution machinery did not go into top gear until after the bomb attack on Hitler had failed – but then it did so with its usual murderous thoroughness. One cannot help thinking that Himmler wanted to leave it to others to strike the blow against Hitler, which for all his 'loyalty' he now considered, in view of the military situation, to be the only sensible way out. After the failure of the assassination attempt the *Reichsführer-SS* made an effort to show his contacts with the resistance in a favourable light. He presented himself as a sophisticated intriguer who had conspired with Popitz on a close, personal level, in order to extract information from him. It is doubtful whether Hitler gave much credence to this interpretation. But the dictator did not ask the question. Even the suspicious Führer could not imagine that his 'faithful Heinrich' would ever betray him.

Hitler was all the more hurt when he found out that in the last days of the Third Reich even Himmler would leave him in the lurch – admittedly at a point when it no longer mattered anyway. On 20 April 1945 Himmler was a guest for the last time in the 'Führer-Bunker' in Berlin. It was Hitler's birthday, the last day of 'celebration' in a Third Reich that everywhere lay in ruins. At the same time, at Felix Kersten's country home, an emissary from the World Congress of Jewry awaited the *Reichsführer-SS*. At 2 a.m. on the morning of 21 April Himmler arrived there with his espionage chief, Schellenberg. The proposal that Himmler came up with was absurd: 'It's time that you Jews and we National Socialists buried the hatchet,' he declared to the dumbstruck envoy, Norbert Masur. Was the hatchet which the Nazis had dug up and which Himmler's SS had wielded now simply to be buried? But Masur was prepared to negotiate with the axeman: 'I hope that our meeting will save the lives of many people.' The Jewish Congress would not and could not enter into peace negotiations but were trying to save the concentration-camp inmates from being dragged down into the abyss along with the rest of Germany, now on the brink of collapse. Masur requested that all Jews imprisoned in places from which it was possible to reach the Swiss or Swedish borders should be immediately set free. In all other camps he called at least for humane treatment pending the peaceful hand-over of the camps. Masur presented a list from the Swedish Foreign Ministry of the names of Swedish, Norwegian, French and Jewish prisoners whom the Germans were holding as hostages. They were to be released immediately, together with 1,000 Jewish women. Himmler, who had up to now been so merciless, showed a willingness to negotiate. Not only would the listed prisoners and the 1,000 Jewish women in Ravensbruck be released, but also the Dutch Jews in Theresienstadt. As the Allied Armies approached, the camps were to be handed over intact. The prisoners, Himmler promised faithfully, would not be evacuated. At that very moment, only a few miles from the scene of the negotiations, the inmates of the Sachsenhausen camp were being herded away on a terrible march that few of them would survive. A few days earlier, Himmler had ordered the Commandants of Dachau and Flossenbürg to evacuate their camps immediately. Not a single inmate was to fall into enemy hands. Surrendering the camps was out of the question because, so Himmler claimed, when the prisoners in Buchenwald had liberated themselves rioting had broken out among the civilian population in nearby Weimar. That too was a lie.

As late as 20 April Himmler had ordered the formation of 'mobile drumhead courts-martial' which, supported by units of the security police and SD, were to cordon off the centre of Berlin and prevent any attempt at escape by the civilian population. Fleeing soldiers or members of Hitler's last-ditch *Volkssturm* were to be hanged immediately if they were suspected of desertion – a grim warning to anyone not prepared to continue the senseless fighting to the bitter end. Privately, Himmler himself had no doubt capitulated already. Taking his leave of Kersten, he declared: 'The most valuable element of the German people will be destroyed with us. The fate of the rest is unimportant.' It was not humanity, nor remorse, but merely indifference that motivated Himmler's 'generosity' in sparing a few people from the fate to which he had already consigned millions of others; indifference and the attempt to acquit himself of guilt: 'I'm the one who will get all the blame for the crimes which Hitler himself committed and which I always tried to prevent.' It was the moment for his ultimate betrayal.

On 23 April Himmler held talks with the Swedish diplomat, Count Folke Bernadotte. From the beginning of that year Walter Schellenberg had been trying to persuade the *Reichsführer* to start peace negotiations with the west behind Hitler's back. Now that Hitler himself had admitted defeat, Himmler abandoned all his former inhibitions. Shortly before an Allied air-raid on the city, he flew to Lübeck where, in the cellars of the Swedish consulate, he made a surprising offer to Bernadotte:

'In order to save as much of Germany as possible from the Russian invasion, I am prepared to surrender on the Western Front – but not on the Eastern Front.' Bernadotte agreed to inform his government of Himmler's proposal. However, he considered the chances of a separate cease-fire to be slender. Himmler would not accept his objections. For him there was no doubt that the Western Powers would negotiate with him. He had lost his grip on reality to such an extent that he was already worrying whether, on meeting Eisenhower, he should shake hands with his victorious opponent. The next day Himmler and his SS colleagues had to flee from approaching Soviet reconnaissance troops. The west had no intention of accepting Himmler's peace proposal. But the offer was released to the press. On 28 April the BBC in London announced: 'The *Reichsführer* claims that Hitler is dead and that he is his successor.' In Berlin Hitler thundered at the 'most shameless betrayal in world history'. Göring's Luftwaffe was to arrest Himmler: reality was breaking down on all sides. Since Hitler's thirst for revenge would brook no delay, a substitute victim had to be sacrificed. The axe fell on Hermann Fegelein,

Himmler's liaison officer in the Führer-Bunker. He was demoted on account of an alleged attempt to desert and summarily condemned to death for being an 'accessory'. It was of no avail to Fegelein that he was married to Eva Braun's sister. In his political testament Hitler removed both Himmler and Göring from office for their 'secret negotiations with the enemy, conducted without my knowledge and against my wishes', and gave orders for the fighting to continue. Finally he himself abdicated from responsibility by committing suicide.

When I spoke to Hitler for the last time, on the night of 29 April 1945, he in turn made a speech to me about the disappointments of his life. He told me how the worst thing he had to experience in his final days was the terrible disappointment of being abandoned by his colleagues. His betrayal by Himmler he described as the most terrible disappointment of all.

Arthur Axmann, leader of the Hitler Youth

Himmler was clearly unimpressed by Hitler's verdict. On 1 May the new leader of the Reich, Admiral Karl Dönitz, met the deposed *Reichsführer-SS* in the naval barracks at Plön, surrounded by U-boat crews – as protection against all eventualities. True, Himmler had been relieved of his office, but no one knew what loyalty the SS would show their leader. Dönitz had a loaded Browning pistol in his desk when Himmler arrived with a large retinue from his last headquarters in Kalkhorst on Lübeck Bay. He showed Himmler the telegram from Martin Bormann informing him of events in Berlin and specifically about Himmler's dismissal. Himmler congratulated Dönitz on his new appointment and declared his willingness, as the second most senior man in government, to continue working under the new head of state. He had begun his career as a Deputy and he wanted to continue in the same role. Dönitz declined. 'On the other hand,' he recalled later, 'I could not sever relations with him completely, since he still had the police under his control.' Himmler made several more

attempts, in personal conversations with Dönitz, to retain a
position in the successor state. But at around 5 p.m. on 6 May
Dönitz informed Himmler that he did not want to see him again.
As he was leaving Dönitz' office Himmler met the new Foreign
Minister, Count Schwerin von Krosigk, to whom he outlined his
future plans: the west would soon have trouble from the Russians.
Until that moment, and it would not be long in coming, he would
go into hiding. Then, when Germany would be in a position to tip
the scales in the conflict between east and west, his time would
come: 'Then we will complete what we were unable to achieve in
the war.' Until that time, which Himmler estimated was two or
three months away, he would go underground. He lectured his
last few loyal followers about wanting to turn Schleswig-Holstein
into an SS state.

It was 22 May 1945, a warm spring day. Two weeks after the
end of the world war in Europe, chaos reigned in Germany. Its
cities lay in ruins, refugees from the east and those who had been
bombed out of their homes were streaming along the dusty
country roads. The remains of Hitler's Wehrmacht were being
taken prisoner by the Allies. Many attempted to escape this fate by
dressing as civilians. For others a German uniform meant
protection, for they hoped that, as 'simple soldiers', they could
avoid responsibility for their crimes. Before the war ended, in his
headquarters in Flensburg, Himmler had advised Rudolf Höss to
go under cover: 'Disappear as swiftly as possible into the
Wehrmacht,' was the watchword of anyone who was threatened
with more than just imprisonment. The murderers had to blend in
with the people upon whom they had brought disgrace. Many
members of the second rank of Nazi elite tried to submerge
themselves in the anonymous mass from which, twelve years earlier,
they had risen like scum. Julius Streicher, the one-time 'Führer of
Franconia' had been thrown out long ago and was posing as an
artist in Bavaria, Robert Ley the former leader of the 'German
Labour Front' was hiding behind the name of 'Dr Distelmeyer',
and the high-profile ex-Foreign Minister, Joachim von Ribbentrop,
had dropped out of sight with a lady friend in Hamburg.

Outside the village of Barnstedt, between Bremervörde and
Hamburg, there appeared on this same 22 May a small group of

ragged figures. They were stopped by a British army patrol. A short, thin man introduced himself as *Feldwebel* 'Heinrich Hitzinger', and showed a forged identity document to this effect. The emaciated and sickly looking man bore no resemblance to the mighty *Reichsführer-SS*. The moustache was missing and his left eye was covered by a black patch. No one had any idea of the true identity of this man, dressed in the uniform of an ordinary soldier, who was trying to make his way through the British and American lines, from Flensburg down to Bavaria. On 12 May the men in their shabby uniforms with the shoulder-straps missing had crossed the Elbe in a fishing-boat. They had had to leave their cars behind on the other side. Now they were continuing their flight on foot: Himmler, his bodyguard Kiermeyer, his adviser, *Standartenführer* Rudolf Brandt, his adjutants *Obersturmbannführer* Grothmann and *Sturmbannführer* Macher with seven other men from the SS. They all claimed to be demobilized members of the *Geheime Feldpolizei* (military secret police). Also in the party was Professor Karl Gebhardt, a 'boyhood friend' of Himmler's, who as doctor in charge of the Hohenlychen Clinic had performed experiments on human beings in the Ravensbrück concentration-camp, and equally had every reason to evade imprisonment by the victors. After a long march on foot they hid for several days in a farmhouse near Bremervörde. Their next stage was to be a crossing of the River Oste. But at the first checkpoint the operation failed. British soldiers took the little group into custody and transferred them to Camp 031 near Bramstedt, south of Bremen. The British still did not realize what a big fish had been caught in their net.

To Himmler the treatment that he received as plain *Feldwebel* Hitzinger did not seem appropriate to the importance of the person he actually was. The prisoner requested 'a private talk' with Captain T. Sylvester, the Commandant of Interrogation Camp 031. In the first conversation he immediately removed his eye-patch, put on his glasses and in a weary voice revealed his true identity. Himmler now hoped to be treated with exceptional courtesy. But just the opposite happened: like the millions of his concentration-camp victims he was forced to undress completely. But unlike the SS thugs, the British were not interested in recycling his possessions, only in preventing his suicide. Until he could be taken to the headquarters of the British Second Army in Lüneburg, Captain Sylvester kept his valuable prisoner under personal supervision. After a body-search he was given a British Army uniform to prevent him from smuggling poison capsules into his cell in his clothing.

No one had told me who he was. All I knew was that I had to guard an important prisoner. When he entered the room – not as the dapper figure we all knew, but wearing army underwear and wrapped in a blanket – I recognized him immediately. I spoke to him in German and pointed to an empty couch. 'That's your bed,' I said. 'Get undressed!'

He looked at me and said: 'He doesn't know who I am.' I said: 'You are Himmler. And that is your bed. Get undressed.' He stared at me. But I just stared back. Eventually he lowered his eyes and began to take off his underpants.

The doctor and the colonel came in and searched him. We suspected he might have poison on him. The doctor looked between his toes, all over his body, under his armpits, in his ears, behind his ears, in his hair.

Then he got to his mouth. He asked Himmler to open his mouth. Himmler obeyed and waggled his tongue. But the doctor wasn't satisfied. He asked Himmler to come closer to the light. The doctor tried to stick two fingers into his mouth. Then Himmler pulled his head away, bit the doctor's fingers and crushed the capsule of poison which he had been carrying in his mouth for hours.

The doctor said: 'He's done it!'

When he was dead, we threw a blanket over him and left him lying there.

Sergeant-Major Edwin Austin, Himmler's guard, 1945

On the next day, 23 May, Himmler was brought in for further interrogation. He had still not made use of the ampoule of poison which all the top Nazis carried with them. The interrogating officer, Col. N.L. Murphy, from Montgomery's intelligence section, ordered another body-search. When a doctor tried to examine Himmler's mouth, the prisoner bit on a cyanide ampoule which he had kept hidden in a gap in his teeth. 'We immediately upended the old bastard,' one of the officers present later wrote in his diary. The Englishmen tried to fasten Himmler's tongue with a needle and thread, so as to remove the poison from his body by administering emetics and pumping his stomach. But all their efforts were in vain. After a death-agony lasting twelve minutes the most feared man in the Third Reich was no more. His body was left lying there for a whole day, while American and Soviet officers viewed the mortal remains. A death-mask was made. The Soviets remained sceptical. It could be Himmler, was their cautious verdict. But doubts were uncalled-for. The dead man was Heinrich Himmler, Hitler's enforcer. On 26 May his corpse was buried by British soldiers in a shallow grave. Today his bones still lie, anonymous and unconsecrated, in a copse outside Lüneburg. In this respect at least he shares the fate to which he consigned millions of his victims.

CHAPTER FOUR

THE DEPUTY: RUDOLF HESS

KNOPP/DEICK

I am a stranger to myself.

I want to be the Hagen[1] of the party.

We believe that the Führer is following a higher calling
to shape the destiny of Germany.

I like to describe National Socialism and Fascism as nothing
other than healthy common sense cast in a political mould.

National Socialism has its roots in war.

When we make declarations of peace in our major official
speeches we are not just paying lip-service to it.

You can always distance yourself from me –
declare me insane, if you want.
I regret nothing.

Hess

Everything seems a completely new experience. A little while
ago I was standing at my post, thickly muffled up. The
landscape white with snow, stars sparkling in the sky.

[1] An odd choice of role-model: in the medieval legend of the Nibelungs, on which
Wagner based his 'Ring' cycle, Hagen, though a trusted adviser to King Gunther,
plots against the hero Siegfried, uses black magic to make Siegfried forget his love for
Brünnhilde, and finally kills him on the grounds of his having committed perjury.

Suddenly to my right a bright glow in the sky, then to my left. Burning villages! Breathtakingly beautiful. This is war!

Hess in a letter to his parents, 1914

The Kapp government seems to be finished this time. It's sad. A large section of the population was crying out for a dictator who would create order, take action against Jewish businesses and put a stop to black-marketeering and extortion. But when the man who selflessly wants to take matters in hand for the general good, once appears and acts with the courage of his convictions, lo and behold, the cry of 'trouble-maker' goes up. Our Jewish press, which knows that its co-racials may get it in the neck, naturally does its very best to brand the new men as 'Junkers', 'reactionaries', 'monarchists', etc.

Hess in a letter to his parents, 1920

When will this artificial wall between the workers and the middle class finally be torn down? Certainly not as long as the Jewish riff-raff benefit from it.

Hess in a letter to his parents, 1920

Up to that time I was not an anti-Semite myself. But the events of 1918 and later made things so blindingly clear that I had to convert to anti-Semitism.

Hess, 1940

Hess: the most decent of men, calm, friendly, intelligent, reserved: the perfect private secretary. He is a dear chap.

Goebbels, diary, 1926

I just hope that Hess never has to replace me. I don't know who I'd be more sorry for, Hess or the Party.

Hitler to Göring, 1937

Should anything befall me, then my first successor is Party-comrade Göring. Should anything befall Party-comrade Göring, then the next successor is Party-comrade Hess.

Hitler, 1939

I can still see my husband as though it were yesterday: We had drunk our tea and after kissing my hand he stood at the door of the children's room, suddenly looking oddly serious, brooding, almost unwilling to leave.

'When will you be back?'

'I don't know exactly. It could be tomorrow, but I'll certainly be home again by Monday evening, I should think.'

I didn't believe him.

Ilse Hess about her husband, shortly before his flight to England

Are you trying to tell me in all seriousness that the Führer's deputy is in England? Well, Hess or no Hess, I'm now going to watch a Marx Brothers film.

Winston Churchill, 1941

We all have our graves to tend and become ever lonelier, but we must overcome it and go on living, my dear lady! I too have lost the only two people around me to whom I was really deeply attached: Dr Todt is dead and Hess has flown away from me.

Hitler to the widow of the publisher Hugo Bruckmann, 1942

If my judgement is correct, Hitler never got over the 'breach of faith' by his deputy. Shortly after the attempt on his life on 20 July 1944 he mentioned, in amongst his wildly mistaken assessments of the situation, that his peace conditions would include the handing over of the 'traitor'. He would have to be hanged. When I recounted this to Hess later, he said: 'He would have made things up with me. I'm quite sure of it! And do you not suppose that in 1945, when the end was coming, he sometimes thought to himself: "Hess was right after all"?'

Speer, on Hess' flight to Britain

He is completely detached, has a few sheets of paper on his knees and writes ceaselessly. Göring leans over and points out that it is now his turn. But Hess brushes him aside with a dismissive gesture and continues to make his mysterious notes, paying no attention to what is being said about him.

He is not even wearing headphones, and when Göring subsequently whispers the verdict in his ear, he merely responds with an absent-minded nod.

Joe J. Heydecker, American journalist, Nuremberg 1946

* * *

'False alarm,' duty NCO Felicity Ashbee shook her head. 'Just another dud report from the coast.' The radar station at Ottercops Moss on the north-east coast of Scotland was notorious for mistaking storm-clouds for German bombers. The report on that evening of 10 May 1941 was another one that sounded altogether too fanciful: a lone aircraft over the North Sea, above 15,000 ft and flying as fast as a fighter, heading for Scotland. To an experienced air-plotter like Ashbee this was completely illogical. Admittedly, she knew that at that moment 500 German bombers were flying towards London and that air-raids on this massive scale were often accompanied by diversionary manoeuvres. But now, at nearly 22.00 hours – when the attackers had already penetrated the air-space over southern England – it was far too late for deception. And now that it was dark a reconnaissance-flight by the Luftwaffe had to be ruled out.

At 22.08 two other Scottish radar-stations confirmed the report from Ottercops Moss. A few minutes later the intruder crossed the Scottish coast. Units of the Royal Observer Corps identified the aircraft as a Messerschmitt Bf 110. Two British Spitfires soon began to tail him. However, having no on-board radar the encroaching darkness made this a hopeless undertaking The Messerschmitt now dived down and flew low over the Scottish hills. Later the pilot would write poetically of his impressions: 'A fairy-tale picture. The steep, mountainous islands in the full moon, in the last glow of dusk.'

Only when a Defiant night-fighter was scrambled from Glasgow was he in serious danger. But the German pilot was in luck. When only a few miles separated him from the night-fighter, he opened the cockpit cover and jumped with his parachute into the Scottish night. Had he hesitated just a few minutes longer, world history would have been poorer by one very strange chapter.

It was the first parachute-jump of his life, and the Führer's

Deputy, Rudolf Hess, was drifting down towards Scottish soil, in his last minutes of freedom. Scarcely any other episode in the Second World War has given rise to so much speculation as this risky undertaking. Even today the background to it has not been fully explained. The chances of the riddle being finally solved are not good. All those directly involved are dead and the documents do not contain any definite proof. Even after the extensive opening of British archives in 1992 one question remains: did Hess in fact fly as a doomed angel of peace on a mission of his own, or was he the selfless conveyor of an offer from Hitler, as many historians believe?

Right up to his death in 1987 in the Spandau prison for war criminals, Rudolf Hess remained silent. It is true, in any event, that he was not officially obliged to give any information about the political background to his flight, but even to those people who set aside prison rules and had confidential conversations with him, he gave not a word away. It was not least his self-imposed silence and a pride bordering on obstinacy that made Hess a cult-figure for neo-Nazis all over the world. He himself wanted none of it. He told his son he considered the shaven-haired skinheads in their bomber-jackets to be 'fantasists and idiots'. Nevertheless, his death made him a martyr in the eyes of both the old diehards and the neo-reactionaries. Although there was no solid evidence, it is not only Hess' family who believe that an unexplained murder took place behind the walls of Berlin's Spandau gaol.

However, the guessing-game about his flight to Britain and about his end in prison has distorted our view of the actual life-story of Rudolf Hess. Where are the roots of this man, which led him to become one of the great mysteries of modern history? Who was this man who was at Hitler's side from the beginning of his rise to power and who supported him to the point of total self-abnegation? What qualities turned him into Hitler's credulous henchman, and allowed him to fall so irrevocably under the spell of the demagogue?

The first thing that the seductive leader and his follower had in common was being born outside Germany. Hess' birthplace was the Egyptian port of Alexandria, and thus, like the Austrian Hitler, beyond the borders of the country which both men made the object of their ambitions. From an early age Hess, like Hitler, developed strong feelings towards this distant homeland. For the well-to-do mercantile family in Alexandria the Kaiser's empire meant above all the romantically transfigured rebirth of the nation. It is true that among the so-called *Auslandsdeutsche* exaggerated nationalism was very common – they were 'more German than the Germans', as a later colleague of Hess remarked.

The Kaiser's birthday used to be considered the most important secular festival of the year. Fritz Hess, the paterfamilias, did not go to his office but celebrated at home by opening his best bottle of wine. Far removed from the social problems of the Hohenzollern state, he felt the founding of the German Empire in 1871 to be the greatest good fortune for the nation. And when the Hess family returned home to Germany regularly every summer, they avoided the cities where the miserable conditions of the factory-workers could occasionally be glimpsed behind the showy Wilhelmine façades. They preferred to savour the summer in their country house at Reichholdsgrün, surrounded by the remoteness of the Fichtelgebirge mountains.

As soon as his son was born, in 1894, Fritz Hess was determined that one day the boy would head the family firm. The upbringing he provided for his offspring was no different from that which every well-off *Auslandsdeutscher* enjoyed: local German schools and private tutors, and then, in 1908, boarding school in Bad Godesberg, on the Rhine. Rudolf was bright, though not enormously gifted. He was keener on science and mathematics than on languages. His relationship with his parents was typical of families around the turn of the century. Father Hess ordered the household about in a strict, parade-ground manner, 'which', as Rudolf Hess later recalled, 'nearly made our blood curdle'. To show any tenderness towards his children – Rudolf had a younger brother, Alfred and sister, Margarete – was against the patriarch's nature. The family's origins in Calvinist Switzerland, steeped in an old mercantile tradition, were reflected in the character of Fritz Hess. Despite the wealth he accumulated, Hess Senior remained essentially a stolid, unsophisticated tradesman. Hitler's press-chief, Ernst Hanfstaengel, once met the 'Deputy's' father and remembered him as a '*Kegelbruder*', the sort of man one might play skittles with at the local inn. Discipline and self-discipline, duty and obedience, were the cornerstones with which Hess equipped his son for life – qualities of an age from which Hitler would profit, and not only in the case of Rudolf Hess.

It was left to his mother, Clara, to create a loving home environment. From her Rudolf inherited a love of nature and of music, a faith in herbal medicine and a keen interest in the stars. It was nearly always his mother who wrote to him at boarding school. His awe and admiration towards his authoritarian father on the one hand, and on the other the deep tenderness he felt for his mother – these were the opposite poles which would influence Rudolf Hess throughout his life.

It was typical of him that in the zone of tension between these two extremes he was never really able to establish an independent position of his own. Throughout his life he showed two different faces: the tough daredevil in the brawls of the 'fighting days' was at the same time a highly sensitive animal-lover who literally could not hurt a fly. The moral apostle of the Party, who stood up against corruption and abuse of office, could at the next moment be a malevolent agitator, urging the introduction of punishment-beatings for Jews in occupied Poland. The courageous and quick-thinking First World War officer developed a doglike devotion towards Hitler, which hardly left him any room to use his own initiative. And lastly the Deputy, frozen out politically, who was merely laughed at by the other henchmen for his detachment and unworldliness, but who surprised everyone in 1941 by summoning up the daring and decisiveness to fly over to the enemy in the middle of the war.

Rudolf Hess' youthful years have often been interpreted as holding the clues to the fateful path he took. But in fact there was nothing in that period of his life that went beyond the bounds of 'normality'. His was a rather happy childhood, untroubled by material worries. At boarding school in Bad Godesberg he was one of the most unobtrusive pupils. Rudolf bowed – albeit unwillingly – to his father's wish that, instead of taking his school-leaving certificate, he should aim for a diploma from a college of commerce in the Swiss town of Neuchâtel. He would really have preferred to become an engineer. In less turbulent times he would probably have become a respectable businessman, with a secret longing to follow his scientific bent.

> Rudolf Hess' parents were quite delightful. My sister got on very well with Rudolf's father, though he sometimes appeared arrogant. His wife was very much softer. It was a blow to the father that his eldest son did not become a businessman, so he could take over the firm.
>
> *Ingeborg Pröhl, Hess' sister-in-law*

But these were stormy days. In the late summer of 1914, when the peoples of Europe were overcome by an intoxicating nationalism and were carried on a wave of enthusiasm into a war which was to become a world conflagration, the turning-point came in the life of the twenty-year-old Rudolf Hess. In August, within days of the outbreak of hostilities, he defied his father's will and volunteered for the armed forces. It was the first time that the son had been openly disobedient. The seed of overweening nationalism sown by the expatriate German trader had long since borne fruit. Father and son retained a respect for each other, but from now on Rudolf Hess would look elsewhere for authority.

Initially, however, his road to the Front remained barred. Too many German men had rallied to the flag. For the time being Rudolf Hess had patiently to undergo weapon training on the barrack-square. Waiting for the first posting was torture for him. In the absurd fear that he might not be able to fire a shot before the swift victory that was anticipated, the recruit even hoped for higher German losses: 'So one actually *wants* the poor chaps to cop it in the next engagement,' he wrote to his mother. 'Otherwise who knows how long my suspension between heaven and earth will go on for.'

But then, for four long years, Hess had ample opportunity to witness death on a massive scale and at close quarters. His unit, the 1st Bavarian Infantry Regiment, fought on the Western Front. When Hess the infantryman underwent his baptism of fire, the war in the west had already become a stalemate in the trenches.

Nevertheless he described his impressions poetically, in letters filled with naïve enthusiasm: 'Burning villages. Breathtakingly beautiful. This is war!' Hess possessed the attributes of the 'good' soldier. He had learned military obedience at home, and the decisiveness that he had also inherited from his father soon made a favourable impression on his superiors. In the summer of 1915 he was promoted to NCO, and by 1917 he had been commissioned as a *Leutnant*.

> Right from the start, he showed his mettle and was soon one of the most daring of soldiers. When the call went out for volunteers for the many reconnaissance-patrols and for the shock-troops, he was always among them, always gave it everything he'd got, and in attacks his cool nerve and selflessness were exemplary.
>
> *Comrade of Hess in the First World War, 1955*

His early enthusiasm soon gave way to a sobering realization that the prospect of a swift victory over France had been illusory. But the soldierly Hess was never afflicted by doubts. 'We must fight on and see it through – in the field as well as at home,' he exhorted his parents in 1916 at the climax of the Battle of Verdun and wrote how he himself had inveighed 'vehemently against the slackers'. The senseless death of millions in the trenches and shell-craters, was cloaked by Hess with heavy pathos. It was the only way he could reconcile the war with his image of the world. In a battle-ballad running to several pages the 'fighter at the Front' penned verses about 'proud, victorious charges', 'hellish fire', and 'grey, expectant figures'.

Not even the injuries he sustained in action could diminish his zeal. In 1917, on the Romanian Front, he barely escaped death from a deep bullet-wound to his lung. No sooner had he recovered than the freshly commissioned lieutenant received orders to go with a reserve company to the Western Front. In the same company was an Austrian corporal who had dodged the draft into the Imperial and Royal Austrian Army, preferring to volunteer for service under the flag of the German Kaiser. His name was Adolf Hitler. In this chance encounter, it is true, the officer and the corporal, whom history would cast in opposite roles, exchanged not a word.

In the spring of 1918, after applying repeatedly, Lieutenant Hess was transferred to a new elite branch of the army, the 'Flying Corps'. Hess was full of admiration for the air-aces Baron von Richthofen and *Hauptmann* Göring, whose aerial battles were familiar to every schoolboy, even if they had no effect on the outcome of the war. During his pilot's training Hess proved himself skilful in the cockpit. Though not sent into action until the last days of the war – too late to shoot down a single enemy aircraft – he emerged unscathed and would remain devoted to flying.

The collapse of the Kaiser's Empire in November 1918 seemed to Hess, as it did to most of his comrades, like a national catastrophe. Having no inkling of the crucial part played by the Imperial government in starting the war, he still considered it a justified defensive war waged by the German people. As he saw it, entering into armistice negotiations was a major error: 'Our position is no worse than it was in 1914,' he wrote defiantly to his parents, 'On the contrary; our men only wavered for a short time, as a result of malicious rumour-mongering from back home and cleverly written leaflets distributed by the enemy.' It was the 'stab in the back'. Hess had never doubted who was to blame for the 'failure' of his homeland: the left. In fact it was the *de facto* leader of Germany in the last years of the war, General Ludendorff, who had admitted defeat and had then slunk away from responsibility by resigning. But Hess, like many soldiers at the Front, would hear nothing of that.

The loss of the war was a piercing, personally felt anguish. And what was wrongly interpreted as a betrayal by the politicians in parliament, traumatized millions of hearts. It tore a rift in the new Weimar Republic and created a deep gulf which split the nation in two. On one side of the chasm stood Hess, with but one thought in his mind: 'The only thing which sustains me,' he declared in the summer of 1919, 'is hope for the day of revenge.' Hess saw on whose heads this revenge would fall, just as his subsequent idol did at the same moment: Communists and Social-Democrats, but above all the Jews. He underlined this in a speech sixteen years later: 'Up to that time I was not an anti-Semite myself. But the events of 1918 and later made things so blindingly clear that I had to convert to anti-Semitism.'

For someone who thought along those lines, Munich, where the demobilized Lieutenant had taken up lodgings, proved to be dangerous territory. Under the Socialist Minister-President Kurt Eisner, the Bavarian capital had, along with Berlin, become Germany's second hotbed of revolution. The city's elegant Königsplatz was patrolled by soldiers with red armbands. Almost daily the newspapers carried reports of political murders. To begin with, Hess kept his head below the parapet and calmly reasoned that this 'farcical play-acting' was 'copied from Russia'.

His own personal prospects also looked gloomy. The British had confiscated his family's property in Egypt and the financially carefree years were over. In their country house in Reichholdsgrün his parents waited to see which way the wind would blow. For their twenty-five-year-old son the recent loss of the firm in Alexandria and the turmoil in German politics culminated in a grave personal crisis. In a letter written later he admitted to having toyed with the idea of 'putting a bullet through my brain'.

In his desperation Hess found a first foothold in a back room of one of Munich's grandest hotels, *Die Vier Jahreszeiten* (The Four Seasons). Here conspiratorial meetings were held by the members of a society listed as the 'Study-group for Germanic Antiquity'. This harmless-seeming entry, however, concealed a secret lodge, the 'Thule Society', whose aims were intensely right-wing, anti-Marxist and anti-Semitic. The group combined 'ethnic' ideas with plans for a counter-revolutionary *coup d'état* – an incubator for the fatal ideological epidemic which was to break out fourteen years later.

The emblem of the 'Thule' was the swastika, and one of its ideals was the 'Aryan man'. Hess joined the secret society early in 1919 and soon took on important tasks, procuring weapons, recruiting volunteers and leading sabotage squads. His subversive labours bore fruit in May 1919, when paramilitary *Freikorps* supported by the Reichswehr overthrew the Munich Soviet, the *Räterepublik*. The *Freikorps* 'Epp' set up its headquarters in rooms in the *Vier Jahreszeiten*. Now Hess fought against the left in the service of the *Freikorps*.

In the 'Thule' his vague anti-Semitism and his dream of seeing the nation restored to its greatness hardened into an amalgam of extremist ideas. Even the notion of a 'Führer' who would bring about Germany's rebirth met with Hess' active approval. What is more, in the society's meeting-rooms he got to know future colleagues and men who would become big names in the Nazi Party: Hans Frank, Alfred Rosenberg and Dietrich Eckart. Whether an unknown beer-hall orator named Adolf Hitler was in touch with the 'Thule' at that time, as Rudolf von Sebottendorf, the brains of the organization, later claimed, is a matter of conjecture. What is certain, however, is that the Thule's body of ideas and many of its supporters would later put down roots in the NSDAP.

Rudolf Hess had found his first political home in the Hotel *Vier Jahreszeiten*. In his professional life as well, he struck out in a new direction. As a former front-line soldier he was entitled to study at Munich University without having taken his school-leaving certificate. A university degree seemed the perfect way to escape once and for all from the fate of working in the family firm. Hess enrolled in economics and history – for want of a better idea, and with no specific career in view.

It was in the lecture-theatre that he became acquainted with a man who would have a lasting influence on his life. The geopolitics faculty was headed by a retired General, now Professor, Karl Haushofer, a man of some distinction with connections in Munich society. Hess found in the old warhorse just the substitute he had been seeking for the authority figure that his father had been for so many years. The undergraduate Hess soon become the Professor's assistant, spent more and more time visiting him privately and adopted his mentor's scholarly creed. In truth, Haushofer's theories amounted to a political programme rather than an academic one. His basic proposition ran thus: the German people lacked *Lebensraum* (living space), which could only be found in the east. If the price of realizing this obsession would be rivers of blood, that was something missing from Professor Haushofer's scholarly analysis. Nonetheless, his assistant lapped up the *Lebensraum* plan greedily.

The young man who, at the age of twenty-five, had already made a name for himself in Munich's extreme-right circles, was in private leading a rather Spartan existence: no alcohol, no cigarettes – he did not even go out dancing. Although he was athletic, good-looking and from a wealthy family, there do not seem to have been any young ladies in the early life of this upright individual. The tone of his letters at this time bespeaks a colourless sobriety, which only veered into fanatical obsession when the subject turned to Germany, politics or the war. The few existing pictures of Hess in these years show a taciturn-looking man, whose bushy eyebrows seem visually to reinforce this impression.

In 1920, in a modest boarding-house in Munich's bohemian Schwabing district, he met an officer's daughter named Ilse Pröhl – the first woman in his solitary life. Ilse recalled the first meeting with her husband-to-be:

> Suddenly a young man in a field-grey uniform with the bronze lion of the Freikorps Epp on his sleeve, burst through the garden-door and bounded up the little staircase three steps at a time. He stopped short, not expecting to see me there, gave me a very dark and disapproving look, bowed curtly but politely – and was gone! That was Rudolf Hess.

It was not exactly a flaming passion that was ignited between them. Significantly, Hess took a long time to warm to the idea of having a woman at his side. The way he described Ilse to his parents was scarcely flattering: from a 'pit full of snakes' he had fished out 'the only eel'. Yet Ilse Pröhl became more than just a girlfriend, fiancée and wife. She was one of the first women to join the NSDAP, and in the years before they were married helped him in his political work.

This personal change of fortune was followed one May evening in 1920 by an experience which would transform his life: in a Munich *Bierkeller*, the '*Sterneckerbräu*', Rudolf Hess heard a speaker from the German Workers' Party (*Deutsche Arbeiterpartei* or DAP), one of the many nationalist splinter-groups in Bavaria. An audience of scarcely two dozen had assembled in the hostelry, where a waitress served beer in litre mugs and cigarette-smoke hung heavily in the air. The speaker was a few years older than Hess, wore his hair parted in the middle and had an almost rectangular moustache. A leaflet put out by the DAP announced his profession as 'artistic painter'.

In a strong Austrian accent he began to describe the events of the last few years: the Treaty of Versailles was a crime against the German people, the bourgeois government had 'betrayed' the troops at the Front, and those pulling the strings – the Jews – were to blame for everything. By now his delivery had risen to an ecstatic scream. Hess was enthralled. It was his awakening. This man seemed to be addressing him from the depths of his soul. Late that same night he burst into Ilse's room. 'I've heard a man . . . a man . . . speaking,' he stammered joyfully, 'he's unknown, I've forgotten his name. But if anyone can liberate us from Versailles, then it's him; this unknown man will restore our honour!' As Ilse Hess later described him, her husband was 'a changed man, alive, radiant, no longer gloomy and morose'.

In 1920 Hitler was a long way from being the 'Führer'. For the moment he was still struggling for power within the tiny DAP. Even so, the future force of his oratory could already be sensed. Hess was one of the first people to fall prey to his demagoguery. A few days later he made up his mind to follow the fiery-tongued painter. The reasons for this were complex. Certainly, Hitler's as yet unorganized political ideas largely corresponded to those which his future disciple had privately developed in the nationalistic milieu of the 'Thule'. Both men had fought at the Front. Both had suffered severe injury, and both took the collapse of the Imperial Army as a personal insult. But Hess had succumbed to another deep need, the longing for a source of authority. After breaking away from his father he had continually been seeking a new central focus in his life. In the Army the military hierarchy had filled this vacuum, later it was briefly his teacher and paternal friend, Karl Haushofer.

Now it seemed that this man from the 'Sterneckerbräu' was not only ideally suited to be his new personal authority figure, but even offered a remedy for the piercing pain he felt over the state of the nation – for Hess it was a fateful combination of private and political longings. His own desires were a perfect fit for the Zeitgeist. In numerous books, poems and articles of those years there was talk of the 'one man' who would bring about the nation's salvation. For

Hess this 'one man' was Hitler, and from now on he made it his task
to bring this national 'saviour' to his goal.

> The Hess family were very nationalistic Germans. That is why
> Rudolf was interested in Hitler. Rudolf's father had a big
> picture of Wilhelm II hanging in his study. On the Kaiser's
> birthday he always ordered wine and wished his monarch
> 'Happy Birthday'. When Hitler was elected, I asked Frau
> Hess how things would change now. 'Well', she said, 'it's
> very simple. Instead of someone with a good plan having to
> wait for the government to agree on it, we now have a man
> who says: this is how it will be done, and there's no
> argument.' It was extremely clear to me.
>
> *Stefanie Camola, family friend*

Hitler immediately took a liking to the young helper, who
attached himself like a disciple to his master. Hess was reliable;
from his time with the 'Thule' he knew some influential people,
and he possessed one quality which greatly appealed to Hitler in
his mania for monologues – Hess was a good listener. Within the
still small party people smiled at the ill-matched pair, who usually
even went out to coffee-houses together: Hess, the son of a
middle-class family, well-mannered, reticent – and Hitler, the
agitator from a humble background, who struck others as rather
shifty, as well as gauche. There was nothing to suggest that people
were looking at the future 'Führer' of the Germans and his deputy.

Hess' admiration for the 'People's Tribune' as he reverently
dubbed Hitler, swiftly soared to unbridled fanaticism. 'A man of
splendour,' he wrote to his cousin and launched into this gushing
hyperbole: 'Recently, at the end of a magnificent speech in the Circus
Krone, he managed to get the whole audience of 6,000, from all
walks of life, to join in and sing *Deutschland, Deutschland über alles*.
There were about 2000 communists there who sang as well.'
Naturally, this kind of excess scarcely aroused enthusiasm in Karl
Haushofer, Hess' anxious patron. The cultured general wrinkled his
nose at the upstart Hitler, who displayed neither wit nor education.

Admittedly there was probably a trace of jealousy at work here as well, due to the fact that this beer-hall orator from Austria had succeeded in keeping his favourite student away from university.

> Hitler was his great idol. He got to know him in the very early days and said then that this was the man to get us out of our misery. As such, he always admired and respected Hitler. He would never have done anything behind his back
>
> *Laura Schroedel, Hess' Secretary*

Increasingly Hess took on the role of secretary to Hitler – especially after the latter had seized control of the NSDAP in 1921. Hess made himself useful in various ways; he and Ilse stuck posters up and distributed leaflets. At Hitler's behest, Hess, still nominally an undergraduate at Munich university, organized the first student *Hundertschaft* (100-strong company) in the SA. The young Party official scarcely bothered to attend lectures any more. The outcome of the tug-of-war between Hitler and Haushofer over the future of Rudolf Hess had been decided. In brawls with political opponents in public halls Hess gained a certain reputation for recklessness. The fact that a communist once inflicted a gaping wound to his head with a beer-mug was referred to in speeches by the deputy in the recurring phrase: 'Anyone who has, as I have, collapsed bleeding in front of the Führer . . .'

Yet Hess lacked one ability needed to make a name in the early NSDAP. He was not a public speaker! When Hess stood on a podium his delivery was inhibited and awkward. His listeners got the impression that he was glad when his own speeches were over. In the words of Hermann Esser, a party orator of the early days: 'Faced with a dozen people, Hess couldn't string a sentence together.'

Nevertheless, people in the Party began to take seriously the dependable henchman at Hitler's side. On 31 July 1921, in the new party newspaper, the *Völkischer Beobachter* (*National Observer*), Hess was given the opportunity in a leading article to set out the Party's programme, which already contained the essential points of the later years: it was anti-parliamentarian, anti-Jewish and anti-capitalist – and had as its goal the creation of a 'national ethnic community'. True, Hess was not one of those who had drafted the programme, he was not one of the 'brains' of the Party, and never became one, but even in these early days he gave it a face: fanatical, devout and – to a fatal degree – credible. With care and consistency he began to construct a myth around his 'tribune'. The very title which, twelve years later, every child in Germany would associate with Hitler, was the work of Hess. He was the first person to call him the 'Führer'.

In November 1923, for the first time, this 'Führer' set about making history. The atmosphere in Bavaria was explosive. Inflation had reached unimaginable heights. A loaf of bread cost more than a *billion* Reichsmarks. Hundreds of thousands of lives were ruined by the plummeting value of money. Particularly in the south of the unloved Weimar Republic, the call went up to put an end to 'parliament's mismanagement of the economy'. A year earlier in Italy, Benito Mussolini and his black-shirted Fascists had shown with their 'March on Rome' how power could be seized in a ramshackle state. Admittedly, Hitler was no Mussolini and his NSDAP was still a splinter-party, hardly known to anyone beyond the borders of Bavaria, but he believed in himself strongly enough to take action. On 8 November he risked staging a *coup d'état*.

In a letter to his parents written the same day, Hess described his impressions of the events. It is a document of immense importance. According to the letter, at 9 a.m. the ex-corporal Hitler ordered *Leutnant* Hess (Retd.) to stand by in readiness to arrest all the ministers in the Bavarian government that evening: 'An honourable and important assignment. I promised absolute secrecy, and we parted company until the evening.' Just before 6 p.m. Hess, along with Hitler, Göring and a handful of armed SA men, forced his way into the '*Bürgerbräu*' beer hall, where the provincial government was holding a public meeting. Hess describes how

Hitler jumped up on a chair. We followed his lead, and ordered everyone to be quiet, but they wouldn't. Hitler fired a shot in the air. That did the trick. Hitler announced: 'As of this moment the national revolution in Munich has broken out;

simultaneously the whole city is being occupied by our troops. This hall itself is surrounded by 600 men.'

The very next day the attempted *putsch* proved to be a melodramatic bluff, amateurishly planned and staged like a scene from an operetta. Under the rifle-fire of a police detachment, Hitler's first attempt to seize power came to a swift and bloody end. In later years, the fourteen men who died on 9 November 1923 would be commemorated annually in a sombre ritual, with flaming torches, drum-rolls and all the false emotion that Goebbels, the regime's master-of-ceremonies, knew just how to whip up. The fact that Rudolf Hess, the 'old campaigner', always marched in the front rank, was a deliberate distortion of history. The truth is that on 9 November, in the bloody debacle outside the Feldherrnhalle, Hess was not there.

At that moment he was following orders and guarding hostages from the Bavarian state government, two ministers named Schweyer and Wutzelhofer. When he heard of the failure of the *putsch* he requisitioned a car and fled with his two 'charges' in the direction of Bad Tölz. The remainder of the hostage-taking episode is described by Hess in another letter to his parents: as darkness fell he attempted to find lodgings for the party in a roadside farmhouse. 'When I returned, the car, for what reason I still do not know, had driven off. The ministers turned up later in Munich. Perhaps that was the best solution.' In fact the Ministers' escape from his custody was a poor advertisement for the would-be revolutionary, as was his subsequent behaviour: the same day Rudolf Hess got away across the Austrian frontier to Salzburg.

After the failure of the attempted *putsch* Rudolf Hess initially had to go into hiding. My sister Ilse always used to take him food, because she was the only one who knew about his hiding-place in the Isar valley. Later he gave himself up and was imprisoned in Landsberg. The atmosphere there was not as oppressive as in a normal prison, but much freer. My sister, particularly, visited him regularly.

Ingeborg Pröhl, Hess' sister-in-law

While Hitler and most of the other insurgents awaited their trial in police custody, the Secretary remained under cover. Was this the behaviour of a vassal whose devotion to his master was, in the words of one of Hess' biographers, 'doglike'. From a series of remote hiding-places in the Alps, he enjoyed nature, went skiing, met his girlfriend and devoted himself once more to the study of economics.

For the last time in his life he seemed to waver. He grumbled in a letter to his parents: 'At my age here I am still without a respectable job, without home and family.' Was it for a brief moment possible that he might have returned to a normal, middle-class life? Were doubts arising in Hess' mind that after the catastrophe of 9 November the Party might never be brought back to life again? Was the power of the 'tribune' to attract his assistant waning, now that his rise seemed to have been halted so suddenly by the might of the state?

It was only on hearing the news from Munich's military academy, where a 'People's Court' was to pass judgment on the insurgents, that Hess pulled himself together. Hitler exploited the trial as a political stage for his rhetorical talent – and the judges gave him free rein. To everyone's surprise the Feldherrnhalle fiasco was transformed into a triumph. Passages from Hitler's tirades of self-justification were printed in the newspapers. When Hess was handed one of the cuttings he was jubilant: 'It is probably one of the best and most powerful speeches he has ever made.' The spell was working again. The sentences against those guilty of high treason turned out to be mild. Hitler was given five years' imprisonment and a fine of 200 gold marks. He was granted the prospect that after six months' good behaviour his sentence would be suspended and he would be put on probation.

Like a disciple who had rediscovered his faith, Hess made his way back to Munich. He now wanted to give himself up to the authorities. 'I doubt it will be any worse for me than it was for the Master,' he comforted his parents. Time was pressing. In May 1924 the 'People's Courts' in Bavaria were to be abolished. If the straggler did not succeed in getting himself arraigned before one of them, then he was threatened with the *Reichsgericht*, the high court in Berlin – and harsher penalties. But Hess was in luck. After proceedings lasting a few days he was sentenced to eighteen month's imprisonment and taken to the same gaol as Hitler, Landsberg Castle.

The months that followed had a decisive effect on the relationship between Hess and Hitler. It was only in Landsberg that the close bond beween the Führer and his deputy was finally forged – a bond which would last beyond their 'parting' in 1941. Hess' career began there, as it ended: behind bars. Yet the prison conditions were as benign as was the judges' treatment of the revolutionaries. In a modern, spacious building that was more like a sanatorium than a penitentiary, the political prisoners enjoyed extensive liberties.

When Hess arrived, Hitler already had his own room, the doors of which were never locked. His closest confidants lived with him on the first floor, reverently referred to by the other prisoners as '*Feldherrnhügel*' ('*Generals' Hill*') in allusion to the street-battle at the Feldherrnhalle. Hess was given the room next to Hitler, who wanted to have his acolyte close by him. 'The tribune looks splendid,' Hess reported delightedly to Ilse. 'His face is no longer so gaunt. The enforced rest is doing him good.' But for Hitler the time spent in Landsberg did not just provide physical recuperation, above all it gave him the chance to take stock of his political career. After the failure of his first assault he planned, in luxurious confinement, the future of the 'Movement'.

In all this Hess played several roles simultaneously: as interlocutor, prompter and sounding-board. His direct influence on the intellectual edifice which Hitler developed and which he also formulated in his personal testimony, *Mein Kampf* (*My Struggle*), was probably greater than has hitherto been supposed. Hess was not simply the secretary typing the author's manuscript; he was Hitler's adviser. In particular, the geopolitical theories of his teacher, Haushofer, were eagerly taken up by the 'tribune'. 'Living-space in the east,' which was at the core of Haushofer's geopolitics, was also a central demand in the foreign-policy section of *Mein Kampf*.

Haushofer himself, when questioned about this by the Allies at Nuremberg more than two decades later, understandably wanted to hear no more of his authorship or of anything to do with

'*Lebensraum*'. Only after stubborn insistence by his interrogator did the Professor admit: 'Yes, these ideas came to Hitler via Hess, but Hitler never really understood them and had never read my books.' A few weeks after the hearing Haushofer committed suicide.

In Landsberg the two inmates on the '*Feldherrnhügel*' found common ground not only in politics. A significant scene took place in June 1924: Hitler was reading aloud a few pages from the manuscript of *Mein Kampf*, about the war-fever of August 1914, about the comradeship of the trenches and the death of comrades. The scene in the prison-room lapsed into pathos: 'In the end the tribune was reading more and more slowly and haltingly,' Hess wrote to Ilse Pröhl, 'then suddenly he dropped the page, buried his head in his hands – and sobbed. Need I tell you that I lost all self-control as well?' The two Great War veterans shedding tears together – that is something that welds people together for ever. Hess ends his letter: 'I am more devoted to him than ever; I love him.'

From now on Hess would never be able to escape the influence of Hitler. Whatever road the 'tribune' might lead the Party down, Hess would follow. Hitler had already planned the route while in Landsberg. 'We'll poke our noses into the Reichstag,' he said. 'True, it'll take longer to outvote the Marxists than to shoot them, but in the end their own constitution will guarantee our way to success.' When Hess asked when he hoped to assume power, Hitler replied: 'At least five years from now, at the most, seven.' In fact it took only one year longer.

At the time it seemed a long, slow process: after his release from Landsberg, where Ilse Pröhl picked him up in her car, Hitler re-organized the party and began his 'legal' attempt to realize his goal. With electioneering tours, Party rallies and ever more speeches, the NSDAP launched its long-term campaign to win the favour of the voters. To begin with it was a wearisome undertaking. In the second half of the 'Roaring Twenties' the German economy recovered from the earlier hyper-inflation. The unpopular republic appeared after all to have more staying-power than was supposed in the crisis-year of 1923.

These were bad times for extremists – in all the national elections for the Reichstag up to 1930 the NSDAP never received more than 2 per cent of the popular vote. Nevertheless, the Party

Chief's Private Secretary displayed boundless optimism. 'The day will come,' he prophesied to his parents, 'when the German people will take its destiny in its own hands, entirely in accordance with the constitution, but not in the way intended by those who drafted it!' Furthermore, he wrote, he had read in a 'little book of astrology', that 'all the signs' were favourable to Hitler. This letter is dated 27 January 1927 – the first indication of his incipient stargazing tendencies.

In these campaigning years Hess was close to Hitler nearly all the time. As his secretary he organized Hitler's appointments and travelled with him from one engagement to another. After Hitler had once again turned two speeches to rather subdued audiences into rousing triumphs, Hess commented with both pride and anxiety: 'By the end he had them eating out of his hand. But the tribune was worn out! Deathly pale, gaunt, trembling, so hoarse as to be scarcely comprehensible, he laid his head on the table without a word. Never again will I set up two speaking engagements so close together.'

Even when Hitler spent time at his newly acquired house, 'Wachenfels', in the Obersalzberg mountains, Hess was usually with him. On official occasions the two men addressed each other with the formal *Sie*, but in private it had long been the intimate *Du*. Hitler's other henchmen noted with envy his continuing favour towards Hess. Alfred Rosenberg was one who complained: 'One just can't get near Hitler; that man Hess is always hanging around him.' Other party functionaries, contemptuous of his meek, devout manner, were already calling him '*Fräulein*' Hess. It is a fact that even before 1933 Rudolf Hess seems to have seen himself as the servant of a higher cause. Any attempt to raise his profile by creating a stir or coming on strong, was anathema to him. Goebbels, who got to know him for the first time in 1926, noted in his diary: 'Hess: the most decent of men, calm, friendly, intelligent, reserved.'

Among the German public, however, the name of the man in Hitler's shadow was still largely unknown. The excitement was provided by others in the brown-shirted party, in addition to the leader himself: the egregious and brutal Göring, Joseph Goebbels, who was drumming up support for the Movement in Berlin, and

Ernst Röhm, the former Reichswehr officer, now heading the SA. But Hess was satisfied with his role, in which his influence in fact far exceeded his public profile.

Because people assumed, correctly, that he had Hitler's ear, he was courted and treated with respect within the party. Heinrich Himmler, for example, gradually promoted him to higher rank in the SS, finally making him an *Obergruppenführer* (equivalent to a general), as a Christmas present on 24 December 1932. At the same time Hess made use of his position as mediator between Hitler and the rest of the party, in order to protect his boss from tiresome squabbles and complaints. Without having been formally requested by anyone to do so, the Private Secretary thus created an unofficial Party function for himself, as mediator and agony-aunt.

These tasks scarcely left him any time for a private life. Ilse Pröhl who, after seven years of waiting, wanted something more than the occasional mountain walk with her friend, was planning to take up a job-offer in Italy – for professional reasons, she said, but also to get away from the man who in any case seemed to prefer being with the Führer. It was only then that Hess decided to get married. Yet the impulse came not from him but from Hitler, who was no doubt worried about the talk occasioned by the large number of bachelors in his entourage. The night of decision is described by Ilse Hess: 'We were sitting with Hitler in the "Osteria" [the Osteria Bavaria in Munich, Hitler's favourite restaurant]. When I talked about my Italy plans, Hitler suddenly placed my hand on Rudolf's and said: "Has it never entered your head to marry this man?"'

On 30 December 1927 the couple said 'I do'. It was a simple ceremony. For 'ideological' reasons the bride and groom had decided against a church wedding. Hess justified this to his churchgoing parents: 'As it is, neither of us have anything to do with Heaven in the normally accepted sense.' The witnesses were Hitler and Professor Haushofer, who were still not on particularly good terms. Hess' parents were absent, being away in Egypt, where Fritz Hess had built up his business again. Ilse's mother did not attend either, though this was presumably because, as she wrote to Hess, she stood 'on quite different political ground' to her son-in-law.

> Hess' solemn earnestness sometimes gets on my nerves!
> *Hitler to Heinrich Hoffmann, 1927*

The dream of domestic bliss did not, however, come true for the newlywed Ilse. The couple did move into a small apartment in north Munich, but her husband continued to spend most of his time at his 'tribune's' side. Throughout her life Ilse Hess would only know a love divided. Very soon after the wedding she confided with some disillusionment to a woman-friend that she sometimes felt like 'a convent-school girl'. But at least she could be certain that her husband was not indulging in any indiscreet amours. With his secretive nature Rudolf Hess certainly did have an attraction for women – if we can believe the sparse evidence on this subject. But it is doubtful that his concept of morality would ever have permitted an affaire.

The virtuous husband remained faithful to another old love: his passion for flying. Lack of opportunity had forced him to put this on hold for several years, but when the *Völkischer Beobachter* purchased a single-engined aircraft, he once again had a chance to climb into the cockpit. Hess carried out numerous promotional flights for the Party newspaper. Whenever his boss's timetable allowed, he took part in air-races such as the '*Deutschlandflug*' around Germany, or the '*Zugspitzflug*' to the country's highest mountain peak. As Germany's answer to the first Atlantic crossing by the American pilot Charles Lindbergh, Hess planned to cross the ocean from east to west in the summer of 1927. He sent a telegram to the US automobile mogul, Henry Ford, asking for financial support. Ford's sympathies towards the German Nazis were well known. But Ford graciously declined, and so Hess missed his first great opportunity to make history in the air.

He did at least succeed in finding his way into the legal records as a pilot. In 1931 he 'buzzed' an open-air rally of Social-Democrats in Hanover, and broke it up. The summons he received stated that for two-and-a-half hours he repeatedly roared over the heads of his political opponents and even pursued a march 'in a reckless manner' down a street between tall buildings in the city centre. These were the two faces of Rudolf Hess – the same man who struck his Party colleagues with his calm and thoughtful manner risked his life in highly dangerous aerobatics over crowded streets. This capacity quite suddenly to put aside all inhibition and embark on the most perilous ventures is also the key to explaining his flight to Britain ten years later.

From the letters which Hess later wrote from his confinement in Spandau, it seems that the decade between Landsberg and the Nazi seizure of power in 1933 was the happiest in his life. The Party was forging ahead, he was closer to Hitler than any other man, and the vision of restoring Germany's 'honour' seemed to be coming ever closer to realization. The descriptions of Hess from those years do not show any indications at all of his later mental confusion. At that time at least, he was not the chronically sick man that many of his biographers would have us believe he was.

When the Nazi Party moved into its new headquarters, the 'Brown House' on Munich's Königsplatz, Hess was given his own office whose décor, despite the protests of the architect, was nothing if not Spartan. By now he had for some time been regarded as the '*éminence grise*' of the brown-shirts. The secretary even distinguished himself in the fundraising field, though he still carried no official title. The lucrative contacts among the industrialists of the Ruhr, who were still hesitating because of the 'socialistic' tone of Nazi electioneering, were chiefly established by Hess. 'He gave such an impression of integrity,' recalled a diplomat from the German Foreign Office. More effectively than the 'stirrers' in the Party, sometimes even more effectively than Göring, this businessman's son could gain the confidence of the smokestack barons. It was their generous contributions which finally made it possible for the Nazis to mount a high-powered electoral campaign that put all other parties in the shade.

'If only the Third Reich could come into being very soon. It would be sure to bring redemption to many.' The heartfelt wish of his mother, written on 4 May 1932, reached her son in the middle of a 'year poised between hoping and fearing'. An economic slump, unemployment and the slow death-agony of a succession of governments, had enabled the NSDAP to grow into a mass-movement. With a poll of 37 per cent in the July elections they achieved an overwhelming result. But Hitler's expectations of being appointed Reich Chancellor were not fulfilled. President Hindenburg's aversion to the 'Bohemian corporal' and the justified fears of the conservatives about Hitler's loyalty to the constitution, prevented his triumph in the hot summer of 1932.

The Party plunged into its worst crisis ever. Now that their goal, despite this electoral success, remained as far away as ever, the bond between the Führer and his grass-roots supporters threatened to snap like an overstretched bow. Impatience, despair and a shortage of funds were widespread. The captains of industry were keeping their purses fastened and the Party had debts of nearly 12 million Reichsmarks.

The crisis affected Rudolf Hess' health. In September a severe outbreak of boils forced him into a sanatorium. His mother, who had been staying with him a short time before, saw the cause of his illness quite simply as 'his job'. When Hess returned to his desk, the situation had worsened dramatically. In the November elections the NSDAP had lost 2 million votes. The first loss of votes in a general election! Hitler's aura suffered serious damage.

Even within the Party the authority of the Führer was crumbling. Gregor Strasser, the old comrade who, with his 'Reich organizational management' had guaranteed the smooth functioning of the Party, took matters into his own hands and on 4 December 1932 opened negotiations with Reich Chancellor Kurt Schleicher – to Hitler and to Hess as well this was open rebellion. The fact that Strasser had started talks with the government out of a concern for the cohesion of the 'Movement' was of no importance. 'You attacked me from behind!' Hitler screamed at him. 'You don't want me to become Chancellor! You want to split the Movement!' Strasser was at a loss to understand any of this and left the room without a word. 'It's bad enough that the man's a bohemian,' he said to a colleague, with a sad shake of the head, 'If he's a hysteric as well, then we're in for disaster.'

In the evening Hitler seemed more downcast than he had been at any time. 'If the party ever falls apart,' he mused, 'in three minutes I'll take my pistol and end it all!' After all their successes, after the undreamed-of rise of the Party, a setback simply had not been bargained for. Goebbels noted in his diary: 'We are all very depressed.' That evening in the Hotel '*Kaiserhof*' Hitler had gathered around him only the most loyal Party members. Hess was of course among them.

His Nibelung-like loyalty was soon rewarded. Gregor Strasser, who for a brief moment had held the fate of the Party in his hand, avoided a quarrel with Hitler by escaping on the night-train to Italy. Thus the threatened schism never took place. Later, Hitler was to exact a pitiless revenge on his failed rival for having acted independently. The murder-squads of the SS, who fanned out around the country on 30 June 1934, the day of the so-called 'Röhm *putsch*', shot Gregor Strasser along with the others.

As early as December 1932 Hitler dismembered the power-structure which Strasser had left behind. Along with Strasser's deputy, a hard-drinking apparatchik named Robert Ley, the loyal servant Hess was the real inheritor of Strasser's organization. It was his first official post of any kind in the Party: to be head of the 'Central Political Committee'. Overnight Rudolf Hess had become a kind of Secretary-General with powers which, on paper, reached into every arm of the NSDAP. From now on the entire party press and all elected NS representatives outside Prussia came under Hess' control. Hitler's ulterior motive in appointing his Secretary to be 'overseer' was transparent: Hess' unquestioning loyalty would prevent any Party functionary from ever again rebelling against the Führer's authority.

Externally too, Hitler made a show of upgrading his secretary. Hess was allowed to accompany his chief to crucial talks with Franz von Papen, the devious conservative politician who had the ear of the venerable President Hindenburg. Ironically, it was precisely the crisis in the NSDAP which in January 1933 made Hitler suddenly an acceptable figure. It encouraged Papen, the amateur horseman, in the illusion that he could 'tame' the Nazi leader. It was to be a ride on a tiger.

Hess was only partially privy to the intrigues behind the scenes which led to Hitler's appointment as Chancellor on 30 January. Like most members of the Party Hess was surprised and delighted. He was one of the first to offer his congratulations. The handshake between the two men who had both fought at the Front, been imprisoned together and worked side by side, was long and heartfelt.

The following day Hess sent his wife a note written on the Reich Chancellor's letterhead. 'My dear wee girlie! Am I dreaming or waking – that is what I ask myself! I am sitting in the Chancellor's study in the Reich Chancellery on Wilhelmplatz. Ministerial officials approach noiselessly on soft carpets, to bring papers "for the Herr Reichskanzler".'

Hitler had reached his objective. What followed now was no more than what he had promised – that he would only leave the Reich Chancellery feet first. But twelve years of the 'Thousand Year Reich' and rivers of blood still lay before the final fulfilment of this prophecy. After sneaking into government 'through the back-door' on 30 January, there now followed, blow by blow, the real seizure of power, accompanied by a kind of general mobilization of the whole population. The Reichstag fire, the enabling legislation, the destruction of other political parties and the 'Gleichschaltung' or bringing all of Germany into line – these were the corner-stones of the breathtakingly rapid construction of a dictatorship. There was no resistance worthy of the name. In Germany 'the lights were going out', as one clear-sighted observer remarked.

For Hess, too, it was the beginning of a new period in his career. On 21 April 1933 Hitler appointed him 'Deputy to the Führer'. An auspicious title, that at the time gave rise to misunderstandings – which was probably just what Hitler intended. For with the title there came no real increase in power. The deputyship only applied 'within the Party', where, as head of the 'Central Committee', he already ranked formally second to Hitler.

For Hess this promotion was important for another reason: it meant the end of his reticence in public. The Deputy stepped into the spotlight. In 1933 he even became a member of the government, as Minister without Portfolio. His popularity with the general public surprised even Goebbels, the media-manipulator at the Ministry of Propaganda. Although at that time there was still no opinion-polling system for gauging the popularity of politicians, Hess was soon considered the Nazis' most popular figure, equal with the ebullient Göring – and after Hitler, needless to say.

Now, under the aegis of the 'viceroy without power', the new Party headquarters was created in premises on Munich's

My sister once asked him: 'Rudolf, don't you now think we ought to leave the Church?' He replied: 'No. Imagine how people would react. They would all leave, just because Hess had left. And that wouldn't do. Basically, we *need* the Church. Otherwise people have nothing to hold on to. We're staying in!'

Ingeborg Pröhl, Hess' sister-in-law

Königsplatz. Only part of the massive building could be completed before the outbreak of war. Work was finished on the '*Führerbau*' and on the NSDAP's administration building with its 'Temple of Honour' to those who died on 9 November 1923 – megalomania hewn in stone. Around the 'Brown House' and a number of adjoining houses which had been bought up, arose a complex for several thousand party bureaucrats – with its own power-plant, 'gas-proof' air-raid shelters and a labyrinth of subterranean passageways.

In the new buildings the Deputy's administrative network grew like a weed. The Secretary who had formerly been close to Hitler at all times, now became a sort of Head of the Civil Service. The expanding Party empire controlled hundreds of thousands of 'political managers' from *Gauleiter*, or regional governor, down to the humble *Blockwart*, who supervised a city block. At many points this structure cut across the authority of government departments. Bringing some order to this chaotic growth was actually the Deputy's task. But the life of a functionary did not appeal to Hess.

He quickly looked around for an able secretary of his own. In May 1933 an almost entirely unknown head of the 'NSDAP aid fund' had applied to him for a job. The bull-necked man, a Party member since 1927, appeared to be a reliable worker with a great capacity for getting things done his way. His name was Martin Bormann.

The 'new boy' started in July 1933. By October he had already been given the rank of *Reichsleiter* (national manager) of the Nazi Party. This was an astonishing rise, and one can only speculate as to the reasons for it. What is certain is that Bormann plunged himself into his work to such an extent that from then on Hess was freed from tiresome paper-pushing. Bormann was also consistent in acting the part of devoted lackey to his boss. From the outset, the unsuspecting Deputy must have developed genuinely warm feelings towards his secretary. In letters he would refer jokingly, but without malice, to his 'wee Bormann'. In fact, however, this archetypal technocrat himself developed more and more into a strong-man. He often made decisions in the name of his superior, but without his knowledge. Being unscrupulous, power-hungry and crafty, he surreptitiously succeeded in undermining his boss' power. It seems hard to believe that Hess did not realize what was going on. It is more likely that the Deputy considered a power-struggle with his secretary as beneath his dignity.

> Bormann was an unpleasant man. As we Bavarians say, he would shaft you as soon as look at you. As long he was still working for Hess he was friendly enough. But as soon as Hess had his back turned, he worked against him.
> *Stefanie Camola, friend of the Hess family*

Like Hitler, Rudolf Hess was averse to paperwork. In a speech on 12 September he admitted this quite openly: one should not 'attribute too much importance' to documents, he recommended to his audience of *Gauleiter* and *Kreisleiter* (District Managers). The only thing that counted was 'one's own judgement based on real life and personal impressions'. Nevertheless, just like his idol Hitler, he could become exhaustively involved in small, even trivial details. He spent up to four hours a day listening to verbal reports from his staff on the progress of party matters. The kind of questions that came up might be the proposal of the 'League of Loyal Bavarians in the Eastern Marches' to acquire new banners, or a *Kreisleiter*'s worries about the provision for war-victims in his area.

The most urgent problems he left unresolved. The governance of the Third Reich was gradually becoming an impenetrable undergrowth of overlapping hierarchies. Ministries and Party departments devoted more energy to these wrangles over authority than to their actual areas of activity. In a way this suited Hitler who, true to his motto of 'divide and rule', wanted to make himself irreplaceable; but it led to the paralysis of government and administration. But now his entrusting of the top Party office to Hess would was coming back to haunt him. Party discipline had lost all meaning. Individual *Gauleiter* publicly walked all over the Deputy. The rampant acquisitiveness of the satraps in regional Party posts can be seen chiefly as a consequence of Hess' impotence.

> Bormann was hewn from coarser timber than Hess. He never again allowed the reins of Party government to be dropped, but kept the *Gauleiter* on a tight rein. Most of them gritted their teeth and fell into line.
>
> *Count Schwerin von Krosigk, 1939*

Yet despite this very obvious inability to govern the Party, Hess remained, until the war at least, a central figure in the regime. His effect on the masses was prodigious. With his positively reverential Christmas addresses on the Reich radio, the ritual massed swearing of the oath of allegiance to Hitler, which Hess staged by torchlight with drum-rolls, and the speeches he made with eyes aglow at Party rallies – Hess contributed substantially to the fateful mass-hypnosis. The clichés which he bellowed into the microphone to crowds of over 100,000 at party rallies, sound banal today – such as the formula: 'Hitler is Germany, just as Germany is Hitler.' But at the time such slogans exerted an overwhelming power of suggestion.

As the high priest of the Führer-cult Hess was one of the most effective of his master's 'harbingers', as he liked to call himself. A scene of great significance was the nocturnal mass oath-taking on the Königsplatz in Munich in 1937, illuminated by dozens of bowls of flame. In a voice trembling with reverence Hess, as master-of-ceremonies, pronounced the words of the oath and tens of thousands answered: 'I swear by the guardians of the Movement, unconditional obedience to Adolf Hitler and to the leaders he appoints over me!'

Seen only on film, these scenes have lost much of their haunting quality. Yet even today we are astonished by the extraordinary fervour with which Hess imbued such pseudo-sacred initiation ceremonies – particularly as by his own admission he hated making public appearances. Here, before massed crowds, stood someone who was the first to make his belief in the Führer into his creed. It was his own faith which made him so credible to others. In the cult of the Führer, the fire that glowed within this first protector of the Holy Grail was not an act he put on. It was real.

The zeal with which he played the part of his master's herald sometimes produced grotesque behaviour. Some sections of the film which Leni Riefenstahl had shot at the 1934 National Party Congress turned out to be unusable. So a few months later the scenes had to be recreated in the studio. Albert Speer described the scene:

Hess arrived and was the first to be asked to go before the camera. Just as he had in front of 30,000 people at the congress, he raised his hand ceremoniously. With the emotion of genuine excitement which only he could display, he slowly turned towards the spot where Hitler would have been sitting – but wasn't – and standing strictly to attention shouted: '*Mein Führer*, I welcome you in the name of the Party Congress.'

However, Hess was also thought of as the 'Mister Clean' at Hitler's side, incorruptible, dependable, decent: the good conscience of the Party. It is a fact that on one occasion, when his driver filled the tank of his private Mercedes sports-car at the Party's motor-pool, he reimbursed the sum out of his own pocket. Party propaganda deliberately reinforced this 'clean' image. The encomium in the newspaper *NS-Rheinfront* on the occasion of his forty-fifth birthday, praised him as: 'the warning voice, who sees to it that National Socialism remains pure and unalloyed; and that everything done in the name of National Socialism really *is* National-Socialistic'. In the light of the behaviour of the *Gauleiter* under his authority, this was admittedly a grotesque mockery of the truth.

Nevertheless, Hess' own ironic assessment of himself, as the 'Wailing Wall' of the Movement, had a kernel of truth. Every day hundreds of complaints about abuse of office or misbehaviour by party functionaries arrived on his desk in Munich. The Deputy dealt with many of these himself – it was a fight for justice in the service of the unjust. However, his admonitions to the brown-shirt officials often only gave rise to mirth. For example, at the 1938 Party Congress he enjoined the 'political managers' to give up smoking and alcohol and devote an hour a day to their health, since 'the health of the National Socialist leadership belongs to the nation'.

> Hess was always very careful about what he ate. The whole family were vegetarian, and he very seldom drank wine. When I first started working for him, we had a party and wine *was* served. Göring, who was also a guest, commented: 'Who would have thought there would be such good wine at the Hesses.'
>
> *Hildegard Faht, Hess' Private Secretary*

However, with his rise to the most senior office in the Party, he began to become separated from the close circle around his beloved Führer. The latter was, for one thing, spending more and more time in Berlin. It was in the summer of 1934 that the relationship between the two men received its first severe jolt. Since the Nazi seizure of power, the head of the SA, Ernst Röhm, had become a source of disturbance. His Party-based army was dissatisfied. The promised sinecures had been withheld from the 'brown bruisers'. Röhm now made no pretence about demanding more power for himself and the SA – at the expense of the regular Army, the *Reichswehr*.

After some hesitation Hitler made up his mind. He would still need the Reichswehr, but his close friend Röhm was dispensable. On 30 June he issued orders that the entire leadership of the SA were to be arrested in a surprise pounce – and liquidated. Hess was bitterly disappointed – not because of the murders as such, but because no one had put him in the picture beforehand. Alfred Rosenberg described how Hess strove to regain Hitler's favour with a desperate proof of his loyalty. This was that he would personally execute the imprisoned Röhm, saying 'that biggest of all swine must be got rid of'. However, Hitler entrusted the task to others.

When an SS man read out the list of further candidates for the bullet, the Deputy was suddenly overcome with emotion. His Adjutant, Alfred Leitgen, recalled:

My chief was deathly pale, but outwardly quite calm. But when the name Schneidhuber came up, he made a demurring gesture, threw his head back and murmured something. He leaned towards Hitler and whispered a few words in his ear. Hitler shook his head angrily. Hess suddenly turned green in the face. He went into an adjoining room. When I followed him a short time later, he waved me out of the room. He was bent double with pain, as though he had a stomach-cramp. There were tears in his eyes. Schneidhuber had been a good friend of his.

The double hurt did not, however, prevent Hess, a few days after the shootings of 30 June, from joining in the chorus of justification and from dressing up the liquidation of more than 200 people as 'self-defence by the state': 'As loyal as the old SA man was to his Führer, so loyally does the Führer stand by his old SA. The Führer has punished the guilty. Our relationship to the SA is now once more as it used to be.' Doubts about Hitler's action never entered Hess' mind. Had he himself not written prophetically, in a student essay in 1921: 'To achieve his goal, the dictator even tramples over his closest friends!' ?

The 'good conscience of the Party' was in truth just as extreme and ready for violence as the other henchmen. Only, everything must be done 'by the book'. With as much intensity as Hess had opposed the 'wild' terrorism of the SA in the first months after 30 January, he interested himself in the construction of a 'legal' code of violence in the years to come. He spent hours being shown round the Dachau concentration-camp by Himmler.

The Deputy took an active part in legalized terrorism against the Jews in Germany. The Nuremberg 'Race Laws' of 1935 bear his signature, as does the order banning Jews from practising as lawyers and doctors. However, like some others in the inner leadership circle, he had an ambivalent relationship to Jewry.

Three days after the promulgation of the 'Race Laws', Hess made a private telephone-call to his old friend Haushofer and assured him that his family had nothing to fear. Under the Laws the Professor's wife was classed as half-Jewish. During the war, the Deputy proposed introducing punishment-beatings for Jews in occupied Poland. And he was deeply involved in the 'camouflage' measures. In 1935 he used a cold, bureaucratic language to state: 'National Socialist legislation has taken corrective action against excessive foreign domination.'

At home in the Hess' villa, in the Munich suburb of Harlaching, much was made of their modest lifestyle. Almost alone among the senior dignitaries of the Third Reich, Hess did not try to make money from his office. To celebrate the naming of his son only a handful of select guests were invited. Naturally a church baptism was out of the question for Hess – two years later he would even forbid the sending of Christian literature to soldiers at the Front. Hitler was there as the child's 'godfather'.

The infant was to be named 'Wolf-Rüdiger', 'Wolf' being Hitler's old *nom de guerre* and 'Rüdiger' after the faithful hero in the saga of the Nibelungs. It was a historic day, 9 November 1938. Hess and Hitler wallowed in reminiscence about the attempted *putsch* they had both taken part in a decade and a half earlier. That evening the telephone rang. Hess was informed that synagogues were on fire all over Germany, and that Jews were being maltreated and some murdered. In the trivializing linguistic manner of the regime, this event was later to be known as '*Reichskristallnacht*', the 'Night of Crystal', or 'broken glass', to be more precise.

'When he came back from the phone,' Hess' private secretary recalled, 'his face was livid with anger.' It was another breach of trust. No one had informed the Deputy about the planned pogrom, not even his son's godfather. But this time he was also appalled by what was happening on the streets. If the mob was running amok, that was not Hess' style. This was not 'his' form of violence. The next day, in telegrams sent out to all *Gauleiter*, he tried to put a stop to further excesses. But instructions from the Deputy were no longer taken seriously.

Hess was certainly the best boss I ever had. He was always polite and pleasant, and we had lots of laughs. His sense of justice was also very pronounced. That's why he always protected General Haushofer's wife. And in general, whenever he heard of particular hardship, he intervened and helped those concerned. That's why he was known as the 'agony aunt' of the Party. Many people asked him for help and support. I never saw him lose his temper. Only once was he really angry, about the *Kristallnacht*, which had been organized behind his back. When he heard about the campaign he forbade any Party member from taking part. But by then it was too late.

Hildegard Faht, Hess' Private Secretary

Hess' outrage in this instance was an exception. He usually preferred to avert his eyes. When he received a written complaint from Friedrich Rupp, the deputy head of a clinic in the Hessian town of Stetten, to the effect that mentally ill patients were being systematically murdered as part of a 'euthanasia' programme, the Deputy wrote only the briefest reply. Rupp's complaint would be passed on to the appropriate authority, the SS.

Rudolf Hess had in fact left Germany before the mass-murder of Jews in Germany had begun. Would he have contributed to the Holocaust just as he had to the official ostracizing of the German Jews before the war? Hess saw himself as a 'radical'. 'National Socialism is applied biology,' he had said. In a broadcast speech in 1934 he formulated his concept of 'obedience' which could be taken as an anticipation of the instructions given to the SS murderers in Auschwitz: 'Loyalty in its fundamental sense means unconditional obedience, which does not question the value of an order, does not question the reasons for an order, but obeys for the sake of obeying.' Speeches of that kind were part of the preparations for the crime of the century.

Nonetheless, in the courtroom at Nuremberg Hess appeared paralysed with horror on being shown a film of the liberation of the extermination-camps. He seemed unable to believe what a

No one in Germany at that time thought of Hess as a 'little man'. Only after the Nazi era did it emerge that he had had relatively little authority. He was nonetheless an accomplice. He was someone who never voiced any form of criticism of what was going on in that period. Quite the opposite: he was someone who dedicated himself to the Führer with the loyalty of a Nibelung. And that is not altered by the fact that he flew to Britain. The atrocities which took place in the Third Reich had been planned long before 10 May 1941. The war of aggression against Russia had been planned, the annihilation of the Jews had been planned, the use of forced foreign labour had been planned – they didn't just happen overnight. All those things were based on many years of planning, which Hess knew about and supported. Many of the laws bore his signature. It is not possible for someone to absolve themselves of responsibility by saying, 'when it was finally carried out, I was no longer there'.

Arno Hamburger, participant in the Reich Party rallies

murderous path the 'final solution of the Jewish Question' had taken in his absence. For him there could be only one explanation: the films must be forgeries. Had he not followed Hitler's ideas to their logical conclusion – ideas he had been familiar with since working with him on *Mein Kampf* in Landsberg? Or had he foreseen the consequences and suppressed them mentally? Is it just coincidence that, in those years when the regime's 'race policy' began taking an ever more extreme form, Hess showed pathological symptoms of illness? The only person capable of answering these questions was the prisoner of Spandau.

The Deputy's increasing remoteness from reality was carefully noted by those around him. Hess had always had a penchant for areas of study on the fringes of human knowledge. To astrology, which he had studied with growing seriousness, along with his friend and colleague Ernst Schulte-Strathaus, he now gradually added other obscure interests: dowsers, diviners and geomancers, clairvoyants and interpreters of dreams were all made welcome by the Deputy.

Hess now suffered with increasing frequency from colic of the stomach and gall-bladder. Neither orthodox medicine nor quack remedies and miracle-healers, whom the notorious hypochondriac consulted, could provide any relief. Alfred Rosenberg stated that, on the advice of one of these 'healers' Hess had all the teeth in his upper jaw extracted in order to combat some supposed infection. But even that produced no improvement.

Naturally enough, Hitler did not remain unaware of his Deputy's growing oddness. The following encounter tells us much. When Hess was invited to a meal at the Reich Chancellery he would bring with him a tin bowl containing a vegetarian dish and secretly have it served to him. One day Hitler, also a vegetarian, got wind of this and challenged Hess about it at table: 'I have a first-class dietary cook here,' Albert Speer remembers Hitler saying. 'If your doctor has prescribed you something in particular, she will be happy to prepare it for you. But you cannot bring your own food.' Hess tried to explain away his special treatment as being part of a planned diet, whereupon Hitler suggested he had better eat at home. 'From then on,' Speer noted, 'Hess hardly ever appeared at these meals.'

Even among the other henchmen Hitler would joke about his strange Deputy, whom he otherwise still referred to in conversation in a friendly way as '*mein Hesserl*' (my Hessie). 'I just hope that Hess never has to replace me,' he said to Göring. 'I don't know who I'd be more sorry for, Hess or the Party.' The Deputy was no longer brought into important political discussions. His chief-of-staff, Bormann, on the other hand, was now always present.

Hess was a likeable nutcase. We all knew there were some odd things about him, for instance that he believed in herbalists. He was a devoted follower of Hitler and always announced him in a thoroughly unctuous way. He swore eternal loyalty to him and indeed kept to his oath. Hess was an almost religious National Socialist, a fantasist and an idealist, and he was a man with very high moral principles.

Reinhard Spitzy, adviser to Ribbentrop

Instead, Hess was acting more and more in the role of the regime's roving representative: winter assistance for the poor, coffee-mornings with the young ladies of the *Bund Deutscher Mädel* (League of German Lasses) for the benefit of the newsreels, awarding *Mutterkreuze*, medals for the Reich's most prolific child-bearers, and honouring the war-wounded – the frequency of such appointments in Hess' diary grew as his favour with Hitler declined. 'He hated jobs of that kind,' his Secretary Laura Schrödl recalled. But he never ducked out of them. Doing one's duty was the first commandment and Hess, the son, adhered unshakeably to his father's precept.

The German invasion of Poland on 1 September 1939 came as no surprise to Hess. In the weeks before he had dutifully made speeches in support of the preparatory propaganda. Five days before German troops crossed the border, he was in the Austrian city of Graz, where he declared with his customary emotion: 'We shall stand under the banner of the Führer, come what may.' And added in his inimitable style: 'The responsibility for Poland's irresponsibility lies with Britain!'

Two weeks earlier Hess had predicted to Haushofer that the war would only be 'a brief storm, not a steady fall of rain'. His friend objected that one never knew what 'wave of flooding' might follow a storm, but his words went unheeded. The Deputy now only saw his Führer infrequently. As war-leader Hitler gathered others around him. Nevertheless, Hess was officially given increased status. Hitler, in his speech on 1 September – which must rank as the most cynical non-declaration of war in history ('Since 5.45 a.m. we have been returning fire') – made his succession arrangements public for the first time. As the first man to inherit the mantle of Führer, he nominated Hermann Göring, and then: 'should anything befall Party-comrade Göring, his successor is Party-comrade Hess!' He was now the third man in the Third Reich – in truth this honour was not intended seriously, but as a tribute to his popularity with the people. Hermann Göring, who showed little enthusiasm for his potential successor, was told by Hitler: 'If you were to become Führer of the Reich, you could throw out Hess and nominate your own successor.' In addition, Hitler appointed his deputy to be a member of the

'Ministerial Council for the Defence of the Reich' – a position which would be held against Hess in the Nuremberg War Crimes Tribunal. In fact the Defence Council was a committee of no importance and Hess never attended any of its sittings.

> My father was an idealist and a convinced believer in Germany. His aim was always the well-being of his country. He certainly was not a typical power-figure like Göring, for example. When the war came, everything non-essential was got rid of at home. So we were left with just one car for the whole, very extensive family. Like Hitler he led a very austere life.
>
> *Wolf-Rüdiger Hess, son of Rudolf Hess*

On 3 September, when German units had already fought their way deep into Poland, the Deputy was admittedly back at the Reich Chancellery once more. It was the day when news of Britain's declaration of war was received. Now it no longer looked as if it would be a 'brief storm'. In uncontrollable rage Hitler roared at his Foreign Minister: 'Now what?' Ribbentrop had repeatedly assured him that the British would never enter a war.

'My whole life's work is now falling apart,' Hitler lamented. 'My book was written for nothing.' It was indeed true that one of the core theses of *Mein Kampf*, friendship with Britain, was now null and void. The men in the Reich Chancellery who had set Europe ablaze now experienced a moment of fear. Göring murmured dully: 'If we lose this war, may Heaven have mercy on us.' In an access of misplaced heroism Hess now, with military punctilio, requested permission to go to the Front as a fighter pilot. He was a man of forty-five. Hitler looked at his deputy incredulously and brusquely banned him from flying for a twelve-month period. Hess clicked his heels and left the room without a word.

Prior to this he had witnessed a hopeless attempt to keep London out of the war. Through the good offices of a Swedish diplomat Göring had asked the British whether he might fly to London for negotiations. It was the straw to which even Hitler clung like a drowning man. The answer that came back was chilly:

> Hess loved Hitler! Hess was the only real gentleman in Hitler's immediate circle. But his love for Hitler was a kind of enslavement. He would do anything for Hitler, even things which his natural sense of decency and honour must have rebelled against.
>
> *Otto Strasser, Gregor's brother, who left the National Socialist party in 1930 and opposed Hitler from exile, 1973*

'His Majesty's Government has no more time for discussions with Field-Marshal Göring.' As Hess saw it, this was a botched attempt. He would have flown over without prior warning. Since Chamberlain's 'peace-flight' in 1938 was there not a good precedent for bridge-building visits between the two 'Nordic' states?

Now came the days of swift victories. A new word would characterize the year 1940: '*blitzkrieg*' or 'lightning war'. Rudolf Hess, too, rejoiced at the unexpectedly successful campaigns in which Hitler's *Wehrmacht* subjugated half of Europe: Poland, Denmark, Norway, Holland, Belgium and France. But the war against Great Britain remained a 'misfortune' in the Deputy's view. Did he already suspect that against the stubborn island nation Germany was on a losing game?

When the British Army escaped by sea from Dunkirk, the Deputy believed he saw a deliberate sign of Germany's willingness to make concessions. Hitler had repeatedly offered London the chance of peace, both officially and through discreet diplomatic channels. It would have been a peace which gave him a free hand in Europe, in exchange for which he would leave the British Empire intact. But Churchill had no thought of a peace treaty with Germany, the country which had subjugated its neighbours and made undisguised terrorism a byword in its state policy. Others in the British government, most of all the Foreign Secretary, Lord Halifax, would probably have been ready to talk – at least until the start of the German air offensive, with which Göring had promised to bomb Britain into submission.

Churchill's attitude destroyed all the calculations which, ever since *Mein Kampf*, had underlain Hitler's plans for conquest. To the Deputy especially, this was all a tragic misunderstanding. That the war was seen by the west as having become a struggle for freedom against dictatorship, was something he simply could not grasp. Surely communism was their common ideological opponent; that was a widespread misconception which, until the very end of the war, would raise false hopes in Germany.

In the summer of 1940 a new idea began to mature. Possibly the decisive moment came at a dinner at Hitler's Berghof retreat, at which Hess was present. Rochus Misch, a soldier in Hitler's retinue, the *Führerbegleitkommando*, recalls: 'Suddenly Dietrich, the Reich press chief, came in and announced: "*Mein Führer*, Britain has turned us down." Whereupon Hitler said in desperation: "My God, what else am I supposed to do? I can't fly over and throw myself on my knees in front of the English!"'

Hess now began to make foreign policy on his own initiative. He sought advice from his old teacher Karl Haushofer. After a visit from Hess at his family seat on 31 August, Haushofer wrote to his son Albrecht, that it was now vital to avert something which would have 'infinitely serious consequences'. This was extremely cryptic in its phrasing – he knew the SS would read the letter – but it seems to mean that Haushofer wished to dissuade his friend from taking rash action, which would produce no possible benefit but might be fatal both to Hess and to the Haushofers.

Albrecht Haushofer, an academic like his father, said, on the other hand, that he *was* prepared to help. He felt under an obligation to Hess, who held a protecting hand over his 'non-Aryan' family. But this was a dangerous game, for any contact with the enemy without Hitler's knowledge was considered high treason.

On instructions from Hess, Albrecht now attempted, through a middleman in Portugal, to make contact with Britain. The objective was to set up a meeting on neutral soil with a high-ranking British representative. As the person to whom this message should be addressed, Hess selected the Duke of Hamilton. Precisely why the choice fell on this Scottish nobleman, is a matter for endless speculation. What we do know is that Albrecht Haushofer knew him slightly and that as a keen amateur pilot himself it seemed that Hamilton would, at a basic level, be well-disposed toward the Deputy. In 1936 Hess had once met him briefly during the Olympic Games in Berlin. Whether they exchanged more than a few polite words is doubtful. In any case, Hamilton was anything but an influential politician. As Commanding Officer of the anti-aircraft defence in Scotland, he had a military position but had scarcely any contact with the politicians in London. However, relying on a rather romantic conception of politics, the Deputy considered the Duke would provide an ideal channel of communication to the British royal family, whose true importance Hess, as an amateur in foreign affairs, had far overestimated.

> In the autumn of 1940 Hess told me he had to focus all his strength on doing something that would bring salvation to Germany. When I asked him what he meant by 'salvation', he replied that he couldn't talk about it, but that he was preparing for an act of historic importance.
>
> *Felix Kersten, Himmler's doctor and masseur, 1940*

The role of Albrecht Haushofer in Hess' peace probe has never been made clear. It is probable that he was playing a double game. Given his good contacts abroad and also with the opposition to Hitler, collaboration with the politically naïve Deputy was a two-edged sword. At all events he considered a successful outcome unlikely. In a letter he warned Hess that 'any British of any importance' would consider a treaty signed by the Führer to be a 'worthless scrap of paper'. Yet Hess had become obsessed with his idea. If he were to succeed in bringing about a settlement, then surely with this he could win back Hitler's respect – or so he hoped. Misguided notions of foreign policy were blended with irrational emotional motives.

Albrecht Haushofer's attempt to establish contact failed. The British secret service intercepted the message. Hess now decided to go it alone. He himself would fly to Britain as a representative of the German government. Once again his objective would be the Duke of Hamilton, who had the practical advantage of owning an airstrip on his family estate. It appears that Karl Haushofer,

Albrecht's father and Hess' mentor, strengthened him in his resolve. On a walk in the forest he apparently told Hess about a dream he had, in which he had seen Hess walking through 'palaces with tapestries on the walls', to bring peace to two great nations. For Hess, who believed in 'more things in heaven and earth . . .', this was a good omen. Even when he was in prison in England, he wrote with melancholy to his counsellor: 'I often think about that dream.'

The final months of preparation lifted him out of his apathy. After a meeting with Hess, Goebbels noted in amazement: 'He is back on form. Hess makes the best of impressions on me.' But no one was to find out what was afoot – not even Hitler, whose goodwill the enterprise was intended to promote. People have puzzled a great deal about whether Hitler had information about his Deputy's planned flight, and was secretly behind the whole operation. Numerous historians have tackled this question, but none has managed to find any proof that the Führer was implicated. On the contrary, the circumstances in which the mission was prepared, and his reaction after the flight show clearly that Hitler would never have given his approval for this risky enterprise.

From the end of 1940 I knew my boss was involved in something which he was hiding from his closest colleagues. Herr Hess seemed to have a secret which we deliberately kept away from.

Alfred Leitgen, Hess' Adjutant, 1955

Hess' very first attempt to obtain an aircraft was significant. He asked Ernst Udet – his old Flying Corps comrade and now Göring's *Generalluftzeugmeister*, in charge of equipping the Luftwaffe – to put at his disposal 'a Messerschmitt for pleasure-flying'. But Udet said he would have to get Hitler's agreement to this. Hess immediately back-pedalled and withdrew his request. Two years later Hess stated: 'In all innocence Udet insisted on obtaining the permission of the Führer – whose ban on my flying had only just expired. He might just as well have put me under arrest there and then.'

It was only in the Messerschmitt factory in Augsburg that the 'Messenger of Peace' found what he wanted. Under the pretext of wanting to carry out some test-flights, he obtained a Bf 110 fighter, which he gradually had converted for his long-haul flight. No one suspected anything. 'If the Führer's Deputy wanted an aircraft,' recalled test-pilot Fritz Voss, 'we had no reason to wonder why.'

In the autumn he began to hone up his English. He dictated to his secretary a speech to be delivered to British officers, and made her give her word of honour to speak to no one about it. Discreetly he got hold of weather-reports and charts of interdicted airspace over the North Sea. On 10 January 1941 he made his first test-flight. Before taking off he handed his adjutant, Karl-Heinz Pintsch, two envelopes: a farewell letter addressed to Hitler, and a letter which was only to be opened four hours after he had taken off. Two hours after take-off the weather deteriorated and Hess turned back. On his return to Augsburg he found to his horror that Pintsch had read one of the letters, saying that he, Hess, had just flown to Britain. He now had no alternative but to take the adjutant into his confidence and make him give his word to say absolutely nothing. For giving that promise Pintsch ended up in a concentration-camp.

Following a second abortive attempt, Hess returned to Berlin in early May. At this time Hitler had only one thing on his mind: preparation for the invasion of the Soviet Union. Hess naturally knew about it and saw the dangers of a war on two fronts looming in front of his eyes.

That evening he spoke once more to Hitler in the Reich Chancellery. There has been much speculation as well about what was said in this last conversation. According to a police officer who was standing guard outside the door of Hitler's study, the meeting lasted four hours. At the end of it the two men apparently parted on good terms and Hitler said: 'You are and always will be a stubborn old so-and-so.' What we can be certain of is that Hess was making sure once more that nothing about Hitler's dream of peace with Great Britain had changed. A hitherto unpublished document

In those days I would often type for Hess. Once when we were all having a few days' rest at a friend's house in Karlsbach, he dictated a speech to me in the garden there. He planned to give it before British officers. What it said was roughly this: 'We want to come to a gentlemen's agreement with you; we've worn you out and you have worn *us* out; now we must stand together and face the Russians.' While he was dictating the speech, all I could think was: I'd love to know how he thinks he will get near any British officers. I couldn't make head or tail of it, but he made me swear not to mention the speech to anyone. It never occurred to me that he was planning to fly to Britain on his own.

Laura Schroedel, Hess' Secretary

confirms this: among the papers found at Hess' house after his flight there was a sixteen-page manuscript relating to political negotiations. In this Hess offered, unaltered, the same deal which Hitler had formulated a year earlier, before the air-battle for Britain: a free hand for Germany in Europe and the east in exchange for leaving the British Empire untouched. It was an offer with no hope of being accepted, and one which Churchill had curtly dismissed more than once. However, in his manuscript Hess expressly refers to its identity with the views of Hitler: 'No interest in breaking up the Empire. My discussion with the Führer. The last on 3 May.' On the other hand, there is no mention in the document of his having made Hitler aware of his planned flight – just as Hess, when questioned in England, consistently denied that he had been sent by Hitler.

An astrologer had described the stars on 10 May as favourable. That morning Hess devoted a generous amount of time to playing with his four-year-old son at their villa in Harlaching – so much time in fact that his wife was rather surprised. She herself had felt unwell that morning and had stayed in bed. Towards noon her husband appeared in pilot's uniform and said goodbye to her. 'When are you coming back?' When he replied 'Tomorrow', Ilse said with dark foreboding: 'I don't believe that. Come back soon. The boy will miss you.' – 'I'll miss him too.'

Hess drove with Pintsch to Augsburg. At 5.45 p.m. he took off in the Messerschmitt. Shortly before 10 p.m. he jumped with his parachute into the Scottish darkness. It was the moment in which everything came to an end. It was the end of an obsession, the end of a career as the most devout of all Hitler's henchmen, and the end of freedom for Rudolf Hess. The Deputy spent the second half of his life in prison. On the night of 10 May 1941 his detachment from reality reached its completion in an act of muddle-headed heroism.

I was just having dinner with the Duke and Duchess of Hamilton when suddenly there was a phone-call for the Duke. The caller said a German aircraft had crashed. The pilot had landed by parachute somewhere near Glasgow and insisted on speaking to the Duke of Hamilton. He gave his name as Alfred Horn. The Duke said he didn't know anyone named Horn and that he would come over tomorrow. The officer on the line said: 'There's something odd about the man, sir; I really think you should come tonight.' The Duke did go and didn't get back until two in the morning. Then he said: 'I know you'll say I'm mad, but I think Rudolf Hess is in Glasgow. What do we do now?' We discussed it and thought that first of all the Duke should somehow get a message to the Foreign Secretary, Lord Halifax. The whole thing put the Duke in a very awkward situation, because people would obviously say: 'What's going on? Does this mean he's on good terms with the Germans?'
    Sandy Johnstone, British Air Vice-Marshal and friend of the Duke of Hamilton

In the tense international situation the news of the winged knight-errant, Rudolf Hess, burst like a bomb. At first Hitler refused to believe it, then he had one of his fits of frenzied rage. 'How could Hess do a thing like this to me?' he screamed. Goebbels wrote in his diary that he could only explain it as resulting from Hess' 'grass-guzzling and get-well prayers'. The same day Hitler had Hess' adjutant and secretary arrested. Then he hesitated. For a moment it seemed that he had been expecting news from England. It was just possible. Albrecht Haushofer was brought to the Berghof and made to write, under supervision, a paper entitled: 'Is there still a chance of peace with Britain?'

When the first reports from England made it clear that Hess' mission had never had the slightest chance of success, damage limitation was called for. What should Germany's Axis allies be told? Together with Bormann Hitler drafted a radio news item which declared that Hess was mad and referred to his farewell letter, which in its 'confused nature unfortunately shows signs of a mental breakdown, which leads to the fear that Party-comrade Hess was sadly the victim of delusions'. The way the affair was dealt with was anything but consistent. A confidential circular from the Propaganda Ministry to the district managers of the Nazi Party, dated 4 September 1941, announced that the Deputy had flown to Britain with the 'most honourable of intentions'. Within the Party at least the impression had to be avoided that there was any room for madmen in the senior ranks of the Movement.

A few days after Hess' arrival, the German-language service of the BBC made the mocking comment: 'No further ministers of the Reich have flown in today.' But to Goebbels' delight there was no great propaganda offensive by the British. 'Think what *we* could have made of that,' the propaganda boss remarked with relief.

The regime now did everything possible to ensure the unpleasant episode was quickly forgotten. The newsreels for the second week of May were withdrawn from cinemas because the Deputy could still be

After Hess' flight to Britain Bormann's power of course grew immeasurably. Long before that even, he had succeeded in isolating Hess almost totally, which was without doubt one of the reasons behind Hess' crazy flight. Afterwards Bormann, who incidentally behaved quite appallingly towards Hess' wife, very quickly – within days – took over all his functions and had himself appointed Secretary to the Führer.

Speer, 1979

seen in two extracts. Hospitals which had been named after Hess were renamed. Hess' Adjutant had to undergo months of interrogation and was then sent to a concentration-camp. Even the astrologer Ernst Schulte-Strathaus was arrested.

The dreams of Martin Bormann, who had immediately distanced himself from his former superior, did not come to fruition. It is true, he was now officially assigned the tasks which he had already been carrying out anyway, but Hitler did not nominate any new Deputy. He probably never forgave Hess. Albert Speer gave an account of a conversation in 1944: Hitler had apparently insisted that if Hess were ever handed over he should be hauled before a drumhead court-martial and executed immediately. In one of his dinner-table conversations Hitler uttered the threat that if Hess ever returned there were only two alternatives left for him: 'the firing-squad or the madhouse'. Only in the final days of the war did the failed dictator again seem to remember his one-time colleague in a different way. The Führer's driver, Kempka, told Ilse Hess after the war that in one of his last nocturnal monologues Hitler had spoken warmly of her husband as the only 'thoroughgoing idealist in the Movement'.

The history of Hess after his parachute-jump is above all the description of his pathological condition. Churchill never had any intention of treating Hitler's Deputy as a representative of the German government. For him, too, the Hess flight was most

It was clear to all of us that Churchill had absolutely no interest in peace negotations. Our Foreign Secretary, Lord Halifax, was not seriously interested either, but still had a somewhat different view. He was certainly willing to listen to peace offers. But since Churchill ultimately had the power to decide, we did not imagine that any peace negotiations were possible. What is more, Great Britain was just in the process of gaining allies and so was by no means isolated. Thus there was no reason to entertain a German peace offer.

Sir Frank Roberts, diplomat in the British Foreign Office in 1941

unwelcome. It was essential that no impression should be given either to Washington or Moscow that peace-talks with Germany were starting. The Duke of Hamilton said in amazement: 'It is astonishing how little the Nazis understand us.' After many interrogations in which Hess stated woodenly that he had come on 'a mission for humanity', but in which he made no proposals whatsoever, the British dispatched the envoy behind bars without further comment.

To the great disappointment of the British government he betrayed nothing about the date for the invasion of the Soviet Union – not even when he had been administered a truth-drug. The interrogators reported to London that Hess probably *was* no longer fully in touch with reality. From his cell he wrote yet another farewell letter to Hitler – a document that shows how ossified his mind had become:

> Scarcely ever was it granted to people to serve so successfully a man and his ideas, as it has been to those under you. Please accept my thanks, from the bottom of my heart, for everything that you have given me and that you have been to me. I write these lines in the clear knowledge that no other way out is left to me – hard as this end will be. In you, *mein Führer*, I greet our Greater Germany which is advancing towards undreamed-of greatness. Perhaps my flight, in spite of my death or precisely because of it, will bring peace and understanding with Britain. *Heil, mein Führer*.

A day later he threw himself down a prison staircase. But this attempted suicide, the first of three, ended in failure. Hess only broke a leg.

While the most prominent prisoner of the Second World War languished in prison in south London, the armies of the anti-Hitler alliance prepared to storm that 'Greater Germany' that Hess had so fervently praised. Psychiatrists had to take regular care of their famous inmate. His stomach-cramps became chronic. The guards were instructed to prevent any further attempts at suicide. Letters of complaint from the prisoner showed definite signs of persecution mania: 'They put corrosive acids in my food. The skin of my gums was hanging down in shreds.' Or: 'The food always tastes of soap, washing-up water, manure, rotten fish or carbolic acid. The worst was like the glandular secretions of camels or pigs.'

From the paranoid symptoms of his illness Hess finally took refuge in the dark night of oblivion. One of the doctors treating him made this diagnosis: 'Hess is suffering from hysterical amnesia. It is comparable with that form of amnesia which many soldiers develop under severe stress in war.'

Before the War Crimes Tribunal in Nuremberg he also initially appeared to be suffering from memory-loss. Hess was indicted on all counts in the trial: conspiracy, crimes against peace, war-crimes and crimes against humanity. Judicially speaking this was a questionable approach – for the Deputy had left Germany before the mass-murder had actually begun, nor did he have any part in Hitler's conduct of the war. In the end the last two counts were dropped. But all the hopes of his family and his defence counsel for a suspension of proceedings due to his unfitness to plead, were shattered when the accused declared in a muddled protest that his 'pretence of a loss of memory' had been 'of a purely tactical nature'.

After this statement he sank back in the dock and followed events with dull, empty eyes. Was this intervention a fit of pointless pride or merely an attempt to draw attention to himself? At no time in the trial did Rudolf Hess show any attack of

Hess was an extremely complex personality. There was a great deal of discussion at the time about the circumstances in which Hess flew to Britain. These were of course really odd. We also discussed whether Hess was even capable of following the case and getting through it. The question of his loss of memory was certainly justified. A committee of doctors then decided that his mental faculties were adequate for him to follow the trial.

Sir Hartley (later Lord) Shawcross, British Prosecutor at Nuremberg

remorse. Introverted, arrogantly dismissive towards the court, his mind was stuck fast in the world which he left in 1941.

The Soviet prosecutor demanded the death penalty for Hess, like the others, while the Americans wanted a limited prison sentence. In the end they agreed on imprisonment 'for life'. Perhaps the sentence would have been more lenient, had Hess dispensed with his closing speech. With eyes fixed on some distant horizon he mouthed the confession of a man who had learned nothing. When Göring whispered to him that he would do better to remain silent, his one-time rival barked at him: 'Don't interrupt me.' Then he said:

> It was granted to me for many years of my life to work under the greatest son that my people has ever produced in its thousand years of history. Even if I could do so, I would not wish to erase this period from my life. I regret nothing. One day I will stand before the Judgement Seat of the Everlasting God. I will answer to Him and I know that He will acquit me.

The last sentence matched almost word for word Hitler's closing statement to the People's Court in Munich in 1924. In the Germany of 1946, bombed out and starving, the words went unheard. Yet for Hess they were his attempt to be reinstated, his request to return to the circle of the Disciples. After the failure of his absurd demonstration of love on the night of 10 May 1941, he was once again Hitler's henchman. To the end he held fast to this fatal anachronism.

As you know, Rudolf Hess flew to Britain on 10 May 1941 in a last-ditch attempt to prevent another world war. If I judge the matter correctly, Hess at that time had the status of a member of parliament. Parliamentarians are protected under international law and so he ought not to have been imprisoned by the British. He should have been allowed to fly back to Germany.

Dr Alfred Seidl, Hess' Defence Counsel at Nuremberg

For Hess, the four decades in the war-criminals' prison at Spandau in West Berlin, were simply spent waiting for death. When still in Nuremberg he asked a guard: 'Why don't they let me die?' From 1966 onward he was the sole prisoner in the world's most expensive gaol. All the rest of Hitler's 'champions', even those with life sentences, had been released. In Hess' case all attempts failed due to the veto of the Soviet Union, although many voices had been raised publicly and privately in favour of releasing the venerable prisoner – including the governments of the three victorious western powers and the Chancellor and President of Federal Germany. Throughout the decades of incarceration Hess remained what he had always been – a loner. Not until 1969 did he allow his family to visit him.

In the end Hess, locked up in a prison which had survived into the Cold War as the last relic of the anti-Hitler coalition, became a martyr for neo-Nazis all over the world. Whether after his release from prison he would have found his way around a world that was so foreign to him, is very much open to doubt.

> You'll see, this apparition will disappear and within a month you will be the Führer of Germany!
> *Hess to Göring about the Nuremberg trial, 1946*

His death on 17 August 1987 brought an end to a great mystery of modern history. To this day there are those who prefer not to believe the official statement by the Allies that the Deputy committed suicide. The blame for this lies in no small measure with the clumsy behaviour of the 'Four Powers'. The destruction of evidence, contradictions in official statements, a sloppily performed autopsy and not least the secrecy imposed on papers and interrogation reports – all this contributed to the mystification and conspiracy-theories. The death of Hess, effected by an electric cable in a garden-shed in Spandau, has attracted self-appointed experts and dubious witnesses.

The facts tell a different story. The last prison chaplain, Michel Röhrig, stated that the rapid decline in Hess' health in the spring

Hess tried several times to commit suicide. I heard of one attempt during his imprisonment in England. He tried again when he was left as the only prisoner in Spandau. Then his prison conditions improved.

Tony Le Tissier, Director of Spandau Prison

of 1987 finally destroyed the prisoner's will to live. When Röhrig wanted to take a holiday at the beginning of August, Hess apparently begged him: 'Don't go, I'm going to need you.' A farewell letter found on the dead man also contradicts the murder theory: 'Written a few minutes before my death,' Hess wrote on the back of a letter from his daughter-in-law and thanked her for her years of attentiveness. His son, Wolf-Rüdiger Hess, nevertheless believes the letter to be a forgery, since its style does not match that of his father at the time of his death. However, an expert analysis that was commissioned found no evidence in support of this theory.

We dealt with the matter of Hess' death very carefully – being aware of his historic importance. The post-mortem was carried out with the greatest care by Dr Cameron, a British pathologist. Various envoys of the Allies took part in it. The cause of death was lack of oxygen to the brain. This was somewhat unusual for a person who had been hanged, since in this case his neck was not broken, as would be expected. The flow of blood *from* the brain had been blocked. Hess must very quickly have lost consciousness through the swelling of the brain. All signs pointed to this and to it being a suicide.

General Blank, US Army Doctor in Spandau

The last person entrusted with caring for Hess in Spandau was a Tunisian named Abdullah Melaouhi. A few weeks after the death of his charge he went to the press and told them about two unknown men in American uniforms who were standing beside the body and looked 'like murderers'. Admittedly, Melaouhi only arrived at the garden-shed in which Hess had been found half an hour after his death. The two men in US uniform were probably the guard officer Al Ahuja and his orderly. According to Ahuja: 'He couldn't have known who we were; we had never met before.' This is a plausible explanation since the guard company, which changed every month, as a rule had no contact with the permanent staff at Spandau. Incidentally, Abdullah Melaouhi only agreed to be interviewed in return for a fat fee.

A second post-mortem, ordered by the family, also served to support the argument against the Allied version of events. It is a fact that the report by the renowned Munich pathologist, Wolfgang Spann, contradicted the Allied report by the British Professor Cameron and accused him of careless investigations. But the criticism of his colleague related chiefly to procedures in forensic medicine. Spann found no reason to suspect murder. When questioned he said: 'This is not shown by our analysis. We cannot prove that another hand was involved.'

Yet questions still remain in the Hess case, questions which will probably not be answered until the relevant archives are opened.

I am convinced that my father was killed, and killed by the British. What can have been the crucial motive for this? My father knew too much! There was a risk that in the end it would be revealed that Britain shared the blame for the war. And there were many other things which pointed to a murder: (a) my father knew that the Russians wanted to release him, (b) he was a man of ninety-three, not physically capable of tying his own shoe-laces, let alône taking his own life. Then there was the second post-mortem by Professor Spann, who actually wrote in his memoirs: 'the death cannot have taken place in the way the British described'. Then the business of the farewell letter, which was obviously forged, as one can see particularly from its contents. So the suicide theory has no foundation.

Wolf-Rüdiger Hess, Rudolf Hess' son

Even the files of the British secret service relating to the flight to Britain remain closed for the time being. Thus the gaps in the archives still nourish speculation about the two great riddles in the life of the Deputy.

The effect of such mysteries on a minority of diehards was apparent once again at the burial of Hess in Wunsiedel, only a short distance from his boyhood home of Reichholdsgrün. The ceremony had to be postponed because thousands of right-wing extremists besieged the cemetery. Year after year these incurables make a pilgrimage on the anniversary of the Deputy's death, where they keep a sizeable police detachment occupied. The deluded belief to which Rudolf Hess clung to the very end has still not gone with him to the grave.

To my mind Rudolf Hess was certainly neither mad nor senile. On the contrary, he was intelligent and very focused on anything that interested him. He took a lively interest in everything going on around him and during his imprisonment occupied himself with many things. For example, he became an expert on the American space programme. Physically, too, apart from the usual minor ailments, he was in good shape until shortly before he died. He was definitely capable of stringing himself up.

General Blank, US Army Doctor in Spandau

For Rudolf Hess the clock stopped in 1941. Nevertheless, his relationship with his fellow-prisoners was always good. Speer and von Schirach always looked after the old man and Speer even made his bed. In the end he outlived them all.

Eugene Bird, governor of Spandau gaol

CHAPTER FIVE

THE ARCHITECT: ALBERT SPEER

KNOPP/ADLER

I admire Hitler without reserve.

At those times when he was functioning as an architect, he really was completely relaxed and at ease.

Most of all – and that was definitely the greatest mistake of my life – I felt that he was human.

You could also say that *I* meant something to *him*.

For a great building project I would, like Faust, have sold my soul.

All in all I have a really clear conscience, in that I never did or said anything anti-Semitic.

I know nothing about Jews.

Anyone who rents out a Jewish-owned house without my authority renders himself liable to punishment!

I never thought that it was any of my personal business, if someone else talked in my presence about how all Jews ought to be beaten to death.

Speer

In my view there are two types of responsibility in public life. One responsibility is for one's own sector, for which one is of course fully responsible. Beyond that, it is my personal view that there is and must be an overall responsibility for absolutely decisive matters, insofar as one is a member of the leadership, because otherwise who is to assume responsibility for the course of events?

Speer at Nuremberg, 1946

Just imagine if someone were to say to you: it is my unshakeable will that from now on Beethoven's Ninth may only be performed on the harmonica.

Speer to the conductor, Wilhelm Furtwängler, 1939

Our children hardly knew him. Perhaps he knew the older ones a little. Before the war he sometimes took a day off now and then. But the two youngest practically didn't know him at all. Basically, the children had no father.

Margret Speer

Where Speer is concerned, one must certainly not forget that he has not really got our old National Socialist blood in his veins. He is after all a technocrat by nature and has never bothered much about politics. That is why, in these serious crises, he is rather more liable to crack than the real Nazis.

Goebbels, 1944 (Diary)

Mein Führer, this is the first time for me that you have been dissatisfied with the achievements in my sphere of work.

Speer to Hitler, spring 1944

Tell Speer I'm fond of him.

Hitler to Generalfeldmarschall Milch, spring 1944

Mein Führer,
. . . . Until 18 March my belief in a favourable turn in our destiny was unbroken. I cannot believe in the success of our

good cause, if in these critical months we destroy the foundations of our national life.

I therefore beg you not to take this step yourself in bringing destruction down on the people.

God protect Germany.

Speer, 1945

In this war the German people has shown a steadfastness which in some future time will earn the just admiration of history. This is not the moment for us to grieve and weep over what is past. Only by dogged labour can our lot continue to be borne.

Speer, 3 May 1945

Prosecutor Jackson: You knew about the Nazi Party's policy and the government's measures against the Jews, didn't you?

Speer: I knew that the National Socialist Party was anti-Semitic, and I also knew that the Jews had been evacuated from Germany.

Jackson: Surely you took part in carrying out those evacuation measures, didn't you?

Speer: No.

Examination of Speer at the Nuremberg Trial, 21 June 1946

I have to say that I have not read the book *Mein Kampf* from beginning to end.

Examination of Speer at the Nuremberg Trial, 21 June, 1946

I tried several times to have Himmler and others removed from the government and force them to take responsibility for their actions.

Examination of Speer at Nuremberg, 20 June 1946

Speer not only knew what methods were used for deporting the population of the occupied territories into slavery, but he also took part in meetings at which decisions about the deportation of millions of people were taken. Speer was in close contact with Himmler: and Himmler provided him with prisoners to work in armaments factories; in many factories under Speer's control, branches of the concentration-camps were set up. This is the true face of the defendant Speer . . .

General R.A. Rudenko, Chief Prosecutor for the Soviet Union,
1946

The planning of the Berlin project took over my life, and as I have remarked, I still cannot tear myself away from it today. When I search deep down for the cause of my rejection of Hitler today, then beside all the dreadful aspects he revealed, there is also something of a personal disappointment: that his political power-game drove him headlong into war and thereby destroyed the plans I had made for my life..

Speer, 1953

Whether I would have acted differently if I had known everything, is a question I have asked myself a million times over. The answer I give myself is always the same. Somehow I would have gone on trying to help that man win his war.

Speer, 1979

* * *

The smell of beer blending with cigarette-smoke was part of the atmosphere of the 'New World' just as it was of 'the longest pub-crawl in German history'. The shabby 'ballroom' in the Hasenheide, the main street in Berlin's working-class district of Neukölln, had certainly seen better days.

On that evening of 4 December 1930, however, the audience was drawn from a 'better class' of people. On this occasion the joint wasn't jumping, there was no communist agitation. This time the front row of tables near the stage was dominated by starched shirts, stiff collars and dark suits. Behind them, military-style caps and colourful pennants. This is where the university teachers and students were sitting, who were told by the chairman of the meeting that two more SA men had just 'fallen victim to the murderous Red beast'.

The notes of the old Badenweiler march rang out. The young man up in the gallery who was attending his first political meeting rose to his feet, as did the young men around him, whom he had brought along: architectural students from the technical university. The tall, elegantly dressed man was their Professor's assistant.

Hitler spoke. He had adapted to his surroundings, wore a dark suit and tie. His voice was soft but penetrating. What he asked of the assembled academics was unambivalent: 'It is your task to establish among the German people an organization of those of greatest worth, an organization of idealism.'

The wolf, as always in such situations, was wearing sheep's clothing. That evening he omitted to mention those he considered inferior – and what he had in mind for such people. There was no polemic. But almost every sentence contained an invocation of nation, people, Fatherland: 'Happy our people if one day the spirit of the SA and the SS man will have become the spirit of 40 million.' At this point there was 'a storm of applause'.

A few months later, on 1 March 1931, the elegant young man joined the NSDAP and was given his membership number, 474481. Why did Albert Speer become a National Socialist? 'I did not choose the NSDAP, but joined Hitler, whose presence affected me subtly at our first meeting and from then on never let go of me.' Was there really not a more calculated motive involved?

Gerhard Kosel remembers Speer well from those days. Kosel also studied architecture, but he was a communist. At university Speer was his greatest opponent: 'A whole group had organized itself under his leadership.' According to Kosel, Speer had even made his debut as a speaker. After a discussion forum in the Berlin suburb of Nikolassee the two became closer. Speer, his young wife Margret, and Kosel, strolled up and down the banks of the Wannsee Lake until the early hours of the morning.

'Speer was convinced that the future belonged to Adolf Hitler,' Professor Kosel explains in his apartment on Berlin's Strausberger Platz. From there he has a good view of the television tower which he designed. 'He told us about his conversations with Hitler and the superb prospects for the future of architecture, when Hitler came to power.' Is Kosel quite sure about this? Speer claimed at the Nuremberg trials (and on numerous other occasions) that he did not meet Hitler until 1934. The conversation beside the Wannsee took place in 1931. 'Yes,' says Kosel, 'it was clear from the details he gave me that he had had quite a number of talks with Hitler about architecture and art.'

Was this just a newly converted Nazi showing off because he wanted to impress a communist? At all events it is the case that Albert Speer received the first building contract to be issued by the Berlin Nazi Party in 1932: the conversion of their newly acquired '*Gauhaus*' or regional headquarters, located in Voss-Strasse, in the heart of the government district. When the job was completed, Speer's client, Joseph Goebbels, expressed to the architect in writing his 'great appreciation and warmest thanks'. 'We were especially pleased to find that, despite the very short time allowed, the conversion was so punctually completed that we were able to launch our election campaign from the new offices.'

A man who could get jobs done swiftly and reliably – that was the reputation which laid the foundation-stone of Speer's career. Hitler had scarcely been Reich Chancellor for three months when Albert Speer received his next assignment – a rather out-of-the-ordinary one for him: he was to design the décor for a Nazi Party rally.

The date, 1 May 1933, was one of strategic importance for the new regime. The day that had traditionally been used by the Left as an occasion for demonstrations was subverted into a holiday in celebration of the *Volksgemeinschaft*, or 'national community'. Hitler chose Berlin's Tempelhof airfield as the site for the first mass rally of the Third Reich. Hundreds of thousands were expected. It was intended as a demonstration of power, to further demoralize the stricken Left and to discourage any resistance to the 'brown' terror.

Albert Speer was to provide the stage for the grand entrance of the Führer. The still unknown architect had an opportunity to enlarge on his plans in a radio interview: 'In view of the length of the field, about one kilometer, we became convinced that the central point, from which the Führer speaks, must be so strongly profiled that even those furthest away will sense the special impact of it.'

To present the Führer with special impact – the young Speer had clearly recognized the purpose of his commission. And Hitler showed his enthusiasm for Speer's concept. Immediately afterwards, Goebbels appointed the young architect to be the

> It was of course perfectly clear to me that he was striving for world domination. What many people do not understand today is that at the time I could not have wished for anything better. That was after all the entire purpose of my buildings. They would have looked grotesque had Hitler remained sitting in Germany. My whole intention was for this great man to rule the globe.
>
> *Speer, 1979*

regime's 'producer', the 'head of the department for artistic design of mass demonstrations'. This was a first step on the career-ladder, but not what Speer had dreamed of for himself.

Responsibility for the design of buildings lay with someone else: Hitler's architect was Professor Paul Ludwig Troost. Hitler admired Troost and called him 'the greatest architect since Schinkel (Germany's leading neo-Classical designer), yet when visiting the Professor's Munich studios, Hitler merely assumed the role of student – not an ideal feeling for a man who considered himself a genius in all things.

For the Führer wanted to become known as an architect himself. Even back in the 1920s he had sketched the monumental buildings of his future Reich. In 1936 Speer quoted Hitler as describing architecture in his *Mein Kampf* as 'the queen of the arts' (though he later claimed he had never really read the book). The young architect had also apparently learned from *Mein Kampf* that Hitler believed that 'my beautiful dream of the future would yet become reality, though it might take many long years. I was always convinced that one day I would make a name for myself as an architect.'

Now, though Hitler was perhaps not the architect, he was the architect's patron. He turned his attention first to the 'capital of the Movement': 'The *Haus der Deutschen Kunst*' [House of German Art] and the Führer-buildings on the Königsplatz are the first fine buildings of the new Reich,' Hitler announced at the laying of the foundation-stone. While Troost was at the top of the heap, there was no room for another architect.

For the ambitious Albert Speer no end of backstage jobs for

Hitler's demonstrations came his way: banners, eagles, searchlights, stages. It seems odd that all this could have happened without Hitler being involved. Speer even appears to have received the commission for the 'Party Victory Congress' in 1933 without meeting the Führer in person.

The closest he got to a real construction-site was at the end of 1933 when, at the age of twenty-eight, he was allowed to work as a sort of site-manager under Troost, on the conversion of the Reich Chancellery in Berlin. It was there that Hitler apparently 'noticed' him for the first time, as Speer describes it in his memoirs.[1] The Füher apparently came upon him, as if in search of a 'a young, gifted architect, like a blank sheet on which he could write'.

> The relationship between Hitler and Speer was different from that with his other colleagues. Speer occupied a special place, as we could tell from Hitler's remarks about him: it was more than an official relationship, more a kind of friendship or spiritual affinity. Hitler valued Speer's passion for architecture particularly and shared it with him. It was in this area that the two became very close. Speer was the only one in the circle with any creative leanings and Hitler saw him as an artist. Hitler always said that Speer was the only man with whom he could really talk about these things.
>
> *Traudl Junge, Hitler's Secretary*

Speer would later have us believe that this was the first time he allowed himself to be *seduced* by power. But didn't the same thing happen to a great many Germans? We hear not a word from Speer to say that he deliberately sought a way to Hitler, that he early on and quite consciously recognized in him the chance of a lifetime.

'Like Faust, I would have sold my soul for a major building-project,' wrote Speer in his memoirs about the meeting on the building-site in Berlin. 'Now I had found my Mephistopheles.' Only now? This Faust had for a long time done his utmost to

[1] Speer, *Inside the Third Reich*, (London, New York 1970)

present his Mephistopheles in the best light – in the hope of being richly rewarded for it.

Early in 1934 Ludwig Troost died 'suddenly and unexpectedly'. Whether deliberately or coincidentally Hitler now shifted the focus of his construction mania to Nuremberg. It was now that Hitler and Speer got together: the first task was to develop the terrain where party congresses were held. One of the rare pieces of evidence on film from this period shows the two men, Speer and Hitler, walking around a building-site. First Speer speaks, explaining his plans. Then it is Hitler's turn. He puts on his glasses, and has someone pass him a drawing-pad and pencil. Resting the pad on his knee he begins to sketch. Speer, with his hands placed respectfully down the seams of his trousers, watches the Master. That's how it should be done, Speer, the Führer says, thrusting the sketch into his hand.

Speer, who 'only wanted to be an architect', wrote at the time:

The Führer must build as a National Socialist. As such, just as he determines the will and expression of the Movement, so does he also determine the clean line and purity of the building style, the hardness of expression, the clarity of architectural thinking, the high quality of the materials and, the greatest and most important aspect of all, the new inner sense and thus the inner meaning of his buildings. For the Führer, building is not a hobby, but a serious matter whose purpose is to give high expression, in stone as in everything, to the will of the National Socialist Movement.

Only when Hitler demanded that one building should be 100 metres long did Speer contradict him, as Gerdy Troost, the rather resentful widow of the Munich architect, tells us. Speer's counter-proposal was: 200 metres, *mein Führer!*

The podium of the Zeppelin Field, Speer's first great 'stone building' actually measured 490 meters long – making it twice the length of the Baths of Caracalla in Rome, as Speer proudly notes in his memoirs. The purpose of the building, as he commented later, had rather irritated him: 'The indispensable podium of honour turned out to be rather obtrusive, even though I had tried to locate it as inconspicuously as possible at the centre of the terrace of steps.' Speer actually uses the word 'inconspicuously'!

However, what the Party members read in the official brochure which Speer jointly issued was quite different:

> The place where the Führer stands is given particular architectural emphasis and solidity. He stands in front of the assembled people who have marched past in front of him in a pre-arranged sequence. This standing eye-to-eye, the Führer facing the people and the people facing the Führer, is what determines the arrangement. . . . In the centre, thrust far forward into the field, is the Führer's position. This compelling organization of the massed crowds through the architectural arrangements has the effect of showing every participant . . . the powerful, concerted expression of will . . . Only through witnessing this form of parade as a political tool created by National Socialism can this architecture be understood.

Speer's architecture was the demonstration of political might captured in stone, but it was only shown to its best advantage by his stage-management: Hitler's master-of-ceremonies preferred night and the light of searchlights. In this way he could control all the effects. Then came torches and firelight, banners, marching columns – and the music of Richard Wagner: the overture to *Rienzi*, Hitler's favourite opera.

The climax was signalled by a soaring cathedral of light. Speer, with apparent ingenuousness, later described this acme of Hitlerian seduction as his 'finest spatial creation': 130 of the most up-to-date anti-aircraft searchlights were placed at intervals of 12 metres around the assembled crowd of 150,000 people. The beams of light reached as high as 8 kilometres into the sky. 'All who are present on this evening feel, with a shiver of awe in their soul, the myth of Germany which only German blood can fully comprehend,' ran the lyrical official Party commentary.

Speer never uttered a word of regret about the part he played in the seduction of an entire people. 'My assignment was a non-political one,' he would later tell Hitler brazenly to his face, when everything was falling apart. Speer's greatest project in Nuremberg was the 'German Stadium', intended to hold no less than 400,000 spectators at once. As Hitler announced on the construction-site, in future the Olympic Games would only be held here! Anyone who today goes looking for the remains of the 'world's biggest stadium' will find only a lake. Shortly before the end of the war the vast excavation was flooded by the SS.

Certainly Speer had not foreseen such a fate for his buildings. As he prophesied at the time, they were to serve as 'documents of a political will that bear witness millennia from now to the greatness of their age'. To this end he even decreed a special construction process, the 'law of ruins'. In this way Hitler's palaces, even in a state of decay, were still to remain impressive – like the temples of antiquity.

> Speer was an excessively polite and good-looking 'gentleman'. He was certainly also a man who would always have come to an accommodation with whoever was in power. He was no creep, but because of their shared talents and interests his relationship with Hitler was very good. One can hardly reproach Speer for having great plans as a young architect. And then along came a great statesman and gave him the opportunity to indulge himself: money didn't come into it.
>
> *Reinhard Spitzy, Ribbentrop's Adjutant*

Apart from the podium on the Zeppelin Field, only the shell of the 'Congress Hall' was completed before the outbreak of war – the only one of the Nuremberg buildings which Speer not only designed but also supervised the construction of. But even this, the 'first giant among the buildings of the Reich', as Hitler described it when laying the foundation-stone, merely served as a backdrop for Hitler's annual address to the 50,000 delegates of the Party Congress.

Speer's dream was that soon the entire Reich would boast buildings like those in Nuremberg: 'No longer will cities by dominated by department stores or the head offices of banks and industrial concerns, they will bear the stamp of the Führer's buildings . . .' As Speer's patron, Hitler wanted to have his architect close at hand at his Obersalzberg retreat. In 1935 Hitler gave Speer and his family an old villa only a few minutes walk from the Berghof. A drawing-office was built right next door. Speer and his wife Margret belonged to the small private circle around Hitler and were regular guests on the terrace of the Berghof.

Reinhard Spitzy, who at the time was Liaison Officer for the Foreign Minister, Ribbentrop, often found his duties took him to Hitler's alpine residence.

> I knew that Speer enjoyed Hitler's goodwill to the very highest degree. Later I was able to see this for myself, when I was at Obersalzberg with Ribbentrop for the first time: when Speer was there, he had the say-so. He was certainly a personal friend of Hitler. Hitler was as excited as if a mistress were coming to visit him. Then they would both begin to draw and make plans. Models were set up. One had the feeling that in all this both men were equal partners. My boss, Ribbentrop, and the others were suddenly left out of things – they were just part of the furniture. Hitler would take time out from state business for two or three days and draw up plans with Speer.
>
> *Reinhard Spitzy, Ribbentrop's Adjutant*

'The happiest moments in Adolf's life,' Spitzy tells us, 'were surely those he spent with Speer.' The Hitler–Speer relationship, as analysed by the psychologist Alexander Mitscherlich, was 'impelled by a strong homoerotic component. In this bonding it was obvious that Speer took the female role. He was to *deliver* what Hitler inspired, that which Hitler had *fertilized* in him. Hitler lays the world . . . at his feet. This is normally the gesture a man makes to a woman.'

Some time in the summer of 1936 Hitler really did lay the world at the feet of his beloved Speer: 'The greatest architectural commission of all,' was what he had to offer. Only to be compared, he said, with the temples and palaces of Babylon or the pyramids of ancient Egypt. Speer was to build Germania, the capital city of a German world. Early in 1937 Hitler appointed his architect 'General Inspector of buildings for the redesign of the Reich capital' and awarded him the title of 'Professor'.

The new Reich Chancellery in Berlin was the only large building that was completed to designs by Albert Speer. Nothing remains of it but mountains of photographs and some rather unimpressive film footage. It is only from the colour photographs that we can gain some idea of the style and effect of this architecture. In its better features (such as the Mosaic Hall and the Circular Hall), which imitate antiquity and the Italian Renaissance, it displays a cold but impressive grandeur. At its most hideous (the façade and the Court of Honour), there are drab, monotonous expanses of 'Nordic' granite, heavy, inelegant columns and statues on the window-frontages, which clump across the façades like jackboots.

> Went to see Speer. Looked at his new models for the rebuilding of Berlin. They are indeed magnificent. Of a matchless monumentality. With them the Führer will have his memorial in stone. Along with this I urge for the building of social housing in Berlin. Speer will do that too. The model for the great domed hall defies description.
>
> *Goebbels (Diary), 1941*

Hitler saw these building projects as part of his political programme:

> In late December 1937 and early January 1938 I had made up my mind to settle the Austrian question and thereby establish a Greater German Reich. Given not just the purely administrative requirements but also the representational function involved, the old Reich Chancellery could no longer be considered adequate under any circumstances.

Hitler is in a hurry. In the middle of January 1939 he wants to hold a New Year reception for the foreign ambassadors in Berlin and impress them with the potency of this architecture. The official construction contract is awarded to Speer on 11 January 1938. So he has precisely one year to complete it.

> Speer was convincing. He gave the impression of great calmness – of being someone who knew exactly what he wanted, who was decisive, who stood above things and was generally interested in everything. We liked him because he took an interest in us – the kind of man who listens to other people's worries and difficulties and reacts appropriately. He was always positive and looked for the positive aspects in any discussion. And he was tireless in everything he did.
>
> *Manfred von Poser, Speer's Adjutant*

This is the acid-test for Speer: now he can, indeed he must, prove his ability to handle a major building project. Money is no object; bureaucratic and legal hurdles (planning permission, objections) simply do not exist. Within two months every house in the Voss-Strasse has been cleared and demolished. Willi Schelkes, one of Speer's closest collaborators in the General Building Inspectorate of the Reich Capital, recalls:

> He was a great organizer, which is why he didn't bring in just one firm to build the shell, but three, four or five, so that work could start simultaneously in several places. That was the only way it was at all possible to put up such a huge building in so short a time.

In the final phase of building, over 8,000 workers in various trades are employed on the site. Armies of cleaners are sweeping up non-stop, while everywhere men are hammering, sawing and decorating. Speer is determined to keep to his deadline at all costs; he wants to be seen by his Führer as a man who succeeds.

Two days before the deadline expires Hitler is able to drive up to the entrance. Film footage shows him standing beside a Speer who seems almost bursting with pride. Everything is indeed ready and Hitler heaps praise on his architect:

> The fact that this project was successful, and the manner of its completion, are entirely due to the brilliant architect, his artistic talent and his unrivalled organizational abilities. . . . It is a credit to its brilliant architect and designer, Albert Speer.

However, Hitler plans to use the building for a few years only. From 1950 onward, he writes almost as an aside, it is 'intended for another purpose'. This is where his Deputy, Rudolf Hess, will take up residence. The Führer himself will move house yet again, this time to the new centre of the Reich, which is to take shape right beside the Brandenburg Gate. The site where today the cranes are swinging over the new Chancellor's Office and government buildings of a re-united Federal Republic of Germany, is exactly where Hitler proposed to build the centre of the world capital, Germania.

The plans at the time, as Speer conscientiously noted on all his drawings, were produced 'according to ideas from the Führer'. The new 'Palace of the Führer' was to be erected on the 'Great Square' directly opposite the old Reichstag (which Hitler intended to preserve as a museum). It was to be framed by the palatial buildings of the 'Supreme Command of the Wehrmacht' and by the 'Great Hall': the world's largest building, a domed hall 300 metres (984 ft) high and large enough to hold 180,000 people. Perched on the very top would be an eagle, holding the swastika in its claws. In 1939 Hitler commanded the architect to replace the Nazi symbol by a terrestrial globe. Once every year, Hitler decreed, deputations from the subject nations were to come and gaze in wonder. Completion of the megalomaniac city of Germania was scheduled for 1950.

In the workshops of the General Inspector of Buildings on Pariser Platz, work went on round the clock on the models for the Great Square. Late at night, as Willi Schelkes recalls, Hitler would arrive unannounced, having walked across from the Chancellery, and would have to be shown everything. 'I like it!' he is said to have frequently shouted aloud.

On 14 June 1938 the Lord of Germania had given the starting-signal: 'I lay the foundation-stone for the new House of Tourism and herewith ordain the beginning of work on the rebuilding of

Greater Berlin.' It was to become the first building on the 'North–South Axis', the 120 metre (394 ft) wide and 7 kilometres (4.2 mile) long ceremonial avenue of the world capital.

> It will be the first time in history that a leader with superior technical knowledge creates buildings of stone, which in millennia to come will stand as documents of the political will of their age.
>
> *Speer, 1934*

But this time things did not go as smoothly as with the building of the Reich Chancellery. The General Inspector of Buildings first had to clear an extremely large area for the Führer's new buildings: 52,000 homes had to be demolished, nearly 4 per cent of Berlin's entire housing-stock!

Speer was able to offer alternative accomodation to the 'demolishees'. Since the beginning of 1939 Speer's officials had been compiling a register of over 23,000 so-called 'Jewish dwellings'. The responsible department was II/4, headed by the Vice-Chairman of the Inspectorate, a man called Clahes (whose name is never once mentioned in Speer's memoirs!). A document entitled 'Legal Basis' was sent by Göring to Speer on 26 November 1938, in other words two weeks after the notorious '*Kristallnacht*' pogrom. In these 'regulations . . . concerning the removal of Jews from dwellings, shops and warehouses owned by Aryan landlords'. it was laid down 'that a preferential right to purchase and/or make a decision as to the new tenant or new lessee is granted to the General Inspector of Buildings'.

Special forms were issued on which 'dwellings vacated or about to be vacated by Jewish tenants' were to be notified to the Inspectorate. The addresses of homes 'made available' were published in 'lists of dwellings for tenants from clearance areas' in the 'official organ of the General Inspectorate of Buildings'. Speer, who later claimed to have known nothing of all this, issued the following threat to landlords: 'Anyone who rents out Jewish dwellings without my permission is liable to a penalty.'

As early as 14 September 1938 we find noted in the minutes of an internal discussion in the top echelons of the General Inspectorate: '. . . Prof. Speer developed the proposal which aimed at freeing up the necessary apartment-blocks through compulsory eviction of Jews.' However, it was only during the war that the ideas of the Inspectorate were put into effect, albeit then with considerable pressure: even from the comfortable distance of the Obersalzberg Speer personally sent a telex (on 27 November 1940) to his Vice-Chairman, Clahes, enquiring about 'progress in the clearance of 1000 Jewish dwellings'.

After 1938 we Jews were no longer permitted to practise our professions. However we went on working on building-sites and elsewhere – just manual labour to make enough to live on. We actually thought it wouldn't be so bad; after all workers were in demand everywhere. The eviction from our apartment in 1941 really came as a complete surprise, with no advance warning. It would have been pointless to fight it.

Werner Krisch, a Jew from Berlin

The annals of the General Inspectorate, now kept in the Berlin state archives, note on 26 August 1941:

In accordance with instructions from Speer a further operation is under way for the clearance of 5,000 Jewish dwellings. The existing systems are being extended as necessary, in order that the Jewish dwellings can, despite difficulties on all sides resulting from wartime conditions, be made available and can be occupied by demolishees from the areas urgently required for clearance.

The Gestapo combed the city house by house, accompanied by officials keeping records with German thoroughness: clearance-lists were drawn up, names and addresses of all Jewish tenants documented, along with those of the 'Aryan replacement tenants'. Admittedly, those who would enjoy the benefits of a new apartment were unlikely to be ordinary citizens. As a study of these papers shows, the new occupants were mainly SS-men, employees of various ministries (including Speer's own officials) as well as 'meritorious' Party members for whom 'Jewish dwellings' were wangled by the General Inspector of Buildings.

On 27 October 1941 the Gestapo showed up at Bötzowstrasse 53, where a Jewish family of four named Krisch were living in a three-and-a-half roomed apartment. The parents were doing compulsory labour service as solderers in the Siemens electrical plant, and the two sons worked as porters for a coal-merchant. One of them, Werner Krisch, is unable to forget the scene that night: 'We had certainly heard rumours that something might happen – but what *did* happen was something we never expected. It came as a complete surprise.'

The brothers had been out that evening. At about ten or ten-thirty they wanted to bring two girlfriends home with them. They were still on the staircase when two men accosted them.

They stopped us and asked who we were. Then they made it obvious we had to say goodbye to the girls and go up to the apartment. There we were told we could just pack a few essentials in a suitcase. Everything else had to be left behind. That is the way we were evicted from our home.

The same night the family had to hand over the key. Money, jewelry, Werner Krisch's photographic equipment – all were confiscated. The synagogue in Levetzowstrasse served as a transit-camp for the 'dehoused'. There the Gestapo ransacked the luggage and, Werner Krisch remembers, 'anything they fancied, they took out and kept'.

They were then transported by truck to Grunewald station. The train took them from there to the 'Litzmannstadt' ghetto in the Polish city of Lodz. Werner Krisch never saw his brother or his parents again. He himself survived Auschwitz, Sachsenhausen and finally the death-march to Buchenwald.

About these years, Speer wrote:

I must have had the feeling that it had nothing to do with me

> When I think about the fate of the Berlin Jews, I am overcome by an inescapable feeling of failure and inadequacy. Often on the daily journey to my architects' office I would see crowds of people on the platform of the Nikolassee station. I knew they must be evacuated Berlin Jews. As I drove past I was certainly overcome by a feeling of depression; presumably I was aware of murky things going on. But I was a prisoner of the principles of the regime to an extent that is hard for me to understand today. Slogans like: 'Führer, command; we will obey!' or 'The Führer is always right', had a hypnotic effect, even on those of us in Hitler's immediate circle. Perhaps there was an unwitting numbing of the conscience, as we buried ourselves totally in our work.
>
> *Speer, 1981*

personally, when I heard how Jews, freemasons, Social-Democrats or Jehovahs Witnesses were being treated as 'fair game' by the people around me. I thought it enough that I myself took no part in it.

It was 'the people around' Speer who drove Werner Krisch and his family out of their home and to their death. And it is also true that Albert Speer was not seen on the stairway of Bötzowstrasse 53.

The 'annals of the General Inspector of Buildings, Albert Speer' reported in early November 1941: 'In the period from 18 October to 2 November some 4,500 Jews were evacuated in Berlin. A further 1000 dwellings were thereby released and made available by the General Inspector of Buildings.'

'Did you take part in carrying out the evacuation?' prosecuting attorney Jackson asked Speer at Nuremberg.

'No,' replied Speer.

On 28 June 1940, three days after the armistice with France, Hitler with Albert Speer and the sculptor Arno Breker ('my professor'), arrived at Le Bourget airport in Paris. The victors wanted to see the sights in the capital of their traditional enemy, France. Hitler was heard saying that for him it was the fulfilment of a lifetime's dream.

He did not want to share this pleasure with his military commanders, but with his artists. Speer and the sculptor Breker were at Hitler's side when he visited the Opéra and stopped off on the way at the Sacré-Coeur and the Eiffel Tower. He paid his respects to Napoleon in Les Invalides. Paris was 'done' in three-and-a-half hours – from 5.30 a.m. to 9 a.m.

At the Arc de Triomphe the hectic pace of the tour slowed down a little. So that is what it looked like: the structure which Hitler and Speer planned to reduce to a mere plaything when compared with their version. The building of Berlin's own Triumphal Arch could now be put in motion. Back in 1925 Hitler had made some sketches of it, which he later made a gift of to Speer. From the sketches the Inspectorate of Buildings created a 4 metre (13 ft) high model which was presented to Hitler on his fiftieth birthday (20 April 1939) – to celebrate his victory in a war which would only begin four months later!

Hitler had originally considered having Paris destroyed. But now the conquered city was to be preserved, so that it might appear small and pitiful beside Speer's new Berlin. While still in Paris the architect's patron decreed:

> Berlin must . . . as quickly as possible be given the appearance to which the greatness of our victory entitles it. I see in the realization of this building assignment, which is now the most important in the Reich, the most significant contribution to the ultimate guarantee of our victory.

For this purpose, Hitler decreed, the General Inspector of Buildings should be 'given every support he requires'.

Speer, who would later insist that he was far from happy about all this, set about his task. How he did so is revealed in a rare flash of frankness in his 'annals' of the year 1941:

> On Saturday 1 March the Führer visits the model-building rooms on Pariser Platz. In the company of Schelkes, Herr Speer showed him the new models of the Great Hall and the buildings along the Grand Avenue, which were declared to be ready for construction.

While the boss was on a skiing holiday at Zürs in the Austrian Arlberg, his officials placed orders in Norway and Sweden for 20 million cubic metres of granite. In the middle of the war! In April *Reichsmarschall* Göring paid a visit: 'He was particularly pleased with the model of the Reich Marshall's Office. For the world's largest stairway Breker was to sculpt a memorial statue of the General Inspector of Buildings.'

The Speer annals report of this discussion,

that the Reich Marshall, on taking his leave very warmly, remarked how fortunate it was that Germany had been granted at the same time both a great Führer and a great architect. Speer replied that there had been great architects throughout history, and that while there was no lack of able architects, there had unfortunately been too few patrons with the necessary generosity and energy. The Reich Marshall nonetheless stood by what he had said.

On 12 May Speer had a discussion with the Führer at the Obersalzberg about future processions on the Grand Avenue. The access roads were too narrow:

Herr Speer then suggested that the processions should take place from north to south. The Führer said he was in agreement with this. Only when troops returned from a campaign would the marches proceed from south to north, through 'Project T'.

In August 1941, when the Russian campaign had been raging for two months, 'Herr Speer stated his intention to place some 30 of the heaviest captured artillery-pieces between the South Rail Station and 'Project T' and some particular large pieces in the station itself. He also intended to place similar weapons at further points along the Grand Avenue. And in particular, large captured Russian tanks were to be positioned outside important public buildings.'

'Project T' was the cover-name for the Triumphal Arch. On its account 500 allotment gardens had already been bulldozed, a measure which could make a man very unpopular in Berlin.

Among the Berliners, who were suffering more and more from the consequences of the war, there was no love lost for the useless building-schemes of the General Inspectorate.

On 4 September the Speer annals noted:

Herr Speer gave Chief Planning Officer Stephan the job of drafting the script for a film about the planning of the Reich capital. It was particular important to show evidence of how necessary the new planning is, not only aesthetically but also in the general public interest, and what benefits will arise from it for all concerned.

In December Speer displayed his anger over the fact that Göring, who was in charge of the deployment of Russian prisoners-of-war, was not giving due attention in this 'to the measures for redesigning the Reich capital': 'Herr Speer once again made this the subject of a discussion with the Führer and obtained his agreement that 30,000 Soviet POWs should immediately be put to work in the Berlin area.'

Thus ended the year in which Speer claims to have expressed so much criticism, because he feared that Hitler and his commanders might be gambling away the victory. What, one might ask, if the architect had already been the armaments minister? But the Minister for Weaponry and Munitions was Dr Fritz Todt, a National Socialist from the earliest days and a devoted follower of Hitler. It was his '*Organisation Todt*' that had built the autobahns and the Westwall frontier defences.

Todt, however, believed the war on two fronts against Russia and now, since December 1941, against the United Sates, was a national catastrophe. He knew very well that the Reich, with its limited resources, would lose the race against time. On several occasions he urged Hitler to conclude a peace before the tide of history began to flow against Germany. But the warlord turned a deaf ear to his entreaties.

Again, on 7 February 1942, Todt visited the Führer at his eastern headquarters, the 'Wolf's Lair', and tried to convince him of the seriousness of the situation. When he left, he knew his efforts had been in vain. Next morning Todt boarded an aircraft for Berlin. Moments after take-off it crashed. The cause was never explained. It is probable that the despairing Todt had blown himself up in the air. A few days later Hitler appointed Albert Speer as 'Dr Todt's successor in all his functions'.

> By that time I had of course been a member of Hitler's 'court' for several years. But it is impossible to describe how everything suddenly changed. In particular it was our relationship, naturally, which changed from the moment of my new appointment. In the years when I had simply been his architect, the relationship had not just been warm but thoroughly intimate – I mean, as intimate as any relationship with him could be – but from that morning of 8 February 1942 his manner towards me was cold and remote. The informality and of course the light-heartedness disappeared completely.
>
> *Speer, in 1979, on his appointment as head of the Organisation Todt and Reich Minister for Armaments and Munitions*

'The success of our work is critical for Germany's victory. I have promised the Führer to devote all my strength to this goal alone . . .' With these impressive words Albert Speer, at just thirty-seven years of age, took up a post for which, as he himself stated, he brought only two essential prerequisites with him: his organizing ability and his unconditional loyalty to Hitler. As to the 'armaments miracle' which Speer promised his chief on his first ministerial visit, as to the 'self-policing of industry', as to the production figures for guns, tanks, aircraft and U-boats, Speer has written and spoken repeatedly and at length.

> He was beside himself with joy. He was triumphant: the world belonged to him.
>
> *Annemarie Kempf, Speer's secretary, on Speer's appointment as Head of the Organisation Todt*

Speer had very little to say when asked later 'what I knew about the persecution, transportation and annihilation of the Jews'. He replied as much to himself as to others: 'Whether I knew or did not know, and how much or how little I knew, becomes unimportant when I think of what horrors I ought to have known about . . .' That may sound very honest, but is no more than sophistry. Speer concludes from this: 'I can no longer give an answer.' What Speer had never even asked himself was: how great was his involvement in all these crimes?

On 30 March 1943 Speer visited Mauthausen, a notorious concentration-camp in Austria, not far from the city of Linz. It was there that Simon Wiesenthal survived until his liberation. What was Speer doing there? The prisoners were worked to death mainly in a quarry which was reached by a 'path of death' hewn out of the rock. The quarry belonged to the *Deutsche Erd- und Steinwerke GmbH* (German Earth and Stone Works Co.). The owner of this 'business' was the SS.

Günter Wackernagel was an 'employee' of this firm. As a communist he was arrested in 1937 and dragged off to the Sachsenhausen concentration-camp just outside Berlin. In 1939 work began on clearing a site right next to the camp for the *Deutsche Erd- und Steinwerke*, on which were erected a clinker-brick factory and a stone-dressing plant for the 'Führer's buildings'. For transporting the materials to Berlin the SS had their own docks built on the nearby canal.

He was so arrogant. Some of the top dogs would talk to us, even Göring. But Speer never did.
  Rochus Misch, radio-operator in the Führer Bunker

The correspondence and supply contracts between the SS and officials of the General Inspectorate of Buildings have been preserved and can be seen in the Berlin State Archives. Late in 1941 a special labour-force, the *Arbeitskommando Speer*, was formed in the camp. 'Any prisoners who had anything to do with building were to be drafted into it,' Wackernagel tells us, 'but especially stonemasons. Prisoners were expected to volunteer for this trade.'

In this way 10,000 inmates from the Sachsenhausen camp hoped to escape from their wretched conditions. They were transferred to another branch of the SS firm, the Flossenbürg concentration-camp in northern Bavaria, east of Nuremberg. Only briefly was their labour required in the quarry for Speer's Nuremberg buildings. Very soon they had to start dynamiting tunnels in mountain ranges right across Europe, for Speer's underground factories and Hitler's command-posts. 'For five months on end we couldn't even have a bath,' recalls Günter Wackernagel, prisoner no. 1245. 'Changing our underwear was out of the question. We didn't just have lice, the lice had *us*. And we had epidemics in the camp; typhus and typhoid.' Of the original 10,000 'volunteers' in the *Arbeitskommando Speer*, only 200 survived.

So Speer's visit to Mauthausen was as a business client. However, what he saw there prompted him in 1943 to write a letter to 'Dear Party-colleague Himmler':

> While we lack not only steel and timber but also manpower for the immediate requirement of expanding defensive works at the Front, on the occasion of my tour of the Mauthausen concentration-camp I could not help noticing that the SS is working to a regime which, under today's conditions, appears to me to be over-generous.

Dr Flächsner: On your visit to Mauthausen or on some other occasion did you learn anything about the atrocities which took place there and in other concentration-camps?

Speer: No.

Speer under cross-examination at Nuremberg, 19 June 1946

Speer demanded from the SS that they 'devise a more sensible deployment of available manpower in the concentration-camps in the framework of the overall armaments programme' – for example, in the construction of defensive lines (what that means has been described by Wackernagel; we will later learn about the '*Dora/Mittelbau*' example). Speer then reached this conclusion:

> We must therefore draw up new plans for the expansion of the concentration-camps, with a view to achieving the highest level of efficiency using the minimum resources, with the objective of maximum success in meeting the *current* demand for war materials. This means that we must immediately switch to a very crude method of building.

Following on from this Speer assigned 'one of my people, . . . to make on-the-spot inspections of all the concentration-camps'.

Speer's letter provoked outrage in the SS. *Obergruppenführer* Oswald Pohl, responsible for labour deployment in the camps, sent a confidential memo to Himmler's office. The letter was 'pretty rich', Pohl ranted. Speer, he pointed out, 'fails to mention that every building-project in the concentration-camps has been reported by us in accordance with orders and that he himself issued the approval on 2.2.1943'.

So Speer not only knew of the existence of all the concentration-camps, he was responsible for all the building that went on in them, as Pohl tells us, 'in detail'! 'It is, however, completely mistaken,' Pohl goes on, 'to suggest that we switch immediately to crude building methods in the camps.' In contrast to Speer, the SS man puts in a plea for more humanity. He complains that his men

> are constantly fighting against disease and high mortality, because the accommodation of the inmates, including sanitary arrangements, is wholly inadequate. I am therefore duty bound to point out here and now that the switch to crude building-methods will probably cause a hitherto unseen level of mortality in the camps.

Speer's inspectors, Desch and Sander, had by now returned from their tour of Himmler's concentration-camps. The reports they submitted to Speer have not survived. But they prompted Speer to write once again to his 'dear Party-colleague', but this time with a hand-written postscript: 'I am glad that the survey of the other camps produced a thoroughly positive picture.'

Only for the expansion of Auschwitz did the Reich Minister permit a special shipment of building materials and water-pipes, over and above the approved quantities. When Speer later wrote and spoke about Auschwitz, he simply saw his guilt as 'deliberate blindness' and 'approval through ignorance'.

> But you lot joined in all that stupid anti-Semitism without protest! I remember you telling me in 1938 that you had asked Himmler to set up brick-works at Oranienburg [concentration-camp] for the rebuilding of Berlin, and I remember how, with the cold-bloodedness with which you dealt with moral problems, you quite calmly said: 'Even back in ancient Egypt the enslaved Yids made bricks!'
>
> *Hermann Speer to his brother Albert, 1973*

On 5 June 1943, only a few days after Speer's letter to Himmler, Speer and Goebbels jointly staged a rally in front of 'armaments workers' in the Berlin Palace of Sport. The event was broadcast on radio. Speer spoke first and reported on the successes of his 'total war economy': 'The Führer expects that for us at home no sacrifice will be too great when it comes to forging new weapons for the soldiers at the Front.' This would be 'a decisive contribution to the achievement of ultimate victory'. Goebbels then followed him on to the rostrum, while Speer sat in the front row of the audience:

> Faced with the worldwide threat from Jewry, sentimental feelings have no place . . . The complete removal of Jewry from Europe is not a question of morality, it is a question of the security of nations. The Jew will always act according to his nature and his racial instinct. He can do no other. Just as the Colorado-beetle destroys potato-fields, indeed *must* destroy

them, so does the Jew destroy nations and peoples. Against this there is but one remedy: drastic eradication of the danger.

Was it now of any significance to know whether Speer was present at Himmler's 'Final Solution' speech in Poznan, Poland, on 6 October 1943, or whether he left shortly beforehand, as he claimed?

In his minutes of the armaments conference in the Führer's headquarters on 22 August 1943 Speer noted:

> The Führer orders, on the basis of a proposal, that all measures be taken in order to push on, jointly with the *Reichsführer-SS*, and by deploying more manpower from the concentration-camps, with the building of the necessary production facilities and with the actual production of the A4.

Hitler ordered 'production at secure locations and in a secure manner through the use of caves'.

The Führer expects of us that no sacrifice for our homeland is too great, when it comes to forging new weapons for our front line. We vow to our soldiers at the front not only to continue doing our duty but to put the utmost effort into our work and to raise our output continuously month by month.

Speer, 1943

On 10 December 1943 the Reich Minister for Armaments and Munitions visited what was then his most important building-site: the subterranean factory known as '*Dora/Mittelbau*' near the small town of Nordhausen in the Harz Mountains. Since the end of August thousands of concentration-camp inmates had been working on extending and rebuilding a system of more than 12 miles of underground bunkers. It was here that, at the end of the year, the first 'miracle weapons', the V1 pilotless flying bomb and the V2 ballistic missile (then still designated as A4), were to go into series production.

During the construction phase the prisoners had to live and work in damp caves that were permanently filled with dust. Alexander Samila (prisoner no. 28831) from the Ukraine describes the conditions at the end of 1943:

> There was continual drilling and shot-blasting. The lights in the tunnel were never switched off. The prisoners were beaten for any trivial offence. If you tried to get some sleep down there you couldn't, because some other guy was screaming. It was always 25 strokes with a rubber truncheon. I was lucky. I only got seven beatings the whole time I was there.

Visitors to the memorial there today are told that at least 23,000 prisoners lost their lives in the period between October 1943 and March 1944. When the machinery for rocket production was installed, the situation of the remaining 20,000 prisoners improved a little: they were now 'allowed' to sleep in barracks at the tunnel entrance, as inside the mountain every spare inch was needed for the rockets.

There was one evening which Leon Pilarski from Bromberg in Poland can never forget:

> We were just going into the tunnel for the night-shift, when we were ordered to go to the assembly-area. There was a string orchestra playing there. Then the SS brought on 30 men; all had their mouths covered with sticking-plaster. They were all hanged in front of our eyes.

They had infringed some regulation or other.

One of those who had to work for twelve hours a day in the rocket galleries was Ewald Hanstein, prisoner no. 74557.

> The Nazis still hoped to win the war with this weapon. That's why they shoved everything they could on to the prisoners. The ones who couldn't take it were shot, or else shipped off – back to the other camps. Then a new batch of prisoners was ordered. No one who was not there can have any idea of what went on.

To my mind 'Dora' was a death-camp, where people died from overwork. Anyone who couldn't work ended in the crematorium. We were maltreated until we were finished. For example, there was almost no water. Sometimes they gave us salt herring to eat, and we got dreadfully thirsty. There was only one water-tap for all those prisoners, so most never got to it. Anyone who fought for a place and drank a lot then got dysentery. The food was often stale and mouldy. Many, whose resistance was lower, died. We were often beaten. There was little hope and everyone wondered: 'When am I going to die?'

Alexander Samila, concentration-camp victim

Ewald Hanstein survived three camps including Auschwitz. 'For me Dora was the worst camp. People there were worked until they dropped dead.'

The fact that Speer personally inspected this camp was not known to the investigators at Nuremberg. Speer was able to lie to the court without contradiction. It was only the investigation prior to the 'Dora Trial', at which Speer was obliged to testify in 1968, that brought the truth to light.

In his memoirs published in 1969 in Germany (and in English the following year) Speer described 'the conditions for these prisoners' as 'barbaric indeed'. His biographer Gitta Sereny noted that 'in his entire life he had never been so appalled'. Speer claimed that the same day he put everything in motion to have a proper barrack camp erected.

In the final years Speer was certainly the most powerful man after Hitler. As head of the entire war production he was conscious of his power. He made very sure that his prominent position was respected too. Basically, he was a courteous and obliging man, but when it came to power, he could get very tough.

Willy Schelkes, one of Speer's architects

Speer was unable to produce documentary evidence of any humanitarian reasons for his action – but we can have no doubt that the Minister for Armaments was very anxious not to endanger the output of this highly important production facility through disease and consequent down-time. No less significant was the fact that some of the Third Reich's leading scientists and engineers were regular visitors to 'Dora'.

Since the late 1930s German rockets had been tested at Peenemünde, on the Baltic island of Usedom. Speer had known the development team, headed by Wernher von Braun, since 1939. The two men got on well. In 1942 Speer succeeded in arousing Hitler's interest in this new type of weapon.

On 7 July 1943, at the 'Wolf's Lair', Speer showed Hitler a colour film of the launch of a V2 rocket missile – with the hoped-for result: 'The Führer has decided that work on the A4 [i.e. V2] is to proceed with all urgency. He considers this measure to be decisive for the outcome of the war,' the armaments minister noted.

Originally Speer favoured the development of ground-to-air missiles. They were small, cheap and were urgently needed to combat the ever faster and higher flying Allied bombers. However, he knew that Hitler's enthusiasm could only be aroused by weapons of aggression. 'The Führer stresses,' the ministerial archive of 13/14 October 1942 tell us, 'that this development only makes sense if initially at least 5,000 missiles are simultaneously made available for mass-deployment.'

Speer was now certainly acting as an 'architect of armaments' but his relationship with Hitler had changed since the time when both men were immersed in plans and models for new buildings. The reason for this was obvious: Hitler had been a soldier in the First World War, whereas everything in Speer's life, manner and appearance marked him out as a non-combatant. 'He always looked like a civilian dressed up in uniform,' is how Hitler's Secretary, Traudl Junge, described him.

So it was that in the middle of war and war-production the Minister continued to meet his colleagues at the General Inspectorate of Buildings. There he could speak openly. Willi Schelkes remembers a conversation one evening over a bottle of red wine:

When he was just an architect, he was on the same level as Hitler. They could talk to each other on the same level on a subject which interested them both – architecture. Now he was a cabinet member and Hitler was in charge, and even Speer had to take instructions from him, which he wasn't used to. So then he complained that he was being treated quite differently from how he had been before.

Nonetheless Hitler took every opportunity to heap praise and appreciation on his Armaments Minister. Late in 1943 the word went round among Hitler's entourage that Speer had ambitions to succeed Hitler. In his memoirs Speer delights in describing how Hitler would reply to his '*Heil, mein Führer!*' with '*Heil, Speer!*'

I believe that very early on he ceased to believe in victory, but dutifully did everything he possibly could toward achieving it. I also believe that for him Stalingrad was the decisive moment, when he realised that the tide had turned against Germany.

Willy Schelkes, one of Speer's architects

But to the 'old campaigners' in the Party Speer lacked the true 'smell of the stable'. They saw him as no more than an ambitious arriviste. Here was a man who had the audacity to threaten them openly, at the *Gauleiter* conference on 6 October 1943 in Poznan, that they would get the 'Himmler treatment' if they did not turn all civilian plants in their *Gaue* over to arms production within two weeks.

The manufacture of refrigerators or radio-sets, Speer barked at the top men in the Nazi regime,

is the manufacture of products whose only purpose is bribery. These products are today being reserved for all sorts of prominent people, admittedly not as gifts, but for private purchase . . . But an article which is no longer generally available, . . . is, as far as I am concerned, given the present situation, something to be used for bribery. I have asked *Reichsführer-SS* Himmler to make the SD available for searching out products of this kind . . .

In January 1944 Speer became seriously ill for three months, and the Party bigwigs did everything they could to badmouth him with Hitler. When Speer then started thinking aloud about resignation, Hitler dispatched an emissary to mollify him: 'Tell Speer I'm fond of him!' were the words with which the Führer sent the Luftwaffe chief Erhard Milch on his way.

After the 20 July attempt on Hitler's life Speer himself spoke to the Führer. He was protecting his ministries from attack, since staff who were not Party members were suspected of being involved in 20 July. Speer told him: 'We are professionals, we are not tied to any party; we do the best we can for the German people. We had nothing to do with 20 July.'

Manfred von Poser, Speer's Adjutant

Hitler may have had an inkling that without the organizing capacity of his Minister it would not be possible to continue this insane war for much longer:

I would really like to say here, Speer, without wanting to sing hymns of praise, that you and Herr Saur [Speer's Deputy] have achieved miracles; that in spite of the air raids, in spite of the continuous need to take evasive action, again and again you and your employees in industry have made it possible to find new ways to keep going!

'Without my work the war would perhaps have been lost in 1942–43,' wrote Speer in his last letter to Hitler. He was Hitler's 'minister for holding out'.

As early as February or March 1943, as Speer admitted to his American interrogators just after the war ended, he had 'taken the view that the war was lost'. In May 1944, when a new Adjutant named Manfred von Poser was assigned to the Minister, Speer's first question to him was whether the war could still be won.

Von Poser decribes this unexpected situation:

> For a moment I was quite taken aback. But then I pulled myself together and said: "I don't believe the war is winnable now." He took this answer calmly and said nothing. I gathered from this that he liked to hear the truth, and that was the basis between us, which lasted the whole way through.

Wherever Speer made an appearance in the last year of the war, he mobilized efforts that had become pointless. He devised 'keep-it-up' slogans, which he later said were the result of 'a particular kind of mental aberration'.

The 'miracle weapons', production of which had started at the 'Dora' plant in the spring of 1944, were what Speer chiefly threw into the propaganda battle. In early July he suggested to Hitler that the well-known camera-man, Walter Frentz, should be asked to film the test-launches of the V2 rocket. Hitler agreed but at the same time ordered that in any public showing of the film the launching-structure should not be recognizable – which amounted to complete censorship.

Speer was therefore only able to show the film to a small group of people. Goebbels, who was one of them, was thrilled. 'If only we could show this film in every cinema in Germany, I wouldn't need to make another speech or write another article . . .'

But as it was, Goebbels had to go on writing – and Speer had to make more speeches. The scripts of those speeches were not to be found among the papers which Speer handed over to the Allied investigators at the end of the war. However, a tape-recording of one of them has been preserved. Speer stated before the Nuremberg Tribunal that he had actively opposed the 'miracle weapon' propaganda, yet on 5 December 1944 (at a time when the Americans had already captured the German border city of Aachen!) he made a speech to railway workers, which was relayed on radio:

> Our reprisal weapons V1 and V2 will have demonstrated unmistakably to the world that in spite of everything German

arms technology has a clear lead. I can assure you that the
enemy is in for similar surprises from us in other areas of
warfare.

Then Speer came to the subject which most concerned those on
the bomb-shattered home front – the impotence of the German
anti-aircraft defences:

> Here too we have operated successfully up to now and, I may
> say, as continues to be the case in some key areas, have operated
> in silence. I can assure you that in quality and quantity of the
> necessary means of defence we have today once more reached a
> position which, in the near future, will be recognizable from its
> visible successes. [Loud applause] . . . We know that at the end
> of this road lies victory.

Those were the words of a man who, months before this speech in
memoranda to Hitler, repeatedly reached the conclusion that
following the destruction of Germany's oil-refineries, 'we lack the
resources necessary for carrying on a modern war'. By now the
Luftwaffe could count on less then 10 per cent of the fuel it
needed!

'The useless continuation of the war and the needless
devastation will make reconstruction more difficult. The German
people are beset by privation and misery.' This statement was
made by Speer in his closing words to the Nuremberg Tribunal on
31 August 1946. He went on: 'After this trial [the German
people] will despise and condemn Hitler as the demonstrable
author of their misfortune.'

As for his own responsibility for having prolonged and
organized Hitler's war to the bitter end, long after it had been lost
– he had nothing to say.

> I agreed with him one hundred per cent. If we could no
> longer believe in Hitler, what were we left with?
>
> *Speer on the last years with Hitler*

At the beginning of August 1944 Hitler's henchmen gathered for the last time in Poznan Castle for a 'conference of *Reichsleiter* and *Gauleiter*'. The Russians were already in East Prussia, British and American troops were marching on Paris. It was the gathering dusk, the *Götterdämmerung*, of the Third Reich. Himmler took the floor: 'We all have but one ambition: that when world history makes its judgement on these times, . . . it will say of us and of his [Hitler's] followers: his champions were loyal, they were obedient, they kept the faith, they stood firm . . .'

This time – and not even Speer disputed it – he was present. And eight weeks later a telegram arrived on the *Reichsführer*'s desk, addressed to 'Dear Party-comrade Himmler'. It read: 'You may be sure that, in the difficult events that lie ahead of us, I will always remain bound by loyalty to you. Heil Hitler! Yours, Speer.'

But by this time Speer no longer had any intention of meeting a glorious end with the other 'paladins'. An article in the British Sunday newspaper, the *Observer*, encouraged him to perform a dangerous balancing-act. The anonymous journalist wrote:

In Speer is the very epitome of the managerial revolution. . . . He might have joined any other political party which gave him a job and a career. . . . He symbolizes a type which is becoming increasingly important in all belligerent countries: the pure technician. . . . This is their age; the Hitlers and Himmlers we may get rid of, but the Speers, whatever happens to this particular man, will long be with us.

People were mostly brought to Treblinka by train, but the Jews from neighbouring towns and villages were brought on trucks. The trucks were marked: 'Expedition Speer' [Speer Dispatch Department].
Samuel Rajzman, survivor of the Treblinka death-camp, 1946

Speer knew of this article and it seemed to be giving him a broad hint. He now set about building the bridge that he hoped would carry him into a prosperous future. He was not yet forty years old.

The 'Thousand Year Reich' was not to be the only thing in his life.

The (western) victors would not approach Speer empty-handed. Unlike the Eastern Front, where the Wehrmacht destroyed everything as they retreated, the Armaments Minister blocked any 'scorched earth' policy, first in Italy, then also in France and Belgium. His Adjutant, Manfred von Poser, described the ruses with which Speer sold the idea to Hitler.

> That was Speer's skill; he could get through to Hitler. He told him – and this was what he most liked to hear – that when he reconquered those territories their industries would have to be put back on their feet, so now they should only be crippled, not destroyed. And he agreed.

Crippling often meant no more than removing fuses or cutting fuel-pipes. This was a symbolic action intended to be noted by those on the other side of the front line.

However, on his own side he demanded a 'fanatically growing belief' in final victory and more and more 'last sacrifices'. As the cities burned and old men and boys were thrown into the slaughter, Speer intoned: 'No matter how difficult the situation and how hopeless the chances of improving it may at first seem – we must on no account tire.'

Brave words for those at the Front. Behind the lines in those last months his actions were intended to prevent the destruction of German industry. He promised this on 27 February to a small group of Ruhr industrialists, at Landsberg Castle, the seat of the Thyssen family. This too was an investment in the future – a future in which Speer saw himself as a kind of 'minister of reconstruction' in post-war Germany.

When Hitler attempted to frustrate these plans with his 'Nero order' of 18 March, Speer was 'furious, genuinely furious', his Adjutant von Poser tells us. He travelled to Berlin to see Hitler and demanded the withdrawal of the destruction order: 'I can only continue to work intelligently and with my conviction and belief in the future, if you, *mein Führer*, declare your faith, as before, in the preservation of our national strength.'

Speer threatened his Führer with resignation. In those days

many thousands received the death penalty for refusing to obey orders or for openly criticizing Hitler. However, Speer was received in the Reich Chancellery. Once again he had to swear allegiance to the Führer who was 'fond of him'. But in return for this Hitler gave Speer a free hand until the very last days.

> To the extent that Hitler gave me orders and I carried them out, I bear the responsibility for this; but I certainly did not carry out all his orders.
>
> *Speer at Nuremberg, 1946*

What was he to do now? Was this a 'leave-taking' or was he 'putting himself at the disposal' of Hitler? Of the many riddles which Speer poses, his trip to Berlin on 23 April 1945 is one of the most fascinating. One thing is certain: after Hitler's final birthday in the catacombs of the Führer-Bunker, Speer – like almost all the top Nazis – made his way out of Berlin. There followed a two-day odyssey to northern Germany. Then on 23 April he showed up in Mecklenburg, at the Luftwaffe's test centre in Rechlin. Everyone there knew him; he had acted as host at countless air displays. The Armaments Minister and his Adjutant chartered a small, twin-engined 'Fieseler Storch' aircraft.

They flew back to Berlin and landed on the 'East–West Axis', between the Victory Columns and the Brandenburg Gate. Six years earlier Speer had converted the road for Hitler's parades; now it served as an airstrip for the encircled capital. 'As far as I can see, Speer must have had a good reason for flying to Berlin,' Manfred von Poser tells us. In the last year of the war he saw more of the Minister at close quarters than anyone else; he drove thousands of miles with him, latterly just to the rear of the retreating Front:

> It is my opinion that there must have been something behind it all, that made him think the flight was necessary. One possibility could be that he was worried about being appointed Hitler's successor. That would have been an additional burden for him,

either because of the way the Allies would judge him, or because it would later take him away from the job of rebuilding Germany, which at the time was what he still hoped for.

The fear of being nominated as successor – was this what drove Speer back to the Reich Chancellery, to what he later described as 'the ruins of his life'? The exploit paid off: it was to Admiral Dönitz, not to Speer, that Hitler bequeathed responsibility for the nation he had led to its ruin. There is no mention whatever of Speer in Hitler's will.

Had Speer not flown to Berlin, Hitler would certainly have included his top technocrat in the list of a new cabinet – and perhaps even designated him as his successor. At least that poisoned chalice was not passed to him.

Initially Speer took the blame on himself – whether for publicity reasons or out of actual remorse, I do not know. In fact, he scarcely had a choice. Later, however, he took the wise precaution of very cleverly pushing on to Sauckel all the guilt for atrocities against foreign workers, for enslavement, murder and so on. Sauckel was a crude, rather simple man whom everyone loathed. Speer, on the other hand was educated and from a good family. I think these undercurrents came out in the press and were not lost on the judges either.
Susanne von Paczensky, observer at the Nuremberg Trial

A year later Albert Speer was the only one of the principal defendants before the Nuremberg Tribunal who accepted an 'overall responsibility' for the deeds of the man to whom he had sold his soul. However, he maintained to the end of his life that he knew nothing about the crimes committed by the regime.

The court sentenced Albert Speer to twenty years' imprisonment. In 1966 he was a free man. He died in London in 1981.

CHAPTER SIX

THE SUCCESSOR: KARL DÖNITZ

KNOPP/MÜLLNER

Attack – let 'em have it – sink 'em.

It is sheer nonsense to try and say that an enlisted man
or an officer should be non-political.

Had we not been given a Führer, there would be
no one left in Germany.

We are all pretty sorry specimens compared to the Führer.

The armed forces must stick fanatically with the man
they have sworn allegiance to.

Anyone who expresses the slightest defeatism weakens the
nation's will to resist and consequently must be rooted out.

I would rather eat dirt than see my grandsons brought up in
the filthy Jewish mentality and poisoned by it.

I am and remain the legal head of state. Until the day I die.

Merely earning money is not a satisfying goal in life.

Dönitz

He works quickly and dependably. Expresses himself with ease
both verbally and on paper. Has a very lively mind and takes
an interest in all professional matters. Very ambitious and

anxious to stand out and make a reputation for himself; finds it difficult to be subordinate and to restrict himself to his own sphere of activity. He must, more than hitherto, allow the officers of the Admiralty Staff the independence they require. While he has a strong temperament and inner drive, he often appears restless and, for a man of his age, lacking in equanimity. Must be persuaded to take things more calmly and not to make excessive demands, especially on himself. His frequently apparent restlessness is probably in part attributable to his unstable health (stomach troubles).

Admiral Wilhelm Canaris in a report on Dönitz, 1931

Make no mistake, it will last a long time and we will be happy enough if it ends in a settlement.

Dönitz on the coming war, 1939

I would like to see how things would look in Germany without National Socialism, with dozens of political parties, full of Jews exploiting every opportunity to criticize, damage and fragment. We owe it all to the Führer; National Socialism has brought the German people everything. Therefore there is only one task for the serviceman: ruthless action in support of our Führer, in support of our National Socialism.

Dönitz, 1944

In a year at the latest, perhaps even this year, Europe will recognize that in Europe Adolf Hitler is the only statesman of any stature.

Dönitz, April 1945

To all commanding officers:
1. All attempts to rescue crews of ships sunk, even picking up swimmers and taking them aboard lifeboats, the righting of capsized lifeboats, and the issuing of food and water, must cease. Rescue goes against the most basic requirements of warfare, to destroy enemy ships and their crews.

2. The orders concerning the picking up of captains and chief engineers remain in force.
3. Shipwrecked seamen only to be rescued if they have information important for U-boats.
4. Be tough. Remember that in air-raids on German cities the enemy shows no mercy to women and children.

Orders from Dönitz, 1942

Our lives belong to the state. Our honour lies in doing our duty. None of us has the right to a private life. It is up to us to win this war. We have to pursue this goal with fanatical dedication and rock-hard determination to win.

Dönitz. 1943

When a sailor is given the order to fight, it doesn't matter a damn whether he thinks the fighting serves any purpose or not.

Dönitz, 1944

Since surrender must in any case mean the destruction of Germany's national resources, it is right from this point of view as well that we go on fighting.

Dönitz, 1945

We in the Navy know what we have to do. Our military duty, which we fulfil unerringly, whatever may be going on to our left and right and all around us, makes us stand like a rock of resistance, bold, hard and true. Anyone who does not act like that is scum; he should be strung up with a sign round his neck saying: 'Here hangs a traitor, who through low cowardice has contributed to the death of German women and children, instead of protecting them like a man.'

Dönitz, April 1945

The most important thing is this: we have to guard with the utmost zeal the finest and best thing that National Socialism has given us, the solidarity of our national community. Despite today's complete military collapse our nation looks very different from the way it did in 1918. It has not been torn apart. Even though we ourselves may abolish many aspects of National Socialism and many other aspects may be abolished by our opponents, nevertheless the best element of National Socialism, the community of our people, must be preserved under all circumstances.

Dönitz, 9 May 1945

I believed that Germany was taking the right path.
Dönitz in 1958, on the Nazis' seizure of power

* * *

It was 8 May 1946: a breathless hush hung over courtroom 600 in Nuremberg's Palace of Justice. The defendant stepped up to the microphone, stood to attention and then declared in the precise and calm tones of a man who was displaying a sense of duty rather than showing remorse: 'I acted according to my conscience. I would have to do exactly the same again.'

Later, people would call him 'the Devil's Admiral'. But this emotional epithet could not be less appropriate to Karl Dönitz, the man who acted out of cool conviction. How does one do justice to someone who carried in himself both good and evil? The man who rescued over 2 million refugees from the east? The cold technocrat of a murderous war? To the victorious Allies, there was no doubt at all that he was first and foremost a war-criminal – a man who waged a pitiless war with 'his' U-boats, who caused the deaths of 30,000 Allied seamen and three out of every four German U-boat Captains; a man who as late as 30 April 1945 sent a telegram to Adolf Hitler expressing devotion to an absurd degree:

My loyalty to you will always be inalienable. . . . If destiny compels me to lead the German Reich as the successor designated by you, I will conduct this war to its end in the way that the uniquely heroic struggle of the German people demands.

Not until the following day, on 1 May 1945, did the Grand Admiral learn of Hitler's death. Now he officially took up the office which would thrust him into the spotlight of world publicity at Nuremberg. He was now Hitler's successor – the executor of the ruined 'Thousand Year Reich'. Only twenty-three days remained for his attempt to 'rule' as head of state. Dönitz, as always, did what he was ordered to do, and he showed every sign of a clear conscience, although he must have known how murderous was the regime at whose head he finally stood. Dönitz was both an accessory and a perpetrator. However, he never saw himself as anything but a 'non-political serviceman'. He claimed he had obediently done his duty and nothing more. Dönitz – a servant-figure?

The roots of this authoritarian cast of mind stretch back to his childhood in Berlin at the turn of the twentieth century. Dönitz' mother died when Karl was four years old. His father, an engineer, brought up his two sons alone and preached obedience as the first commandment. Service to one's Kaiser and Fatherland was considered the primary duty in the Dönitz household. Personal happiness came a very poor second. Even as a child and still more as a youth, Karl Dönitz came to know what was meant by Prussian discipline and military drill. He was considered reserved but versatile; and he shared the enthusiasm of the masses for the Imperial fleet, the pride of an adolescent German nation which was impatiently pushing for a 'place in the sun'.

In this atmosphere of overweening national arrogance he made the decision to serve as an officer in the Imperial Navy. His career ambition matched the spirit of a restless age. To be an officer on one of His Majesty's battleships was a guarantee of the highest prestige and furthermore was the ideal way, as he wrote in his memoirs, to combine his 'leaning towards a life in the forces', with 'an urge to see distant parts'. On 1 April 1910 the eighteen-year-old Karl Dönitz' dream of a service life at sea was fulfilled. In the very first lessons at the Mürwik Naval College near Flensburg, the instructors swore the young cadet to abide by the elite class ethos of the Navy: 'Attitude' and 'impeccable behaviour' were as important a duty as 'decency' and the vow to do nothing that 'offended against the moral principle of good conduct'. Here in the massive redbrick buildings of the Mürwik Naval College began the career of Karl Dönitz. It was here that it would also end.

Drab theorizing had never interested Dönitz. He longed for action, for service on the high seas and the comradeship of a crew – a desire which grew greater when, in the summer of 1912, his father died. After the death of his mother, his father had been his only security. In search of a substitute, for a paternal friend who would support and encourage him, he met *Kapitänleutnant* (Senior Lieutenant) von Loewenfeld, his idol and mentor. Von Loewenfeld had requested that the aspiring officer be assigned to his ship, the light cruiser *Breslau*. 'Are you pleased?' he asked Dönitz.

'No, sir, I'm not at all pleased. I wanted to go to the Far East with the cruiser squadron!'

Loewenfeld liked the young midshipman's forthright manner. True, he called him an 'ungrateful toad', but did not mean it seriously. Friendship prevailed and Dönitz' resentment was anyway quickly allayed when contrary to expectations the *Breslau* set course for distant seas. The dream of journeys to foreign lands was finally coming true. Dönitz had the opportunity to prove himself on the high seas. He carried out his duties as Signals Officer to von Loewenfeld's complete satisfaction and completed his training with the mark of 'excellent' – a rare assessment which in naval regulations was reserved only for outstanding achievement. Not for the last time was Dönitz to be among the best in his class. The highest military praise runs like a scarlet thread through the personnel file on this Prussian, who even in his early years as a rising officer in the First World War, gained the reputation for extraordinary courage – a man who risked his life because he considered it his patriotic duty to do so.

When the First World War broke out, Dönitz saw his first action in the Mediterranean, on board the *Breslau*, which, together with the battle-cruiser *Goeben*, was to be placed under Turkish command. The ships were an inducement to bring the Ottoman Empire into the war on the side of the Central Powers. Until a decision was reached, the *Breslau* had to remain moored in harbour. The crew were condemned to idleness and it was Dönitz who suffered more than anyone during this 'time of inglorious waiting'.

The only welcome diversion was provided by a visit from the German commander of the Dardanelles fortifications, General Weber. Less than two years later Dönitz was again facing the much-decorated, monocle-wearing General, this time not as a junior officer but as a suitor for the hand of his daughter Ingeborg, who was working as a nurse in a field-hospital. The following year the couple went to the altar in Berlin.

His second great love was a new weapon: submarines offered a promise of fame and hope of victory in the war. They were the German Empire's last trump-card. After the stalemate of the Battle of Jutland, Berlin put in hand an extensive submarine-building programme, with the intention of bringing Britain to its knees through a blockade. In January 1917, as soon as he had completed his training-course in watchkeeping, Dönitz' rapid U-boat career was launched. His first commanding officer on U-39 was *Kapitänleutnant* Walter Forstmann – a U-boat ace and one of the war's most successful captains. Under his command, in the stuffy confines of a steel tube far below the surface, Dönitz first experienced the communal spirit and cohesion of a submarine crew. It was a crucial experience for the young officer which, ten years later, he looked back on with enthusiasm. His motto from then on was:

> One for all and all for one. We were one big family, completely isolated in the depths of the sea. That way a U-boat crew shares a common destiny, and there can be few things finer than that. To be a member of one is of the highest value and something you never forget.

Three months later in February 1918 he took over his first U-boat command, the UC 25 and felt by his own admission 'as mighty as a king'. Dönitz would be sure of the Kaiser's gratitude when, on a daring foray into enemy waters, he managed to penetrate the Italian naval base at Porta Augusta – a risky operation which earned Dönitz the coveted Knight's Cross of the Hohenzollern Order. He seemed to have a monopoly on success, and was given command of an even faster boat, the UB 68. But shortly after midnight on 4 October 1918, while attacking a British convoy, his luck deserted him. Fifty nautical miles off the coast of Sicily the UB 68 was forced to surface. After receiving a direct hit, Dönitz finally had to give the order to abandon ship. The submarine sank within seconds, dragging four crew members down with it. *Oberleutnant zur See* (Junior Lieutenant) Karl Dönitz and most of his comrades were picked up by the British warship, HMS *Snapdragon*. Her captain greeted his prisoner with a handshake and remarked laconically: 'Well, Captain, now we're quits. Tonight you blew one of my convoy ships out of the water and now I've sunk *you*.'

The first stage of his imprisonment was spent in Fort Verdalla camp on the island of Malta. It was hard for this dedicated seaman to get over the fact that the war had ended in such shame for him, and it was like a punch in the stomach when he read in British newspapers of the defeat of Germany and the collapse of the monarchy. His world had fallen apart and, as if that was not bad enough, it was mutinous sailors, of all people, who had triggered the revolution! On the streets of German cities there was anarchy. Upheaval, disorder, disobedience – it was Dönitz' worst nightmare. He recalled in his autobiography:

Only a few weeks earlier I had been fighting as a sailor, 'In my modest role I had my duty to do and it was not my job to worry about the broader political situation. Now I realized for the first time how things stood for Germany. My faith in the political wisdom of the men in government became uncertain. A change came over me.

On the voyage as a prisoner-of-war from Malta through the Mediterranean and then in a British camp near Sheffield, Dönitz was struck by 'what enormous superiority in material and forces [the Allies] could draw on in order to force us into submission'. However, in the prison-hut nicknamed 'Hohenzollern', among a group of fellow-officers loyal to the Kaiser, he cultivated the legend of the 'unvanquished army' that had been stabbed in the back by red revolutionaries.

Dönitz wanted at all costs to get back home. He pretended to be seriously ill, was briefly admitted to a mental hospital and then in the early summer of 1919 returned once more to Germany.

'The consideration weighed heavily with me,' he wrote later, 'that as a serving officer one could not abandon the German state, whatever form it had taken on. To do so would have gone against the German-Prussian principle of selfless service to the cause.'

For the new republic of President Ebert and his ilk, the returning warrior felt nothing but hate and abhorrence. Dönitz missed the old authoritarian certainties. The new freedoms seemed strange to him. Like other disillusioned servicemen, he swore: 'There must never be another November 1918!'

He had once gone to war for the Kaiser and his Empire. There was now nothing left of either. Wilhelm II lived in exile in Holland, and Dönitz saw himself surrounded by powerful enemies: at home the political opposition, headed by the Workers' and Soldiers' Councils, had plunged the country into violence, hunger and chaos; he felt the peace treaty to be a 'diktat of shame', since the German Navy was reduced to the strength of a mere 15,000 men. Although shortly after being taken prisoner Dönitz had announced he was 'finished with seagoing and with the Navy', and briefly toyed with the idea of taking up a civilian profession, he remained true to the sea. 'Merely earning money is not a satisfying goal in life,' he wrote. 'Man's ambition must be to carry out his duty decently.'

Dönitz served his Fatherland, not the system. He was still drawn to 'that unique U-boat comradeship'. For a while, however, that had disappeared. The Treaty of Versailles had categorically forbidden Germany to possess any U-boats. Its Navy was to consist of precisely six small battleships, six light cruisers, twelve destroyers and twelve torpedo-boats. But in a situation that was so discouraging for Dönitz, some glimmers of hope showed themselves very early on. In the summer of 1919 he was asked by *Korvettenkapitän* (Lieutenant-Commander) Otto Schultze whether he would go on serving; he replied with another question: 'Do you believe we'll soon have U-boats again?' Schultze retorted: 'I certainly do. Things are not going to stay as they are.'

The conversations with his old and his new superiors encouraged Dönitz to tackle a new assignment in Kiel with energy. The *Oberleutnant zur See* was now responsible for the selection of naval officers, a key position. As a convinced opponent of the republic he admitted no one into the officer corps who was not a loyal monarchist. True, that made no difference to the wretched material inadequacy of the Navy. The Imperial fleet, once the nation's pride, now lay at the bottom of the sea off Britain's Scapa Flow naval base: in order to save the 'honour of flag and nation' the German Navy had scuttled its own ships in the summer of 1919.

The new age held no promise for Dönitz. In the autumn of 1919 the political situation in Germany was becoming even more chaotic. The smell of civil war was in the air. Soldiers of the 'Red Army' fought to overthrow the government, and the 'democrats' looked on with approval as *Freikorps* brigades, like that of his mentor von Loewenstein, opened fire on insurgents.

Dönitz was sure that Germany would only be able to recover its former greatness when the 'age of system politics' had been overcome. He was driven by fears: fear of impoverishment, fear of the victory of the left-wing revolutionaries. Since the republic he detested seemed unable to bring calm and order, Dönitz saw this as a legitimate reason to declare war on it. 'We rejected the Marxist state,' he recalled in 1944, 'because it was a negation of our nation's military prowess and of everything the fighting man holds sacred.'

As early as March 1920 when mutinous army units tried to overturn the republic, the monarchists scented change in the air. Dönitz, by now in command of a torpedo-boat, also secretly hoped that the *Freikorps* would succeed in their bid. It was only they who could be trusted to guarantee 'protection against another revolution, this time a Bolshevik one'. His hopes were dashed; the 'Kapp *Putsch*' failed and the economic situation became even worse – not least for Dönitz, who now had three children to feed. Not that the ambitious officer took much time off for his wife and children. Dönitz had other things on his mind. From June 1920, as a *Kapitänleutnant*, he once again had a command of his own and on tactical exercises learned the techniques of detection, shadowing and surprise attacks. Later he was to call these 'wolf-pack tactics' and claimed they were his own idea.

His character and temperament make him a valuable naval officer, who will be suitable for any post commensurate with his age. Off duty he is a generally popular and valued comrade, who despite his economic difficulties never loses his cheerfulness and sense of humour.

Kapitän Werth in a report on Dönitz, 1925

His rise continued relentlessly. In March 1923 he became the Navy's expert in Berlin on 'political and organizational matters in the Defence Department (A1)', which was in fact a camouflage for the naval staff, outlawed by the Treaty of Versailles. For four long years he made a strong case to government for the Navy's interests and applied a fiery zeal in persuading the civilian authorities of what he saw as military necessities. Dönitz proved himself a skilled negotiator and his head of department was lavish in his praise: 'He is adept in his dealings with other ministries and authorities and thanks to his down-to-earth and personal style of negotiating extracts the best result possible for his department.'

However, he was soon to leave his desk and get back on board ship. Here he was able to revisit his past: as navigating officer on the cruiser *Nymphe* he once again met his old benefactor von Loewenfeld, who gave him a final ideological polish. Dönitz absorbed the articles of faith of this extreme reactionary, with whom he was on first-name terms, and among his brother-officers he stirred up feeling against Bolshevists and Jews. The economic plight of Germany, which was reflected in his own family circumstances, only served to stoke his hatred.

The political and economic crises provided the ground on which one man laid the foundation-stone of his career, someone who went around the country picking up votes with the promise of being the strong-man who would create order and clear up the chaos. The seductive slogans of Adolf Hitler had their effect, too, on the naval officer Karl Dönitz. Here was a man who promised what Dönitz so fervently wished for: a strong Germany and the prospect of a Navy that could match that of any great power. For Dönitz, Hitler was the personification of hope. After the war he wrote: 'I believed that Germany was taking the right path.' Because, of course, this path held out advantages for him in his professional career. Hitler's back-door accession to power was for Dönitz 'a welcome new beginning for the nation'. At last, here was someone who 'took drastic measures'.

> He was every inch the imperial naval officer – with everything that entails. He was one hundred per cent patriotic, that's to say, he saw himself as a servant of his people and his Fatherland.
>
> *Otto Kretschmer, U-boat Captain*

While Hitler was grabbing the levers of power in the Reich, Dönitz found himself on a long trip. The Hindenburg Travel Scholarship, awarded to him by the President of the Reich, enabled him to travel for five whole months through South-east Asia and the 'miraculous land of India'. Meanwhile, back home in Germany the SA and SS were bringing order through terror. Dönitz delighted in the beauties of exotic cultures and the 'harmony of a fairy-tale country', which prompted the voyager to ponder 'whether at heart the Balinese did not have just as much inner decency and culture as Europeans'.

As he boarded the steamship bound for home, his thoughts were already in Germany again and the 'restrictions of space' – Dönitz was on his way to the Third Reich, the political system he had always wanted, at whose head the long-awaited strong-man was preparing to fulfil maritime hopes as well. Hitler approved the expansion of the fleet, and by the autumn of 1933 Dönitz had been promoted to *Fregattenkapitän* (Senior Commander), and commended, in November of that year, as 'an officer with outstanding intellectual and personal qualities, a healthy ambition and clear leadership qualities'. He had known for a long time that loyalty to the Führer paid dividends. When the SA boss, Ernst Röhm, and other political undesirables were murdered, Dönitz would still excuse this decades later as 'necessary in defence of the state'. The Navy subordinated itself unreservedly to the new head of state. Like all members of the armed services, the ambitious Dönitz swore a personal oath to Hitler, and promised 'unquestioning obedience'. Until Hitler's death he felt himself bound by this oath.

Dönitz was on his way. Hitler's seizure of power gave his career the decisive push. As captain of the light cruiser *Emden* he would prove his 'leadership qualities' on tours of duty abroad. On 2 November 1934, shortly before the *Emden* weighed anchor, Dönitz was introduced to Hitler. The dictator was impressed by the rigorous attitude of the rising naval officer; and Dönitz was also affected by the appearance of his Supreme Commander. The image he had conjured up of the Führer was fully confirmed. The following day he told his sailors effusively: 'We all want to serve our admired Führer!'

While the *Emden* cruised the seas around Africa for several months, Hitler's diplomats achieved something hitherto considered impossible: on 18 June 1935, after tough negotiations, the Anglo-German Naval Treaty was tabled for signature. In it the Reich undertook not to build up its surface fleet to more than 35 per cent of the strength of Britain's and in the case of submarines to maintain a relative strength of 45 to 100 in Britain's favour. Later Germany would even be allowed complete parity. Britain believed it could afford to make this concession. It was assumed that ASDIC, Britain's acoustic underwater detection system, made it secure against German U-boats.

> According to British press comment, Britain apparently believes they can cope with the U-boat danger because of their detection methods. Our goal must be at all costs to see that Britain continues in this belief. The detection-proof U-boat and also the joint operation of several U-boats against a convoy must be as much of a surprise to Britain as possible.
>
> *Dönitz, 1938*

With the construction of U-boats secured by treaty, a new phase in Dönitz' life began. Hitler had great respect for Dönitz' technical expertise and appointed him '*Führer der U-Boote*' (FdU) – with orders to rebuild the U-boat arm from a standing start. Dönitz set about his task with zeal and determination. The FdU observed with suspicion how Hitler could get much more excited about big battleships than about submarines. Dönitz considered great big tubs like the *Bismarck* outmoded and vulnerable. He ceaselessly pointed out the advantages of 'his' subs. 'The U-boat,' he propounded, 'is wholly and essentially a weapon of aggression. Its large operational range makes it ideally suited to operating in distant enemy waters.' Only U-boats could succeed, he insisted, in cutting off vital supply-routes to Britain and starving Germany's perennial enemy to death. But Dönitz was preaching to deaf ears. He was still only in the second rank.

To begin with he had no more than eleven U-boats at his disposal. But he knew how to fire his young crewmen with enthusiasm. They came to regard themselves as an elite within the Navy. Dönitz hammered home the notion of 'selfless combat-readiness' in his captains and crews. 'Don't be afraid of ASDIC!' The Royal Navy's method of locating submarines was thoroughly overrated. He would get the better of the British convoys by using his 'wolf-pack tactics'. His boats would attack enemy shipping 'like wolves', true to his slogan 'attack – let 'em have it – sink 'em!' In saying this he was well aware of the dangers of being located by their radio transmissions and by enemy aircraft, nor did the naval warfare staff remain oblivious to these risks. His concept got the thumbs-down. The Navy chief, Erich Raeder, remained sceptical about the U-boat weapon, yet Dönitz considered his tactics to be the royal road to victory in a war against Britain.

> Dönitz proved again and again how quickly he could adapt to new situations and he then immediately developed a clear idea of what the new situation demanded.
>
> *Horst von Schroeter, U-boat Captain*

Meanwhile, this war was getting ever closer. The international outlook was changing apace. The *Anschluss* of Austria and the blackmail applied by Germany to the 'solution of the Sudeten question' forced London and Paris to close ranks, while Hitler steadily accelerated Germany's re-armament spiral. Raeder's staff vehemently advocated the building of battleships and cruisers. The 'Plan Z' of January 1939 was tantamount to a declaration of war against Britain as a sea-power. Hitler approved the increased construction of surface ships, while U-boats still languished in the shadows. But Dönitz was convinced that the great moment would soon come for 'his' submarines. He expected that Raeder's big warships would overstretch the arms budget and reserves of raw materials. U-boats could be built far faster and far more cheaply. The chances looked good. In the long run, he calculated, his ideas would have to be accepted.

Dönitz continued working on his U-boat strategy, as though Raeder's divergent notion of naval warfare did not exist. In his book *Die U-Boot-Waffe* (*The U-Boat Weapon*), published early in 1939, he summarized his views on how U-boats, in combination with the rest of the fleet, had to wage a blockade-war against Britain. Although Raeder tried to calm things by claiming that war was not to be expected in 1939, Dönitz worked at high pressure on his theoretical and practical scenarios. For a war he required 300 U-boats. Yet on 1 September 1939, when the battleship *Schleswig-Holstein* started the war by opening fire on Poland's Westerplatte fortress, near Danzig, Dönitz still possessed no more than fifty-six submarines. 'My God! So it's war with England again,' he stammered. 'He left the room,' a staff officer, Victor Oehrn, recalls, 'and came back half an hour later. He was a changed man. "We know our opposition. Today we have the weapons and a leadership which can take this opposition on. The war will last a long time. But if everyone does his duty, we will win it. Now get to work."'

Dönitz was appalled by the outbreak of war, not through any love of peace, but from a concern about Britain's vast superiority at sea. He shook hands with each of his U-boat captains as he sent them into battle. The war-diary spoke of a 'particularly confident mood among the crews'. But this was an optimistic picture. The submariner Otto Kretschmer, who later became the most successful of all U-boat captains, remembered how the men in the subs feared they would now get 'a good hiding' from the enemy.

Dönitz was deeply impressed by Hitler's personality – he trusted him completely. Nevertheless he said: 'I am responsible for the Navy. There I will not be told what to do by anyone, not even Hitler.' His military competence was beyond any doubt. In addition he had a clear leadership style which everyone could understand.

Hans-Rudolf Rösing, Commander-in-Chief U-Boats West

Nonetheless, on the very first day of the war Dönitz' U-boats went out aggressively in pursuit of the enemy. Hitler still hoped he could do a deal with Britain. However, on the third day of the war a torpedo put paid to any last hope of an 'agreement' at this 'thirteenth' hour. The Captain of the U 30, Julius Lemp, sank the British passenger-liner *Athenia* without prior warning. Lemp thought he had an armed merchantman in his torpedo sights; 112 people lost their lives. Pictures of the survivors went round the world and triggered a wave of hate against Dönitz' men. German propaganda tried to have the last word. 'The *Athenia* must have been sunk in error by a British warship, or have hit a floating mine of British origin,' sneered Josef Goebbels; and Dönitz also played a part in the cover-up. When the U 30 returned to port at the end of the month, the FdU gave her captain and crew a severe talking-to. They all had to swear they would say nothing to anyone about the attack on the *Athenia*. Dönitz even had the relevant entry removed from the U 30's log-book.

From the outset Dönitz required his crews to flout international regulations for the capture of vessels at sea. The U-boat war only had a prospect of success if his 'wolves' could sink merchant ships without prior warning. But for political reasons Hitler did not want to abandon these rules. They were progressively eroded and finally thrown overboard in 1940. However, it was not just international law that was causing Dönitz headaches. He tirelessly demanded what no one would or could give him: more U-boats. Hitler still considered the war at sea as a sideshow. U-boat construction only progressed sluggishly; each month no more than two U-boats left the slipway. Dönitz, visibly frustrated, sought an opportunity to prove the effectiveness of his weapon. What he needed was a surprise strike.

On 13 October 1939 just such an opportunity came along. In search of the enemy, *Kapitänleutnant* Günther Prien in the U 47 slipped unnoticed into the Royal Navy's 'holy of holies', the heavily protected anchorage of the Home Fleet at Scapa Flow in the Orkney Islands. There he sank the battleship *Royal Oak*, with most of her crew – an act of effrontery, at which Hitler, as Dönitz wrote, 'was beside himself with joy'. In Berlin the heroic Prien was fêted as no one but the Führer himself had been. Hitler personally received the captain and his crew. A wave of confidence in victory swept the country. The Scapa Flow attack made Dönitz famous overnight in Britain. 'From then on he was permanently in the headlines,' recalled Ludovic Kennedy, who commanded a destroyer in the Royal Navy. 'He became as well-known as Göring or Goebbels. Karl Dönitz was one of the most famous men in the war.' And Prime Minister Winston Churchill admitted after the war: 'The only thing that kept me in constant fear was Dönitz' U-boats.'

Prien's daring coup was mainly a psychological success. From a strategic point of view it was a mere flash in the pan, albeit with the effect that Hitler now looked on a struggle against Britain with more confidence. Dönitz was now appointed *Befehlshaber der Unterseeboote* (BdU), or Commander-in-Chief of U-boats. The prestige of the U-boat service rose considerably and it was now the Navy chief Raeder who pressed with increasing urgency for an 'unrestricted U-boat war'. Dönitz backed him fully. In early December 1939 he issued order 154:

No one to be rescued or picked up. Do not worry about ship's lifeboats. Weather conditions and proximity to land are unimportant. Just worry about your own boat and do your utmost to score the next success as soon as possible! We must be hard in this war. Our opponent started the war in order to wipe us out, so nothing else matters.

However, enormous shortcomings in war equipment were becoming apparent. Torpedoes missing their targets were almost a daily occurrence. 'At least 30 per cent of all torpedoes launched, fail to detonate,' Dönitz confided to his war-diary on 30 October 1939. 'The captains' confidence in their weaponry must be dwindling. Their keenness for action and attack will suffer in the long run. The removal of the causes of misfiring is currently the most pressing problem for the U-boat service.' The problem grew into an out-and-out 'torpedo crisis', which brought with it the U-boat arm's first disaster. During the assault on Denmark and Norway, in thirty-six attacks on warships every torpedo misfired. Dönitz now recalled his boats in order to have the 'fish' checked over with a fine-toothed comb. Even he was shattered by the findings: 'I do not believe,' he complained on 15 May 1940, 'that in the history of warfare fighting men have ever had to be sent against the enemy with such unserviceable weapons.'

For Hitler what mattered most of all were victories on land. With the defeat of France the way to the Atlantic ports lay open. Dönitz had long dreamed of being able to use these as a base. Finally he had free access to the world's oceans. In the port of Lorient in Brittany he had a headquarters built, known as 'Sardine Castle', which was the operational nerve-centre for the Battle of the Atlantic. Along the coast vast bunkers were constructed. With concrete roofs up to 7 metres (22 ft) thick, these submarine-pens were intended to protect the boats from the bombs of the Royal Air Force. They were fortresses of steel and concrete, gloomy and oppressive. The pens at Lorient alone cost 400 million Reichsmarks.

No sooner was the 'torpedo crisis' brought under control than the next round in the war on Britain's supply-routes began. Attack followed attack on the British convoys. Britain was to be starved to death and for the first time Dönitz was able to use his hunting-pack tactics successfully. Like wolves, several U-boats would attack simultaneously. On 15 August 1940 Germany had declared 'unrestricted submarine warfare' and two days later the total blockade of the British Isles. The Battle of the Atlantic was approaching its first climax – a pitiless duel, not only with weapons but with words. 'German U-boats hunt the enemy,' boomed the newsreels, 'Their watchword is: attack – let 'em have it – sink 'em.'

To begin with, the hunting-pack tactics proved to be decidedly successful. The British ASDIC system was ineffectual against

> He was a good organizer, a good leader of men. But only so as to lead his men to their death. That must never be forgotten. Dönitz was a war criminal, of that there is no doubt. He just had a lot of luck – and a very good defence lawyer.
>
> *Lothar-Günther Buchheim, submariner, and author of* Das Boot *(1973), filmed in 1981*

submarines attacking on the surface, and by the end of 1941 German U-boats had sunk nearly 4.5 million tons of enemy merchant shipping. Over 10,000 British seamen lost their lives – choked by the oil from their sinking ships, dying of thirst or sunstroke adrift in the trackless ocean before they could be rescued. And yet, with his operational skill, Dönitz gained the respect of his opponents. In the judgement of the British monitoring expert, Sir Harry Hinsley:

He was an exceptionally able man, Dönitz was such a capable operator that I could tell just from the signals exactly when it was Dönitz himself issuing orders to his boats. He was really astonishingly active and able. He was the Rommel of the war at sea.

In order to keep his crews' spirits up, the Commander-in-Chief had some bright ideas. He organized trains to take the sailors back to Germany on leave from their bases in France. For particularly successful crews he laid on wild parties in commandeered châteaux and country houses – these became known as 'U-boat grazing'. Dönitz made an effort to get close to his crews. As far as time allowed he would stand on the quay as each boat came in or left harbour, and would let no one stop him drinking a toast to successful sorties with 'his' submariners. 'He grew fond of every last man on the boats, stoker or ordinary seaman,' maintained U-boat captain Horst von Schroeter. Nearly every sailor got to meet Dönitz face to face at least once. In this way he gave the crews the feeling that he took a personal interest in their worries and problems – being literally 'in the same boat' as them. Occasionally Dönitz gave them a taste of his abrasive sense of humour. '"I need to be with you, to talk to you and look you in the eye. And anyone who doesn't believe it will get a clout over the head with this!" and with that he would raise his swagger-stick', recalled *Kapitän zur See* Hans Rudolf Rösing, Commander-in-Chief of U-Boats West.

There is no doubt that in the ranks Dönitz was not just well-respected, he was actually loved. They called him 'Lion' or 'Uncle Karl'. For this man with his Prussian sense of duty, mutual trust nevertheless meant demanding the utmost from each man. According to one of his staff-officers, Eberhard Godt:

> Dönitz seldom gave direct orders. He convinced you, and because everything he wanted to do had been carefully thought through, he really was convincing. He sought a discussion with everyone who had an opinion. Regardless of rank. Anyone who had no opinion soon got left out. He provoked people in order to hear counter-arguments. Only then did he make up his own mind.

Yet for all this discussion his orders remained implacable right to the end and frequently amounted to a sentence of death for the crews who, confined to the little world outside time and space, lived through hell on sorties lasting weeks or months. Behind steel walls only 20 mm thick, fifty men were crammed together like sardines in a can, trapped in the oppressive atmosphere of the marine equivalent of a coalmine, in the knowledge that at any moment they could be crushed to death. In the depths of the Atlantic the crews were entirely at the mercy of their Admiral, who spoke with no more emotion about men than he did about torpedoes or tonnage. To Dönitz, despite all his protestations of comradeship, his men remained one thing only: 'human material', which had to function like a machine: smoothly and without complaining.

The sailors who had to follow his pitiless orders were mere boys, the officers were in their early twenties. Like their Commander-in-Chief, they were meant to hate the British. But none of the U-boat crews had ever seen an enemy face to face. The enemy were no more than masts on the horizon, which the Captain could train his periscope on. The enemy were also depth-charges and the eerie pinging sound of the opponents' echo-sounder. And the enemy were ceaseless air attacks, against which there seemed to be nothing they could do. Again and again Dönitz called upon Hermann Göring, the Commander-in-Chief of the Luftwaffe, to provide some support. But the *Reichsmarschall*, under heavy fire himself, refused.

> Here and there it is being suggested that command of the Luftwaffe should be transferred to Dönitz, in addition to his naval command. Dönitz wouldn't be a bad candidate; at least he would inject new morale into the pretty wretched heap that our Luftwaffe is now, and in my view that is the first requirement for any new success.
>
> *Goebbels (Diary), 1945*

From the summer of 1943 onward, German U-boats were being caught with increasing frequency in the net of Allied radio detection – something which puzzled the German High Command, who had apparently failed to notice that on 8 May 1941 it was not merely the U-boat of Julius Lemp – the man who sank the *Athenia* – that had gone missing. A British destroyer had forced the U 110 to surface and then boarded it. In the stern of the boat the British found a machine that would decisively affect the outcome of the war. Now the 'Enigma', the key to the German naval code, was in enemy hands. With the help of this machine the British decoding experts at Bletchley Park, the code-breaking centre north of London, could intercept the orders given by the Commander-in-Chief to his U-boat captains.

Dönitz had no inkling about the leak that would decide the Battle of the Atlantic. The enemy was listening in, and no one knew. As enemy shipping gave the 'grey wolves' the slip more and more often – even when a U-boat had sighted a British convoy – Dönitz smelt treachery and had his entire staff checked out, without result. Finally only he himself and his Chief-of-Staff Eberhard Godt were left as possible traitors. 'Shall I investigate you?' he asked Godt. 'Or will you investigate me?'

'We hoped that they believed it was due to our superiority in radar technology,' Sir Harry Hinsley stated.

We encouraged the Germans in their assumption that we had developed a kind of wonder-radar with which we could see their U-boats from as far away as 100 miles. In fact they always found a different explanation because they were working on the assumption that no one could decode their signals.

Right to the bitter end Dönitz trusted in the security of the German 'Enigma' encoding, because radio experts reinforced his mistaken belief that the risk of decoding was at best an academic one. Not until the 1970s, when Dönitz was eighty-three years old, did the truth come to light. The British had imposed their highest degree of secrecy, 'Ultra', on the decoded radio messages. Thus the outcome of the battle of the German U-boats was already decided. Dönitz' boats were facing an opponent who possessed a modern detection system, had massive superiority in warships and aircraft and knew, thanks to 'Enigma', what the German U-boat command was planning.

> The British people have a great desire to shed no more blood and to end the war as quickly as possible, before the global situation further alters to their disadvantage. All the more then can we hope to gain from reviving the convoy-war, not just by sinking ships, but psychologically. That divergence of views, those various currents of opinion in Britain, show very clearly where our strength lies, namely in the enormously tough and determined unity of our nation.
>
> *Dönitz, 1942*

The time of brilliant victories was over. Dönitz' U-boats tracked down Allied convoys with increasing rarity. Reports of success became few and far between. However, the entry of the United States into the war on 11 December 1941 raised the spirits of the BdU once more. Dönitz declared open season in American coastal waters. There were German U-boats off New York! 'Operation Drumbeat' began on 12 January 1942. The torpedoing of ships off the eastern seaboard of the United States was like a turkey-shoot for the U-boats. By July 1942 they had sent 500 ships and their crews to the bottom. At this point in time the US Navy had nothing with which to oppose them. On Hero's Remembrance Day (9 November) 1942, Dönitz was promoted to Admiral.

The early successes could clearly not continue; in the course of 1942 the defensive tactics of the US Navy improved and the German U-boats were forced further and further out to sea. Dönitz was dissatisfied; his men were not achieving their targets. Now, in addition to tonnage sunk, the destruction of as many crew members as possible became a high priority. At the beginning of the year Hitler had stressed to the Japanese ambassador, Hiroshi Oshima: 'We are fighting for our existence and therefore cannot allow any humanitarian attitudes to prevail.' The warlord would not permit the rescue of shipwrecked enemy personnel and Dönitz, too, was killing men from the plot-room. In a lecture he gave in May he highlighted the improved torpedo detonators, which 'have the great advantage that, due to the very rapid sinking of the torpedoed ships, the crews can no longer be rescued'.

Like a barometer of the war as a whole, Dönitz also became more extreme. All 'observance of the imperatives of military chivalry', which he himself had demanded in a memorandum in autumn 1939, now fell by the wayside. The prime example of this was the case of the *Laconia*. In mid-September 1942, when the U 156 had sunk this British troopship, the captain, Werner Hartenstein, noticed that there were prisoners-of-war from countries allied with Germany on board the *Laconia*. With four fully laden lifeboats in tow, the U-boat proceeded on the surface, flying the Red Cross flag, but was nonetheless attacked by Allied bombers. The rescue of shipwrecked personnel had to cease.

Churchill once said: 'The only thing I am really afraid of is Dönitz' U-boats.' Churchill was absolutely right in that, and Dönitz shared this opinion: 'The U-boat war was the decisive war.'

Sir Harry Hinsley, Britain's chief code-breaker

Dönitz' reaction was swift: on 17 September 1942 every U-boat Captain received the notorious '*Laconia* order'. In it the U-boat Chief expressly forbade the rescue of shipwrecked enemy seamen: 'Rescue goes against the most basic requirements of warfare, to destroy enemy ships and their crews.' Only the captains and selected officers from stricken ships were to be picked up: humanity was now a dereliction of duty. On the witness-stand at Nuremberg he justified the '*Laconia* order' as having been necessary for the protection of his crews. Rendering assistance, Dönitz claimed, would have meant certain death. Shortly after the *Laconia* episode Dönitz called for the sinking of rescue vessels which were escorting enemy convoys. 'In view of the desired destruction of the steamer crews,' this was 'of great value'. To this end he impressed upon his own men: 'Be tough. Remember that in air-raids on German cities the enemy shows no mercy to women and children.'

It is true, Dönitz gave no direct order to kill, but his men could feel empowered to do so. While he did not expressly order the murdering, he still created a murderous climate in which inhumanity thrived. These dubious 'capabilities' rather served to enhance his career. His prestige certainly rose as the U-boat arm became more important in the war at sea. Hitler, by now on the defensive on nearly all fronts, scarcely trusted any of his Generals, but bound the Admiral still closer to him and on 30 January 1943 appointed him Supreme Commander of the Navy. Dönitz was now one of Hitler's innermost circle. He had stepped into the front rank and became a powerful figure in Hitler's team of henchmen. From now until the final collapse he would never be far from his Führer's side.

* * *

By being given overall command of the Navy Dönitz had, without expecting it, received the highest accolade. It was at this moment, if not before, when he was promoted to be head of an independent branch of the armed forces, that his claim to be no more than a 'non-political serviceman' became illusory. The Wehrmacht was harnessed to a political ideology. And as Commander-in-Chief of one of the armed services Dönitz could not escape this even if he had wanted to. However, his rise also coincided with a central decision in the war at sea: Raeder, Dönitz' predecessor in office, had favoured large warships, but the Grand Admiral preferred to deploy the small, fast U-boat as his weapon.

Dönitz was now master in his own house. His creed became a maxim for the Navy:

> Our lives belong to the state. Our honour lies in doing our duty and being ready for action. Not one of us has the right to a private life. For us what matters is winning the war. We have to pursue this goal with fanatical dedication and rock-hard determination to be victorious.

Of necessity his horizon had to extend beyond the U-boat service. His job was to co-ordinate all the Navy's activities, and it soon became clear at what an inauspicious moment he had been appointed to run the Navy. He could in fact do no more than postpone defeat. Germany had lost the initiative on all fronts, and her forces were under pressure everywhere: in Russia Stalingrad had fallen, and in Italy the Allies had landed at Anzio and were fighting their way north towards Rome. On the home front Allied bombers unloaded their deadly cargo on to German cities with increasing frequency. Yet Dönitz still believed, as he wrote in the first orders from his new desk, that the war could be won.

His remedies against enemy superiority were as simple as they were unimaginative: watchwords like 'fanaticism' and 'ruthlessness' were part of his everyday vocabulary. He described putting out peace-feelers as pointless; and any idea of surrender was, to him, criminal. For better or worse Dönitz linked his destiny with that of Hitler. From 'Koralle', his headquarters in the forest outside Berlin, he maintained close contact with the dictator. Whereas up to this point he had only met his master personally on nine occasions, after his appointment as naval Supreme Commander he paid Hitler a total of 119 visits. The public soon coined a nickname for him: 'Hitler-boy Dönitz'. Dönitz' relationship with Hitler has been tellingly described by one of his biographers as a 'junior partnership': Hitler the master and Dönitz the assistant – a mutually convenient arrangement.

Hitler had found a reliable accomplice and Dönitz got an appreciative pat on the back from his boss. As with all Hitler's courtiers Dönitz' faith in him had more than a touch of unreality: he wrote in August 1943, after a meeting with Hitler,

> The enormous power that the Führer radiates, his unwavering confidence, his far-sighted assessment of any situation, have made it very clear in recent days that we are all pretty sorry specimens compared to the Führer, that our knowledge, the way we see things from our own restricted sectors, is very fragmentary. Anyone who thinks he could do things better than the Führer is a fool.

From his 'Koralle' headquarters, protected by massive concrete walls, Dönitz pushed his unprotected U-boats out into a battle that had long been lost. For now the new British radar equipment was proving lethally effective: in May 1943 Dönitz lost forty-one U-boats in quick succession, and 2,000 crewmen perished, among them Dönitz' own son Peter. Now that 'Enigma' was in enemy hands, the German U-boats hardly stood a chance of getting back to their home ports in one piece. The tide in the Battle of the Atlantic had turned.

In this phase of the war, it was enough if a single convoy was successfully attacked, for Goebbels' propaganda organ to boom out hymns of praise to the heroic submariners. On 6 April 1943 Dönitz was awarded Oak Leaves to his Knights Cross. But he could not prevent the U-boat missions from ending in disaster. The western Allies sent out more and more bombers to provide air cover for the convoys, and when the 'air-gap' over the North Atlantic was closed, nowhere in the ocean was safe for the U-boats. If they did not go to diving-stations in time, they were bound for destruction. Month after month Allied U-boat hunters sank dozens of German boats.

Dönitz was beginning to have his first doubts. 'My great worry,' he wrote in his war-diary, 'is that we will lose the U-boat war if we do not succeed in sinking enemy tonnage faster than their shipyards can replace it.' Only now was Dönitz listened to. Albert Speer, Hitler's new Armaments Minister, gave U-boat

I am not able to equip the Navy on my own; that can only be done with the man who holds the whole of Europe's output in his hands: with Minister Speer. We have placed production in the hands of the minister responsible, Speer, who is now answerable to the Führer and to the German people for delivering the new vessels to us on schedule.

Dönitz on his collaboration with Speer, 1943

construction absolute priority. Dönitz pinned his hopes on new types of U-boat, especially electric-powered submarines, which were faster and could dive for longer. 'Miracle-boats' of this kind allowed him to go on believing to the last that the war could be turned round. The truth was that his 'wolf-pack' tactics had long been rendered obsolete by the technical superiority of the opposition. When the losses became completely intolerable Dönitz called a halt, on 24 May 1943, to the Battle of the Atlantic, though admittedly this was only a temporary measure. His father had taught him to 'finish off what you take on!'

By the autumn of that year the U-boats once again had to go out on their murderous – and often suicidal – missions. 'The German people have felt for a long time,' he wrote to his officers, 'that our [U-boat] weapon is the fiercest and most decisive of all, and that the outcome of the war depends on our success or failure in the Battle of the Atlantic.' However, Dönitz was powerless to fight back against Allied bombers, who posed the greatest threat to 'his' U-boats. Nonetheless, Dönitz did succeed where his predecessor Raeder had failed for years. He forced his recalcitrant rival, Göring, to pull in the same direction as the Navy – but it was a hollow victory. It was already too late to mount a combined operation against the convoys. For a long time Göring had been the target of biting derision in the Navy. The Luftwaffe Chief was known as 'the gravedigger of the Reich'.

Despite all the failures Dönitz continued to dream up pie-in-the-sky plans. He still talked of the victory that 'his' boats would achieve. With implacable fanaticism he goaded his crews into pitiless convoy attacks and always claimed to feel a close bond with his men. Yet above and beyond all his vows of comradeship stood his unquestioning loyalty to Hitler. It was to him that he had sworn an officer's oath; to be a turncoat was not even worthy of discussion. 'It is simply a matter of holding out with all our toughness', he remarked laconically in a lecture in the late summer of 1943.

> Dönitz was a very self-controlled person, very decisive in his manner. We had the impression that he thought things over a great deal, but then acted very swiftly. He knew how to persuade people with quite simple arguments. But he could also be persuaded himself: in 1943 he summoned all the flotilla commanders and asked them whether there was any point in fighting on. He wanted to hear everyone's opinion – from the youngest first and lastly from the most senior. If at the time we had said: 'It's pointless now', then the war would have been over. But we hadn't yet reached that position.
> *Hans-Rudolf Rösing, Commander-in-Chief U-Boats West*

Toughness was the most distinctive of Karl Dönitz' characteristics. Toughness was preached to him as a virtue during his training; toughness was what he showed when Röhm and other political opponents of Hitler were massacred; and toughness was a duty he imposed on his own men. For him there was no such thing as a strategically untenable situation. The worse the position became at the Fronts the more Dönitz set himself up as an apostle of tenacity, who repeated his favourite slogans like a prayer-wheel; it was just a question of 'getting through a bad patch'. As late as April 1945 Dönitz would speak out against Germany's 'premature capitulation', because 'unexpected political developments and other events may, as history has taught us, alter even those situations which are almost hopeless'. Toughness as an end in itself applied in his private as well as his professional life: when told the news of his brother's death in August 1943 he remained outwardly unmoved.

With merciless toughness Dönitz promoted 'total war'. He even issued a decree of his own, on 9 September 1943, denouncing 'habitual criticism' and 'moaning', writing:

The Führer has through the philosophy of National Socialism laid a firm foundation for the unity of the German people. It is the task of us all, in this phase of the war, to safeguard this precious unity through toughness, patience and steadfastness, by fighting, working and saying nothing.

Protest was anathema to Dönitz. He saw criticism as treachery. A cloak of silence was to be spread over the terrors at the Front and at home. Anyone who complained was to be 'called to account before an unrelenting court-martial for undermining our fighting strength'. Why did he issue this decree? Dönitz wanted to counteract rumours about the atrocities of the Wehrmacht and the SS. The fact that the organized murder of Jews, Poles and prisoners-of-war was a matter of daily routine in the east, is something even Dönitz must have known about. The Navy chief stood too high in the Nazi hierarchy to remain ignorant of it. The legendary 'gaze fixed seawards' became a cliché. We get nearer the truth in a report by Admiral Hans Höss on a discussion with Dönitz. The Grand Admiral had frequently been urged by his staff officers to protest to Hitler about the crimes in the east. 'Dönitz replied to us: "I will take care not to put my good relationship with the Führer at risk."'

Dönitz and I had a conversation – it may have been in autumn 1943 – after a visit to the Führer's headquarters, in which we discussed his hypnotic power. We discovered to our amazement that we both had the same reason for only going every few weeks to the Führer's HQ: and that was in order to preserve our inner independence. Because we were both convinced that we could no longer work freely if, like Keitel for example, we were constantly around Hitler. We used to pity Keitel, who was so totally under Hitler's influence that he was a tool in his hands, without a will of his own.

Speer, during the Nuremberg Trial.

The fact that Dönitz was at least partially privy to the 'secret project' of the mass-murder of Jews, is proved by an official trip he

made to Poznan in the autumn of 1943. Dönitz himself addressed
the assembled *Gauleiter* and senior Party functionaries, before
Heinrich Himmler, the *Reichsführer-SS*, took the floor as the
principal speaker. Himmler spoke of 'a page in our history that
must never be written', a secret that all those present had to 'take
with them to the grave'. He complained that it was a 'dreadful
task' and finally came out with what was actually under discussion:
the 'extermination of the Jews'. Himmler's precise words were:

All of you take it for granted that there are no Jews left in your
Gau. Every German, apart from isolated exceptions, also knows
very well that we could not have survived the air-raids and the
strain of the fourth year of war, with perhaps a fifth and sixth
year to come, if we still had this subversive pestilence in the
body of our nation.

His audience was dumbfounded. 'We sat at the table without saying
a word, avoiding each other's eye,' recalled the Hitler Youth leader,
Baldur von Schirach. And what of Dönitz? After the war he insisted
that he had not heard Himmler's presentation, because he had to
leave the meeting early. Naval colleagues covered for their superior
and claimed they had seen Dönitz that very evening in Berlin. Was
this the truth or an attempt at exculpation? There is no conclusive
evidence.

The naval Commander-in-Chief did indeed direct his gaze
mainly 'seawards', where the situation was becoming more acute
by the day. It was now obvious, even to him, that from now on
every boat had to 'bear the full brunt of the opponent's defences'.
Once again he complained about the lack of co-operation from
Göring's Luftwaffe, and once again he pressed Hitler for more U-
boats and increased aerial reconnaissance over the Atlantic. Dönitz
stood up stubbornly for his demands and this made him a rare
phenomenon in the group around the Führer, who preferred to
surround himself with yes-men and head-nodders. The naval Chief
formulated his position with unequivocal emphasis and made it
clear that as a seasoned naval officer he wanted to make the
decisions in his department. Unlike other 'courtiers' Dönitz did
not shrink from presenting Hitler with unwelcome news. 'In one

situation discussion he had something negative to report,' U-boat Captain von Schroeter remembers. 'Hitler listened quite calmly and then said to the others present: "I wish I could always be so properly informed by everyone."'

Hitler could rely on a man like Dönitz. The Navy boss made the unrelenting demand on his men to 'fight until we go down'. Hitler and Dönitz marched to the same beat. 'It is therefore necessary,' Dönitz told a groups of flag officers in late 1943, 'that the fighting man stands, with all his mental and spiritual strength and with his strength of will, behind the fulfilment of his duty. And that requires his conviction, his *Weltanschauung*.' However, strong words were not enough to make up for the declining effectiveness of their armaments. Dönitz resorted to action for the sake of action. He ordered the *Scharnhorst*, the last large German warship still intact, to attack an Allied convoy in the Arctic Ocean – a suicide mission with no prospect of success.

Dönitz had to settle a 'debt of honour' with Hitler. The dictator would really have preferred to scrap the big warships, which Dönitz considered a mistake. On 26 February 1943 the 'junior partner' persuaded the war leader at his headquarters not to send ships like the *Scharnhorst* and the *Tirpitz* to the breaker's yard but to continue deploying them. 'We shall see who is right,' Hitler is reported to have said to his naval Adjutant, Jesko von Puttkamer. 'I'll give you six months to prove that the big ships are still of some use.'

Christmas 1943 finally provided an opportunity, as the war-diary tells us, to make 'an important contribution to taking pressure off the tight situation on the Eastern Front'. Neither unfavourable weather forecasts nor the negative advice from Naval Command North could dissuade Dönitz from ordering the captain of the *Scharnhorst* to go out on this fateful operation. Up to this point the atmosphere on board was still peaceful. The crew were celebrating Christmas. 'We had christmas trees, little presents and letters from home,' recalls artificer Herbert Reimann. 'But there was a mood in the air as if the men knew that something was about to happen. There was an odd uneasiness.' Then, on the first day of the Christmas holiday, came the disaster that Dönitz was solely responsible for. Allied torpedoes hit the stern of the *Scharnhorst*. Two thousand seamen died; only thirty-six survived. One of those was Herbert Reimann, who was never able to forget the last dramatic moments on board the battleship: 'Everything was happening quite calmly, but I heard three cheers which the many sailors in the water gave to the ship, followed by the song "*Auf einem Seemansgrab, da blühen keine Rosen*" ("On a seaman's grave no roses bloom").'

Dönitz appeared 'extraordinarily affected' by the sinking of the *Scharnhorst*, as his Adjutant, *Korvettenkapitän* Jan-Heinrich Hansen-Nootbar, observed. However he refused to admit his own mistakes. Instead he tried to make Hitler believe that the blame lay with the fleet commander, Admiral Erich Bey, who had incorrectly assessed the enemy strength and despite his proximity to the convoy had not exploited 'the advantage of his situation'. Dönitz had found his scapegoat. Hitler's henchman was still on course, and wrote in his New Year orders to the Navy for 1944:

> An iron year lies behind us. It has toughened us Germans like no generation before us. Whatever fate may demand of us in the coming year, we will withstand it, united in our will, unshakeable in our loyalty, fanatical in our belief in victory. . . . The Führer shows us the way and the goal. We follow him with body and soul into a great German future.

Are those the words of an 'unpolitical serviceman'?

The more desperate the military situation became, the more firmly Dönitz bound himself and his men to Hitler. On occasions such as a conference of flag officers in February 1944, he countered 'complaints and grumbles' with promises made on his own authority. Of course they would win, as soon as the new U-boats were put into service. But until then only fanaticism, faith and obedience would do any good. 'Anyone who goes against this and thus against his people, gets broken to pieces by me,' he rasped. Even prospective officers had to be educated in the National-Socialist spirit, since: 'The officer is the exponent of the state; any talk of officers being non-political is plain nonsense.' Dönitz, a 'non-political serviceman'?

Dönitz was an ice-cold man, but even as the highest-ranking officer he didn't have the courage to tell Hitler what he thought.

Hans Lautenbach, Medical Officer

Hitler's retainer had quickly got used to his new propaganda role. His speeches were laden with ideology and he sought every opportunity to serve his Führer as a dependable vassal. Hitler noted this with approval. Since the Führer now shrank from showing himself and speaking in public, he asked Dönitz to deputize for him in giving the traditional address on Heroes' Remembrance Day 1944. The speaker dug deep into his bag of propaganda slogans. In this war that had been forced on them by the enemy, the Navy Chief ranted, it was 'a matter of the survival or extermination of our nation. In what state would the German people be now if the Führer had not, ten years ago, created the Wehrmacht, which alone is in a position to ward off our enemies' assault on Europe?' he asked, only to answer his own question immediately: 'The Bolshevist flood . . . would have wiped out our people and swept away the culture of Europe.' As though trying to outdo Hitler himself, he slavered over the 'corrosive poison of Jewry'. With lies and deceit, smears and cynicism, Dönitz set himself up as the accomplice, prepared to go to any lengths for his boss. The alliance between Hitler and Dönitz was an alliance against reason.

Any facts which might shatter his faith in the genius of the Führer, Dönitz swept aside. He closed his eyes to the reality of impending defeat and imagined that an Allied invasion of western Europe would give his U-boats their big chance to prove themselves. 'Any enemy vessel involved in the landing,' he ordered his captains on 11 April 1944, 'is a target requiring the U-boat's full attention. It is to be attacked even at risk of losing your own boat.' He signed the order which carried the unambiguous heading 'Ruthless attack' – an empty gesture, but one which would appeal to Hitler. The reality was of course different. During the Normandy landings, Dönitz completely avoided putting his boats at risk.

Outwardly Dönitz liked to act the hard man. What was going on inside his mind he seldom let people see. On the evening of 14 May 1944, when he learned of the death of his second son Klaus, he sat at the bedside of his daughter Ursula: 'We sat holding hands and neither of us spoke. The death of both his sons hit him hard.' No word of complaint passed his lips. As Dönitz put it to his grandson Klaus Hessler after the war, his sons had died 'a hero's death in performance of their duty'. Despite these fateful blows, Dönitz got on with his job, as though nothing had happened. It almost seemed as though his toughness towards himself and others gave him something to hold on to.

> Dönitz demanded a great deal from us young men. But he was also very understanding if, for example, we made a mistake. Somehow he managed to collect a lot of men around him who were all very similar to each other. Anyone who didn't fit in properly was soon out again. It was with his U-boat captains especially that he had a unique relationship. I once heard him say: 'I must spend time with you, talk to you again and again, look into your eyes.' He could never be so cordial towards other groups of sailors.
>
> *Hans-Rudolf Rösing, Commander-in-Chief U-boats West*

Finally, on 6 June 1944, when neither his U-boats nor destroyers and fast patrol-boats could prevent the landing of Allied troops on the Normandy beaches, Dönitz nevertheless felt a kind of relief, that at last things had become clear: 'The Second Front is here.' Other officers acted to bring an end to the purposeless slaughter on both fronts, while Dönitz saw a further chance, after the failure of the 20 July attempt on Hitler's life, to demonstrate his unquestioning loyalty to the Führer. 'Sailors of the *Kriegsmarine*,' he proclaimed the very same evening, 'the treacherous murder-blow against the Führer fills every one of us with righteous wrath and bitter rage against our criminal enemies and their mercenary accomplices.' The fact that Hitler was almost unscathed he described as the work of 'Providence' and 'a further confirmation of the justice of our struggle'. His peroration was typical of his fanaticism: 'We will band together more closely around the Führer, we will fight still harder, until victory is ours.' He meant no one to doubt his loyalty. On the very day of the assassination attempt he made the raised-arm *Hitler-Gruss* obligatory in the Navy, in place of the traditional salute.

Not until decades later did Dönitz admit even the vaguest insight. 'We knew nothing of the facts which the men of the Resistance knew and which drove them to act,' he wrote after his imprisonment in Spandau, only to sneer in the same breath at the plan of the 'criminals' to open all the concentration-camps:

They apparently imagined that the camps only held respectable citizens who were unpopular with the government of the time, without knowing that 99 per cent of the inmates were habitual criminals who on average were given a five-year sentence – people whom the previous [Weimar] government had allowed to roam around free, until their next murder, sexual offence or serious act of violence, and for whose incarceration we cannot be grateful enough today, because we have that to thank for the safety of our families and for the whole of public life.

We all knew there were concentration-camps. That was where communists were locked up and then had to work in factories. But the fact that people were being systematically exterminated, no one knew, at least not in the Navy. Not even Dönitz. He was not a man who lied.

Reinhard Hardegen, U-boat captain

In all this Dönitz could not have remained unaware of the consequences of his armament demands. He knew that concentration-camp inmates were the victims not the perpetrators of thousands of death-blows. He was not concerned about the inhuman conditions under which they had to carry out their forced labour in the U-boat dockyards. 'I would rather eat dirt,' he told his flag officers on 15 February 1944, 'than see my grandsons brought up in the filthy Jewish mentality and poisoned by it, and that the purity of today's public art, culture and education . . . should fall again into Jewish hands.' For a long time this speech was missing from the record. Only in the 1950s did a single carbon-copy come to light. It is true that Dönitz made a verbal protest to his superiors about the pogroms of the *Reichskristallnacht* on 9 November 1938. But six years later he made no secret of his hatred of Jews. It was some unusual 'presents' he gave to the U-boat captains that revealed his guilty knowledge. *Leutnant zur See* Adolf Clasen saw with his own eyes a sea-chest containing hundreds of watches:

> On the lid of the closed chest was a small label with the words 'Gift from the BdU for his submariners'. We felt uneasy; it seemed weird, and we couldn't make out where these watches were from. We had the instinctive feeling that this mass of watches had to have something to do with wrongfulness and violence.

The cynicism at the head of the Nazi regime drove Dönitz to his demands for 'the ability to die fanatically'. Anyone who refused 'had to disappear'. Every sailor 'had to perform his tasks at his post ruthlessly . . . and stand fanatically behind the National-Socialist state'. The Wehrmacht had to 'stick fanatically by the man they have sworn allegiance to, for otherwise such a Wehrmacht will be lost. . . . To whom shall we dedicate ourselves with our entire soul? In the end these are the reasons why that element of the General Staff failed,' he said, referring to the 20 July plotters and added, quite accurately: 'They were not attached to the Führer with all their soul.' Many years later he reinterpreted this speech of hatred as an act of solidarity. He wanted to make it clear, he said, that 'it was necessary to have the people solidly behind the political leadership'.

Dönitz' loyalty to Hitler was unquestioning, no matter how hopeless the position at the fronts appeared. In February 1945, when the Armaments Minister Albert Speer pointed out to Dönitz the hopelessness of the overall military position and called on him to take the initiative, Dönitz snapped back: 'I only have to

His relationship with Hitler was characterized by an admiration which to outsiders was scarcely comprehensible. To the very end Dönitz considered him to be an outstanding statesman. That is no doubt also why he never joined any form of resistance movement. I once raised this with him, and he said to me: 'From the Normandy landings, if not earlier, I realized that the war could not be won. But to bring it to some kind of decent conclusion needed a great statesman – and the only great statesman for miles around was Adolf Hitler.'

Otto Kranzbühler, Dönitz' Defence Counsel at Nuremberg

represent the Navy here. The rest is not my business. I am sure the Führer knows what he's doing.'

Dönitz went on fighting for supplies and raw materials, long after there was nothing left to distribute. To Hitler he was untiring in his over-optimistic forecasts and promises. Even when the Reich capital was being pounded by Red Army artillery, Dönitz fantasized about a turn-round in the U-boat war, 'if only we were still in possession of the ports on the Bay of Biscay'. This kind of whitewashing was very much to Hitler's taste. Both he and Dönitz clung to every straw that held the promise of survival.

In March 1945 Hitler, whose mistrust towards his generals was pathological, decided in future only to post naval officers to command strongholds on the Western Front, 'since many strongholds, but as yet no ships, have been lost without a fight to the last man'. While in the west soldiers were deserting in large numbers, Dönitz' forces continued to fight relentlessly to hold positions that were clearly lost. The Grand Admiral was merciless in throwing away their lives – there was no trace now of the much-vaunted comradeship. With whiplash orders he drove the U-boats, patrol-boats and so-called 'guerilla' vessels into battle against the Allies. In the spring of 1945 alone nearly 5,000 German submariners died.

Since the last reserves of fuel were now down to the dregs, Dönitz sent his sailors to fight ashore. Naval infantry divisions were intended to stabilize the Front, but these desperate attempts

Thus our Navy's combat integrity must be preserved. This is the best contribution we can make to turning round the current crisis. There is no situation that cannot be improved by a heroic attitude. What is certain is that the opposite attitude means disintegration and with it chaos and indelible disgrace.

Dönitz, 1945

ended in a bloodbath. 'We in the Navy know how we have to act. Our military duty, which we perform unerringly, whatever may be going on to our left and right and all around us, makes us stand like a rock of resistance, bold, hard and true.'

In the final phase of the war there were few people who Hitler trusted as much as the loyal Dönitz. The dictator saw betrayal on every side. He castigated Göring for his incompetence, Himmler for his readiness to make peace and Keitel for his failure. However, even in moments of greatest distraction, he would always address the Navy chief punctiliously as *Herr Grossadmiral* (Grand Admiral). Dönitz repaid the compliment with speeches of devotion announcing in the middle of April:

In a year at the latest, perhaps even this year, Europe will recognize that in Europe Adolf Hitler is the only statesman of any stature. All the negative brooding is unfruitful and factually incorrect. Since it is born out of weakness it cannot be otherwise, for cowardice and weakness make people stupid and blind.

What a difference between Dönitz and Göring! Both suffered a severe technical setback in their arm of the services. Göring resigned himself to it and that finished him. Dönitz overcame it.

Goebbels (Diary), 1945

This Nibelung-like allegiance to the Führer meant a sentence of death for many of his men. He had once sworn to himself that there must never be another November 1918. With this in mind he now ordered: 'The honour of our flag is sacred to us. Let no one think of surrendering his ship. It is better to go down with honour.' Even the lynching of Germans by Germans met with his 'full acceptance'. When it came to his ear that in an Australian PoW camp the senior German officer had ordered the shooting of communist fellow-prisoners, he promised to promote the man responsible 'with all means possible', just as Hitler had promoted him, Karl Dönitz.

> To begin with I was keen on Dönitz, because I believed him to be a man of principle. I saw him as an admiral in the 'Moltke mould': a strict but loyal and above all an able admiral. But then he turned into a terrifying Nazi. I soon realized he was a bigoted, narrow-minded man with a wretched education. In the end I thought him no more than a death-merchant of the worst sort – the lowest imaginable kind of Party hack. Dönitz was completely Hitler's creature.
>
> *Lothar-Günther Buchheim*

As Stalin's troops irresistably approached the Reich Chancellery, Hitler sent Dönitz to the north of the collapsing Reich. On 19 April 1945 the Grand Admiral abandoned his 'Koralle' headquarters and installed himself in Plön, in Holstein. It was here that Dönitz was to hold his position, and it was here that the naval staff had been working since March, in relative safety. First, however, Dönitz had one more brief visit to pay to the bunker beneath the Chancellery. On 20 April 1945, the Führer's final birthday, Hitler, a 'defeated and broken man', as Dönitz' Adjutant Walter Lüdde-Neurath described him, had a brief conversation with the Grand Admiral. Then Dönitz took his leave and headed for his new command-centre. Hitler calculated that, with Germany now split in two by the advancing Allied Armies, the southern half of the country could be controlled from the Alps. Dönitz was to hold the north. The next day the master and his assistant saw each other for the last time. Then Dönitz left Berlin.

Hitler's governor in the north issued an outright rejection of all blandishments about negotiating a separate peace in the west. Supreme command lay ultimately in Hitler's hands and he still clung to war. Meanwhile Dönitz was fully aware that the Allies would only accept the complete subjugation of Germany. In his opinion: 'Since surrender must in any case mean the destruction of Germany's national resources, it is right from this point of view as well that we go on fighting.'

> That night we jumped out of a window and ran off across the fields. We wanted to leave the Grand Admiral to finish the war on his own. We went through villages where deserters were hanging from the trees. The farmers warned us about naval search-parties: 'They're worse than the SS. They'll shoot you down, no questions asked.'
>
> *Heinrich Jaenicke, U-boat seaman, on the ending of the war, 1945*

However, when Dönitz learnt on 27 April, from the war-diary of the supreme command of the Wehrmacht, that 'the end of the battle for the Reich capital' was very close, even he could see that there was nothing more to be gained. This did not lessen his Nibelung loyalty. If necessary he would show, through his own suicide, that the Navy would not be responsible for another 'stab in the back'. And he became obsessed with the idea that only the honourable death of the Commander-in-Chief could keep away 'any stain from the flag'.

That scenario was never played out. On 30 April 1945 at 19.30 hours he received what was surely the most important telegram of his career. The sender was Martin Bormann, Reich Chancellery, Berlin, and it contained astonishing news. 'In place of the former *Reichsmarschall* Göring, the Führer appoints you, *Herr Grossadmiral*, as his successor,' Hitler's Secretary cabled, without mentioning that the Führer had committed suicide. He went on: 'In order to provide the German people with a government made up of honourable men to carry out the obligation to continue the war with all available means, I, as

Führer of the nation appoint the following members of the cabinet: Reich President Dönitz . . .'

Dönitz still did not know that Hitler was no longer alive. He sent an obsequious cable to Berlin. '*Mein Führer*, my loyalty to you will be inalienable. I will therefore continue to make every attempt to relieve you in Berlin.' Without delay Dönitz kept his promise and dispatched young naval troops into the besieged capital, where they were supposed to liberate Hitler. Most of them paid for this lunatic operation with their lives. What Dönitz considered to be a 'heroic duty' those involved knew to be a suicide mission. Gerhard Jakob, one of the sailors, described their general mood:

> We knew, of course, where the front was. There was no chance of winning. We wondered why we as sailors now had to go to Berlin. But orders are orders, and when we heard they had come from Dönitz himself, we carried them out. That was something sacred for us.

The first of May brought Dönitz the certainty that Hitler was dead. He was now the successor and he was facing his final test. The Admiral remained true to himself and went on doing what he had always done – he sang the praises of the dead tyrant who, he claimed, had died a radiantly heroic death. Suicide was not mentioned. On the same day the German population learned that 'the Führer has nominated me to be his successor'. He could thus be certain that those remaining loyal to Hitler would now follow him. He made it clear to the SS, the *Gauleiter* and the troops: 'The oath of allegiance you swore to the Führer now applies to me as the Führer's appointed successor.' As British tanks pushed into Holstein, Dönitz moved his headquarters from Plön to Flensburg, and to the Mürwik Naval College – the place where it had all begun for him, a long time ago.

Conscientiously Dönitz set about dismantling the 'Thousand Year Reich', which lay in ruins and was as shattered as its people. 'All military and political measures have to serve to preserve the German national character,' he wrote in his diary. His stated objective was now 'in the western areas, where a peace-settlement could prevent our national resources from being annihilated, to reach a partial cessation of hostilities as rapidly as possible'. Dönitz wanted to go on fighting in the east, in order to rescue as many Germans as possible from imprisonment by the Russians. More than a thousand ships, from fishing-smacks to ocean liners, were to evacuate the refugees from the Baltic coast. 'My first task is to rescue German men and women from being wiped out by the advancing Bolshevist enemy . . . For this purpose alone,' ran the daily orders of 1 May 1945, 'the armed struggle goes on.' He asked his Adjutant Lüdde-Neurath:

> Who can guarantee that in a hundred years' time the German people will still exist? That whole layers of society will not be annihilated or uprooted, that through deliberate subversion and swamping an international proletarian mishmash will not emerge, which no longer deserves the name 'German'?

Dönitz knew that the western powers treated prisoners-of-war according to international conventions. He therefore gave orders to his successor as Commander-in-Chief of the Navy, *Generaladmiral* Hans Georg von Friedeburg, that in order to win time a partial surrender in Holland, Denmark and northern Germany was permissible. On Lüneberg Heath Field-Marshal Montgomery went along with Dönitz' tactics and accepted a partial surrender. Dönitz' gamble paid off: over two million refugees finally made it to the west. Yet while he was rescuing some, he was executing others. On the night of 5/6 May, in the seaport of Sonderborg, in Denmark, eleven young sailors were court-marshalled and shot for 'military rebellion', because they had locked up their officers and were heading for home. As late as 5 May 1945 German military courts pronounced death sentences on Lithuanian volunteers in the German ranks. The responsibility for this lay with Dönitz.

After the war, Dönitz described the delaying of the surrender in favour of rescuing refugees, as actually 'the intention of his commission from the Führer'. Hitler had been on the point of bringing hostilities to an end, he claimed, 'and therefore by his heroic death in Berlin laid the way open for such a step'. No

> What a marvellous, imposing impression Dönitz does make.
> As the Führer said to me, he is the best man in his arm of the
> Wehrmacht. One only has to look at the consistently
> satisfactory results he has achieved with the Navy.
>
> *Goebbels (Diary), 1945*

sooner had the guns fallen silent, than Dönitz was weaving the
absurd legend of a peace-loving Hitler.

On 4 May 1945 at 15.14 hours an order went out to the U-
boat captains to lay down their arms. Dönitz wrote:

> My submariners! Six years of U-boat war lie behind us. You
> have fought like lions. . . . Submariners! Unbroken and with no
> stain on your honour you lay down your arms after an
> incomparably heroic struggle. We remember with reverence our
> fallen comrades, who with their death sealed their loyalty to
> Führer and Fatherland. . . . Long live Germany. Your Grand
> Admiral.

In the night of 4/5 May many of the crews destroyed their boats.
Dönitz had expressly forbidden such action but, as Count
Schwerin von Krosigk, a member of the 'Dönitz cabinet', recalled:
'The captains believed that in so doing they were complying with
the true wishes of their Admiral.'

The struggle was at an end. The important thing now was to
leave no traces. Many SS officers disappeared into the Navy. Even
the former camp Commandant of Auschwitz, Rudolf Höss, was
given cover. But Dönitz showed less mercy to those of his
'comrades' who were suspected of desertion. When *Kapitän-
Leutnant zur See* Asmus Jepsen heard about the cease-fire he did
not wait for orders, but headed homewards. Dönitz placed
injustice above clemency. The salvos of the firing-squad could be
heard in his office. In Dönitz' view there could not be 'two moral
standards'.

The executor stuck to his brief. He was not guided by any
insight, simply by the compulsive feeling that he had to go on

Our Führer, Adolf Hitler, is fallen. The German nation bows
its head in profound grief and reverence. At an early stage he
recognized the terrible danger of Bolshevism and dedicated
his life to wrestling with it. His death in Germany's capital
comes at the end of this struggle of his, and of the straight,
unswerving path of his life – a life spent solely in the service
of Germany. His commitment to the struggle against the
advancing tide of Bolshevism was recognized beyond Europe
in the whole civilized world. The Führer has appointed me to
be his successor. Conscious of the responsibility I take over
the leadership of the German people at this fateful hour.

Dönitz' broadcast address to the nation, 1 May 1945

doing his duty. He saw himself as the 'guardian' of 'the finest and
best things that National Socialism has given us'. And it almost
seemed as though to him the Third Reich, so far from being in the
past, was the basis for a re-emergence into a radiant future. He
continued to believe that 'the most important thing' was 'the
solidarity of our people'. This Dönitz wanted to preserve 'in all
circumstances'. Not a word of remorse, grief or sympathy passed
his lips. He denounced reports about concentration-camps as
'propaganda and largely exaggerated'. Later he spoke of 'isolated
perpetrators' who should be tried before a German court of law,
but even years later he could find only words full of hate for those
who survived the concentration-camp hell: 'The camp inmates,
who largely consist of criminals and deserters, are being
compulsorily clothed by decent people who, in these hard times,
have nothing themselves; and these antisocial elements now rule
the streets.' Dönitz had learned nothing.

The second act in the demise of the Third Reich was played out
in the northern French city of Reims. General Alfred Jodl had
received orders from Dönitz to prevent an unconditional
surrender on all fronts and to hold off the Allies. Dönitz' plan was
to surrender in the west but to keep up resistance on the Eastern
Front. But this time the victors would not play ball. Jodl had no
choice: after consulting Dönitz he was forced to accept total

> In many conversations I had with him he always denied
> having known about the concentration-camps. There is
> always of course the question as to what he should have
> known or must have known. He probably knew more than
> most ordinary people.
>
> *Klaus Hessler, Dönitz' grandson*

capitulation on all fronts. Once again Dönitz used the radio to
address the population:

> Men and women of Germany! The foundations upon which the
> German Reich was built have been shattered. We all have a hard
> road ahead of us. I do not intend to lag behind you on this
> thorny path. Should duty call upon me to stay in office, then I
> will try to help you in every way I can. Should duty compel me
> to go, then this step, too, will be a service to the people and the
> Reich.

At that same moment Dönitz' last U-boats were surrendering in
the Port of London.

Dönitz was immersed in the performance of his duty. He wanted
to make no changes to Germany's political system. He agitated with
passion against 'the lunacy of party politics'. Democracy would
always be alien to him. He still dreamed of an 'ethnic state' and it
was no surprise that he crammed his cabinet exclusively with rigid
Nazis. In the classrooms of the Mürwik Naval College he played an
impotent game of 'government'. It was a final piece of Theatre of
the Absurd.

Every day at 10 a.m. sharp Dönitz opened his cabinet sessions.
Albert Speer, now 'Minister of Production', later recalled the
buffoonery that the 'head of state' believed to be government
work: 'We drafted memoranda in a void, and tried to counteract
our unimportance with apparent activity. We were well on our way
to making ourselves laughable, or rather we were that already.'
The Western Allies punished Dönitz by ignoring him. Churchill
saw the executor as, at best, a 'stick' with which the German

'anthill' could be controlled. The victors entrusted the 'statesman' in Flensburg with nothing more than winding up the war.

Not until 23 May 1945 did they bring the phantom government to an end. Two weeks after the surrender Hitler's imitators finally had to stand down. 'Hands up' and 'trousers down' bawled the British soldiers as they stormed the naval college. After an embarrassingly intimate body-search some 300 'cabinet members', staff officers and civil servants were led away in front of whirring newsreel cameras. Dönitz accepted his arrest calmly. 'The Admiral bore himself with great dignity,' observed a British officer. The *New York Times* commented: 'Today the Third Reich died.'

A US Army aircraft took Dönitz to internment in the Luxembourg town of Monheim, where he encountered fifty more of Hitler's henchmen in what the Americans dubbed 'Camp Trashcan'. Dönitz knew what was awaiting him. The Allies were quite determined to bring those responsible for the crimes of the Nazi regime before a tribunal.

In the autumn of 1945 that is exactly what happened. The scene of the trial was Nuremberg, once the symbol of and stage for National Socialist self-promotion. In civilian clothes Dönitz 'was frankly indistinguishable from a sales assistant in a grocery store', as an American reporter put it. During the proceedings it soon became clear that the Admiral saw the trial as 'the continuation of war by other means'. He made no bones about presenting himself as a victim of 'victors' justice'. There was no doubt in his mind that the judge had death-sentences against all the defendants ready in his desk drawer.

He protested on the second day of the trial, after the prosecution had shown a film about the atrocities in the concentration-camps:

How can I be accused of knowing such things? You ask me why I did not go to Himmler to get information about the concentration-camps. But that is ludicrous! He would have thrown me out, just as I would have thrown *him* out if he had come along to investigate the Navy! What in God's name did I have to do with those things? It was only by chance that I rose so high, and I had nothing whatever to do with the Party.

From the very beginning of the trial Dönitz played the innocent. 'None of these charges relate to me in the slightest – they are typical of American humour,' he noted on the charge-sheet, which was drawn up under three main headings: '1. Conspiracy to wage a war of aggression, 2. Conduct of a war of aggression, 3. War crimes.' In Dönitz' case the prosecution did not lay charges of crimes against humanity, since many of the documents which would have implicated him were simply unknown to the court. From that aspect Dönitz was certainly fortunate. His hate-filled speech to his flag-officers after the attempt on Hitler's life was not seen by the court, nor did the judges know that the accused would rather 'eat dirt', than see his grandchildren 'brought up in the filthy Jewish mentality and poisoned by it'. Thus Dönitz was spared the most serious charges and, as it turned out, Hitler's successor was fortunate in the choice of his defence counsel. In naval judge Otto Kranzbühler he had an able champion and one furthermore who was deeply convinced of his client's innocence. 'It was our clear strategy,' Kranzbühler stated later, 'to admit Dönitz' responsibility purely in the sphere of his naval authority and to show that he had done nothing more than that which was permitted by the principles of naval warfare prevailing at the time.'

On 8 May 1946, the first anniversary of the surrender, the military tribunal called Dönitz to the witness-stand for the last time. To the question as to when his political activity had commenced, Dönitz replied defiantly: 'On 1 May 1945 – not before!' The man who had apparently been such a 'non-political serviceman' insisted that he had simply followed the orders of his superiors, and indeed he could now cash in on the *esprit de corps* that he had always drummed into his U-boat men. With the sole exception of Karl-Heinz Möhle, a witness for the British prosecution, who commanded the 5th U-Boat Flotilla in Kiel until the war's end, no other witnesses could recall any criminal order being issued by the defendant. Even *Kommandant* Eck, who was later executed for war-crimes, maintained a stony silence on Dönitz' behalf, right up to the moment he faced the firing-squad. As the military historian Michael Salewski puts it, Dönitz was one of the 'very few leading military figures who even in defeat, a total and bloody defeat, kept the trust of the men he was sending to certain death'.

He was a very charismatic person. Even as a child I noticed the effect he had on others. He was very imposing when dealing with people – but when I was alone with him he could drop all that completely. Then he would suddenly become full of humour and kindness. I have often seen how quite ordinary sailors would travel hundreds of kilometres just to catch a glimpse of him. And – regardless of their rank or background – my grandfather would invite them in for a meal and chat to them. He was family-minded. I noticed again and again how much the sailors loved him. He was more than a superior officer to them, he was a father-figure.

Klaus Hessler, Dönitz' grandson

Did he wage a war of aggression? The only thing that interested him, he said, was his particular arm of the services. Hitler had not demanded anything of him that infringed the law of naval warfare: 'That is why I believe firmly that I ran a clean navy in every respect, down to the last man, right to the end.' Finally, when the prosecution attempted to demonstrate the criminal nature of his conduct of the U-boat war, Dönitz went over to the offensive: attacks on neutral ships which, by sending radio reports to the combatants, had turned themselves into warships, had, he said, been carried out in the same way by the enemy. This was confirmed by no less an authority than the Commander-in-Chief of the US Navy, Admiral of the Fleet Chester Nimitz. Immediately after the outbreak of war in the Pacific in December 1941, Nimitz had minuted his orders for 'unrestricted submarine warfare'. American submarines only gave assistance in exceptional cases to the crews of sinking ships from enemy countries. For a brief moment Dönitz was beside himself with glee. 'That is absolutely splendid evidence!' he chortled at lunch the following day.

Apart from this there was nothing very surprising about his manner inside or outside the courtroom. He attempted to justify his inflammatory speeches as being necessary to strengthen the morale of the civilian population and the armed forces. Any expression of remorse was absent. As to forced labour in the U-boat yards, Dönitz claimed to have known nothing. Yet, as the British prosecutor Sir David Maxwell-Fyfe pointed out, he himself had called for 12,000 concentration-camp workers. That demand was made, retorted Dönitz, 'on the clear understanding that the work would be carried out willingly and under very good conditions'.

And what had he meant, asked Maxwell-Fyfe, when he had referred in his speech on Heroes' Remembrance Day, March 1944, to 'the spread of the poison of Jewry'.

'I could imagine that it would have been very hard for the people in the cities to stand up to the bombing-raids, if such an influence was allowed to have effect.'

'What did you mean by the 'spread of Jewry?'

'I meant that it could have the effect of undermining the people's ability to hold out, and in this struggle where the life or death of the fatherland was at stake, I, as a serving officer, was most particularly anxious about that.'

But why, as the Commander-in-Chief of 600,000 to 700,000 men, Maxwell-Fyfe insisted, did he indoctrinate them into believing that Jews were a spreading poison?

'That statement . . . shows that at the time it was my view that the steadfastness, the strength of the people to keep going, could better be maintained with the composition of the population as it then was, than if Jewish elements had been present in the nation.'

'Do you mean to tell the court that you knew nothing of the measures and the intention to remove and exterminate the Jews?'

'Yes, of course I am saying that. I knew nothing about it, and if I made some such statement at the time, that does not prove I had any idea of any murders of Jews. That was in 1944. . . . None of my men had ever thought of using force against Jews, and no one should conclude from what I said, that they did so.'

These were the words of a man who would learn nothing. Such obstinacy met with sympathy from no one but his co-defendants.

'Oh, now I feel terrific, for the first time in three weeks,' boomed Göring. 'Now at last we're hearing from a decent German officer. That gives me new strength. Now I'm prepared to listen to a bit more treachery.' Göring was referring to Speer.

> The little weakling! The innocent little lamb – says he had nothing to do with the Party? My God, if he hadn't been in agreement with National Socialism, he wouldn't have lasted five minutes.
>
> *Göring about Dönitz during the Nuremberg Trial.*

It was to be expected that even Dönitz' closing plea was simply bursting with self-justification. Indeed, he announced, he had nothing to reproach himself for. Quite the 'non-political serviceman', his closing words had the sober tone of a military communiqué: 'My life was devoted to my profession and thus to service to the German people. As the last Commander-in-Chief of the German navy and as last head of state I bear a responsibility toward the German people for everything I have done and failed to do.'

The agony of a month of waiting followed until sentence was pronounced on Hitler's executor. 'It is not shown by the evidence,' the judge declared, 'that he was an accessory to or participated in the "conspiracy to wage a war of aggression".' In the pitiless German U-boat war the military tribunal did not recognize any transgression of the law, but condemned his express ban on giving assistance to shipwrecked passengers and crew, as in the case of the *Laconia*: 'The orders were undoubtedly ambiguous and deserve the strongest criticism.'

The sentence – ten years' imprisonment – provoked a furious reaction from Dönitz. He flung down his headphones, clenched his fists and stormed angrily out of the courtroom. In fact the court had been relatively lenient in dealing with his case. Apart from three acquittals the sentence passed on Dönitz was among the lightest. For that reason alone the verdict did not go undisputed. The British and Soviet judges had demanded the death-penalty, while the US judge, Biddle, was for an acquittal.

Only after a tough wrangle was the tribunal able to agree on a sentence. Ten years' imprisonment – to many observers of the trial this was a contemptible compromise, though in the eyes of defence counsel Kranzbühler, Dönitz was condemned despite his 'proven innocence'. Dönitz also refused to accept it: 'I will never recognize the verdict as just or reasonable under international law.'

Two weeks after the passing of sentence by the judges of Nuremberg, Dönitz and six other leading war-criminals entered their cells in Berlin's Spandau military gaol. 'He wore a mauve-coloured prison uniform with the number "2" on it,' Dönitz' grandson Klaus Hessler recalled. The order in which the prisoners were admitted dictated their number. But it made sense that Hitler's successor would be prisoner 'Number Two'.

He felt his imprisonment to be a personal humiliation. Like every inmate the former Navy chief had a daily quota of labour. In his free time the 'Number Two' read voraciously – the works of Schopenhauer, for example, or books on ornithology. He seldom had visitors, and frequent contact with his family was forbidden. Klaus Hessler, whose first memory of his grandfather was of seeing him in Spandau, remembers a rather 'good-natured atmosphere', despite strict controls and short visiting-hours: 'we were separated by bars and were not allowed to touch each other. Once he asked me to stand on a chair, so he could see how tall I was.'

I believe to this day that my grandfather never managed to come to terms with his relationship to Hitler as a person. Everything he has written finally comes down against the Führer-principle, against a totalitarian leader. But there is nothing there which might lead me to think that he had worked through his relationship with Hitler.

Klaus Hessler, Dönitz' grandson

Impatiently Dönitz awaited the moment when the prison gates would open for him once more. He assumed in all seriousness that he would be able to return to the armed services. It was just a question of hanging on. As the years went by, grass would grow over the past and, after all, there were still his supporters and comrades who, during his gaol sentence, worked assiduously on promoting the legend of the 'decent officer' – a label which the defence lawyer Kranzbühler had already pinned on his client at Nuremberg. Dönitz maintained that he had only done his duty and until his release he continued to rail against his fate. On 30 September 1956, shortly before his release, he turned on his fellow-inmate Albert Speer, with whom he had worked closely until the end of the war and whom he had appointed to his 'cabinet':

It's your fault that I have lost these eleven years. You're to blame for everything! For my being condemned like a common criminal. What did I have to do with politics? If it hadn't been for you, it would never have occurred to Hitler to make me head of state. All my men have been given commands again. But look at me: I'm like a criminal. My career has been destroyed.

Speer himself claimed to remember the reply he gave:

You and the others here, you talked endlessly about honour. Every other word from you, or from Schirach, was dignity, conduct. Millions of people were destroyed by that war. Millions more were murdered in the camps by those criminals. All of us here were part of that regime. But you're more upset about your ten years here than about the fifty million dead. And your last words here in Spandau are 'your career'!

Even if not quite true, it makes a good story.

Dönitz was in Allied detention for exactly ten years to the day and hour. On 1 October 1956, as the prison clock struck midnight, he stood and faced the Russian prison governor for the last time. 'Sign here, Number Two.' The prisoner obeyed. 'So now it's all over, Admiral Dönitz.'

Once more at liberty, Dönitz immediately set about creating his own memorial for posterity. He would now continue the image-building which his sympathizers had attempted to perform for the

I visited Dönitz in 1973 at his little house in Aumühle near Hamburg. I just wanted to meet this man. Dönitz had actually loved Hitler. He once said to me: 'Hitler was a demon. But I only recognized this demon in him when it was already too late.'

Sir Ludovic Kennedy, author, broadcaster and former officer in the Royal Navy

man 'unjustly condemned'. Dönitz wrote his memoirs – the deceptive self-portrait of a 'non-political serviceman'. The title itself, *Ten Years and Twenty Days*, referring only to his imprisonment and brief period as head of state, makes the author's intentions clear. Once more he sang the song of the obedient sailor, whose head was not filled with politics or ideology. 'His book is a cerebral work, which always seemed to me very pallid, very wooden, very elaborate,' was how Dönitz' grandson described his memoirs. 'I do not believe he ever managed to draw a line under things and come to terms with his relationship with Hitler.' The past would never let go of him. As an old man he felt most comfortable among old comrades who still respectfully addressed him as '*Grossadmiral*'.

After the death of his wife Ingeborg, Dönitz lived in seclusion in his house in Aumühle, in the Saxon Forest outside Hamburg. But he was not forgotten. Old shipmates helped out whenever they could. The political successor to the criminal Hitler had no cause for complaint, and yet it is somewhat surprising that in his dotage Dönitz was able to make something, if not very much, of the positive sides of democratic, postwar Germany, and that he wished to be borne to the grave under the flag of the Federal Republic. However, what the new age denied him was a strong man to idolize, an authority to which he might subordinate himself without reserve. Instead Dönitz sought the comfort of faith. 'Ultimately,' he confided to his parish pastor, 'Christ is all I have to hold on to.'

Karl Dönitz died of old age at his home on Christmas Eve 1980. Shortly before his death he said:

His life was founded on the virtues of the unjustly much-reviled officer corps of the Imperial Navy: a sense of honour, self-sacrificial dedication to duty, love of the Fatherland and steadfast loyalty to the government of the day.

From Rear-Admiral Eduard Wegener's eulogy for Dönitz,
1981

My position would have been quite different had I not been known as Hitler's political successor. But today no one asks: what would have happened if, let's say, Himmler had been in charge during the last days of the Reich, instead of me. At the time, I did all that was humanly possible in a period of chaos.

It almost sounded as if Dönitz was about to repeat his declaration at Nuremberg: 'I would have to do exactly the same again.'

There it was, the one word that excuses everything. The loudspeakers trumpeted it right across the cemetery: loyalty, the great German lie, the general pardon for all blindness, cowardice and irresponsibility.

Heinrich Jaenicke, U-boat seaman, on Dönitz' burial

SELECT BIBLIOGRAPHY

General

Bullock, Alan, *Hitler*, London, 1990
Fest, J., *The Face of the Third Reich*, London, 1979
Graber, G.S., *History of the SS*, London, 1978
Hitler, A., *Mein Kampf*, London, 1998
Kershaw, Ian, *Hitler* (2 vols), London, 1999
Taylor, A.J.P., *The Origins of the Second World War*, London, 1961
Trevor-Roper, H.R., *Hitler's War Directives 1939–1945*, London, 1964
Shirer, William, *The Rise and Fall of the Third Reich*, London and New York, 1960
Veranov, M. and the editors of Time-Life Books, *The Third Reich at War*, London and New York, Robinson Books 1997

On Joseph Goebbels

Elke Fröhlich (ed.), *Diaries 1924–1941*, New York, 1987
Elke Fröhlich (ed.), *Diaries 1941–1945*, London and New Providence, 1995
Reimann, Victor, *The Man Who Created Hitler: Joseph Goebbels* (transl. Stephen Wendt), London, 1979

On Hermann Göring

Gilbert, Gustave, *Nuremberg Diary*, New York, 1947
Hoyt, Edwin P., *Göring's War*, London, 1990
Mosley, Leonard, *The Reich Marshal: A Biography of Hermann Goering*, London, 1974
Overy, Richard J., *Goering: The 'Iron Man'*, London, 1984
Swearingen, Ben E., *The Mystery of Hermann Göring's Suicide*, London, 1987

On Heinrich Himmler

Lumsden, Robin, *Himmler's Black Order 1923–45*, Stroud, 1997

Padfield, P., *Himmler: Reichsführer-SS*, New York, 1990

Smith, Bradley F., *Heinrich Himmler: A Nazi in the Making, 1900–1926*, California, 1971

Smith, Bradley and Peterson, Agnes (eds), *Heinrich Himmler, Secret Speeches 1933–1945*

Smith, Bradley F., *Heinrich Himmler 1900–1926. His Path to German Fascism*

On Rudolf Hess

Bird, Eugene, *The Loneliest Man in the World*, London, 1974

Douglas-Hamilton, James, *The Truth about Rudolf Hess*, Edinburgh, 1993

Leasor, James, *The Utopian Peace: Rudolf Hess' Flight to Britain*, 1978

Le Tissier, Tony, *Farewell to Spandau*, 1994

Nesbit, R.C., & van Acker, G., *The Flight of Rudolf Hess: Myth and Reality*, Stroud, 1999

Padfield, Peter, *Hess, the Führer's Disciple*, London, 1991

On Albert Speer

Speer, Albert, *Inside the Third Reich*, London and New York, 1970

Sereny, Gitta, *Albert Speer: His Battle with Truth*, London and New York 1995

Van der Vat, Dan, *The Good Nazi: The Life and Lies of Albert Speer*, London, 1997

On Karl Dönitz

Dönitz, Karl, *Ten Years and Twenty Days*, London, 1959

Padfield, Peter, *Dönitz: The Last Führer*, London, 1984

Wagner, G., *Führer Conferences on Naval Affairs*, London, 1990

INDEX OF NAMES

316 HITLER'S HENCHMEN